Inspiralize
Everything

Inspiralize
Everything

100 NEW delicious recipes and ingredients to spiralize

Ali Maffucci

EBURY
PRESS

First published by Ebury Press in 2016
www.penguin.co.uk

This edition published by arrangement with Clarkson
Potter Publishers, a division of Random House, Inc.
a Penguin Random House Company, New York. All
rights reserved.

A CIP catalogue record for this book is available from
the British Library.

Photography by Evan Sung

ISBN 9781785035302

Colour origination by Altaimage Ltd
Printed and bound in Italy by Printer Trento S.r.l

Penguin Random House is committed to a sustainable
future for our business, our readers and our planet.
This book is made from Forest Stewardship Council®
certified paper.

10 9 8 7 6 5 4 3 2 1

Ebury Press, an imprint of Ebury Publishing,
20 Vauxhall Bridge Road,
London, SW1V 2SA

Ebury Press is part of the Penguin Random House
group of companies whose addresses can be found
at global.penguinrandomhouse.com

MIX
Paper from
responsible sources
FSC® C018179
FSC
www.fsc.org

'Everything you see here I owe to spaghetti.' – Sophia Loren

To my 'best bud' and
love of my life:
Lu, this one's for you

Contents

Introduction

On a typical Saturday morning, my husband, Lu, and I wake up early, go for an invigorating run outside together, and end up at our local farmers' market. We check in with the farmers about what's fresh, what's coming soon and how life is. Many of our meals begin right there with the very people who plant and harvest our food. We walk through the market, loading up on seasonal, spiralizable (not a word in Webster's dictionary, but definitely in mine) veggies, finding all colours of the rainbow – red onions and peppers, orange carrots and sweet potatoes, golden beetroot, green courgettes and cucumbers, and purple kohlrabi, depending on the season. At that point, I'm already thinking about what we'll be eating for dinner all week – will it be Greek-style Prawn Scampi (page 111)? Turkey Picadillo with Green Pepper Noodles (page 188)? Hot-and-sour Soup with Mooli Noodles (page 200)? The possibilities are limitless.

I still remember the first bowl of courgette noodles I ever ate. My mother, a type 1 diabetic, was experimenting with raw veganism to help regulate her blood sugar levels. She discovered spiralizing, and invited me over to try an Asian-style raw courgette noodle dish. As I spun my fork in the crunchy green 'noodles', I was wary. Growing up in an Italian-American family, I was accustomed to eating heaped portions of spaghetti and dipping crusty, oven-heated slices of white bread into the pool of sauce in the bottom of the bowl. How could sliced courgette hold a candle to those meals? Well, that dinner was one that changed everything for me.

If you're familiar with my story, you know that I actually went home that night with my mother's spiralizer (thanks, Mum!) and started spiralizing non-stop. After three months, I quit my corporate job, launched Inspiralized.com and made spiralizing my new lifestyle. I was blessed to garner an audience fairly quickly, and, before the two-year mark, to write a bestselling cookbook, *Inspiralized*. Fast-forward, and here we are. Who would've thought courgette noodles could be so impactful? I promise, if you haven't already tried them, once you do, you'll be just as smitten as I am. And eventually, you too will *Inspiralize Everything*.

I still adore pasta today, but spiralizing has since transformed family dinners – and the way I cook, eat and live every day. In the past, I would head straight to the living room after I finished at the table so I could lie flat on the sofa, belly up, and let the food coma take over. Now, after a spiralized meal, I go for a walk around the block with Lu, full of energy and feeling nourished and satisfied. We'll breathe the fresh air into our lungs and soak up the day's last minutes of sunlight. Not only does this help us digest our food after a meal, but we're also able to enjoy some quiet time to ourselves, talking about our day and feeling gracious. Since launching Inspiralized, I haven't cooked a bowl of 'regular' pasta at home. When I dine out at restaurants, of course I'll order a plate of piping-hot fresh gnocchi in an aromatic tomato-basil sauce and signal the waiter to bring over more bread – God forbid a drop of sauce goes unslurped! I would never neglect my roots or deprive my taste buds. But on the whole, my eating is more balanced than ever before. (Plus, I can classify these meals as 'research' – consider it a job perk.)

Opting for a clean-eating lifestyle changes everything – your energy levels skyrocket, your mood becomes more positive, your focus improves and your waistline shrinks. Overall, you become a better version of yourself. You'll be grateful for the food you eat, as it not only strengthens your body, but also provides you with the vigour needed to live and enjoy your optimal life. After discovering spiralizing, my whole perspective on eating healthy changed: I started to focus on eating whole, real ingredients and stopped getting caught up in the minutiae of dieting. I discovered moderation, the concept of nourishing your body from the inside out, and, most importantly, committing to a lifestyle rather than a temporary diet. Spiralizing is a way to eat lighter and more nutritiously, but still have the dishes and flavours I love to eat most (like

pasta!). Once I went all-in with spiralizing, I lost 2 stone 2 pounds and was able to finally find the weight my body feels best at and that I can maintain without obsessing over what I'm eating. I was freed from the chains of yo-yo dieting and calorie counting and can honestly say that spiralizing has led me to the healthiest and happiest body I've ever had.

All my success and positive results have only driven me to keep spiralizing. I have new tricks, cooking methods, ingredients and of course recipes to share with you. In writing this cookbook, no rock was left unturned, or, ahem, *unspiralized*. Want a thinner noodle? I can show you how to get that (page 15). Having difficulty spiralizing large, tough vegetables? No problem – I've got you covered (page 16). I even found a new vegetable to spiralize (page 184)! Based on all your helpful feedback, I've included new categories and classifications for the recipes, such as Dairy-free, No Cook and Saves Well (see page 23 for a full list of indicators). You'll find dishes from all different cuisines – Thai, Chinese, Indian, Greek, Cuban, American and, of course, Italian. Every recipe can be easily adapted to suit your preference or dietary needs. And everything here is meant to be a fully satisfying meal. You may have a hearty salad for lunch (like Fried Green Tomatoes with Avocado Ranch Kohlrabi, page 146) and an ample bowl of soup for dinner.

Spiralizing can be used not only to re-create noodle and rice dishes, but also to make everyday meals more interesting. Whether or not vegetables were meant to be this extraordinary, they are now – and when you spiralize, you'll impress yourself and friends with what comes out of your kitchen. Simply put, after reading this book, you'll be able to masterfully spiralize everything from apples to potatoes.

When my grandparents call to invite us over for Sunday night dinner, we grab the keys, run out the door and drive the hour to their house, picking up a bottle of Chianti, Brunello or Montepulciano (my grandfather's favourites) on the way. We know we'll arrive to a delicious home-cooked meal, overflowing with love. We'll toast to good health and do what we do best: eat together. I cherish these moments deeply. But as for Monday night? That dinner will be Inspiralized.

How to Inspiralize Everything

BACK TO BASICS

Regardless of whether you've been spiralizing for ages or you're a newbie, it's important to know what you're doing with this gadget before you start cooking. Here are some simple definitions to get you started:

spiralizer (noun) *[spy-ruh-lahyz-er]*
1 a kitchen tool that turns vegetables and fruits into noodles.

spiralize (verb) *[spy-ruh-lahyz]*
1 to turn vegetables and fruits into noodles with a spiralizer.

inspiralize (verb) *[in-spy-ruh-lahyz]*
1 to make meals healthier and more creative by incorporating spiralized vegetables.
2 to replace traditional pasta, noodles and rice with spiralized vegetables.

inspiralized (adverb)
1 a meal made with spiralized vegetables that's now healthier and more inspired because of it.

What can I spiralize?

For a vegetable or fruit to qualify as spiralizable and for best results, it must be:

- Without a tough stone or an interior with large, tough seeds.
- At least 4cm in diameter.
- At least 5cm in length.
- Not soft or juicy inside.

There are a few exceptions to the above, however. Some vegetables and fruits may go through the spiralizer, but not well – the noodles won't look great, and the process will most likely waste much of the vegetable or fruit. Aubergine seemingly satisfies the guidelines, but due to its spongy flesh, it shreds and produces a seedy, mushy mess instead of noodles. Cantaloupes, persimmons and some other foods are spiralizable, but I wanted to focus on the most versatile produce. However, feel free to experiment and get creative! On the opposite end of the spectrum, we have peppers. They are hollow, but they can be spiralized quite successfully (more on that on page 184).

For a flawless experience, stick to these rules and the vegetables and fruits covered through the book. In developing these recipes, I've tried to include the produce that's readily available at local supermarkets and markets.

Which spiralizer should I use?

Now that your mind is racing with the endless possibilities of vegetable- and fruit-noodle meals, let's talk about your gadget. There are many types of spiralizers out there; each will produce a slightly different result, and each has its pros and cons. But no matter what kind you have, you can make every single recipe in this cookbook. If you *don't* have a spiralizer and aren't quite ready to invest, I have a solution for that, too! Check out the Tip Box on the right.

Everything on the market is primarily plastic and easy to clean and maintain. You can find spiralizers at speciality kitchen retailers, department stores, supermarkets, online – pretty much anywhere these days. They essentially break down into two main categories: hand-held and worktop.

Hand-held: These spiralizers require you to manually spin through the produce. They are small and best used on thinner vegetables like carrots, courgettes and cucumbers. They are a great starting point if you don't want to invest in a larger tool, or simply don't have the room for one in your kitchen. They are also a solid option if you plan to bring your spiralizer with you when you are travelling or if you primarily want to spiralize courgettes.

Worktop: These spiralizers secure to a surface, offering more leverage and, therefore, the ability to handle vegetables and fruits of all sizes and shapes. The produce moves through with a crank of the handle instead of with your hand. These tend to take up more space and take a bit more time to clean (see page 16 for instructions on that).

So which one do I use? After trying out pretty much every model on the market, I decided to take the best features of what was out there and design my own: the Inspiralizer, which can be ordered online. But it comes down to personal preferences – one spiralizer doesn't fit all, so just do your research and choose one that best meets your needs.

If you don't have a spiralizer but do want to enjoy these recipes, you have a few options. A mandolin, julienne peeler, regular vegetable peeler, knife or even the widest holes on a box grater can help you make noodles out of all vegetables. These methods are more time-consuming than spiralizing, but they work.

How do I spiralize?

Now that you've got your gadget, let's break down the steps. Here's how it works.

PREPARE YOUR PRODUCE

First, you'll need to get your vegetable or fruit ready to be spiralized. The opening text in each specific produce section specifies what steps to take for that item. But speaking generally, you'll want to slice off the ends of your vegetable so they are flat and even. Doing so will create a surface area that the spiralizer can properly secure to. Without this step, the vegetable will misalign, wobble, fall off and ultimately cause your noodles to come out improperly. You don't have to slice the ends off apples, beetroot (if they're perfectly round), peppers or pears – the spiralizer will just latch right on.

Next, if the outer skin is inedible or unpleasant to eat (like with a knobby, hairy celeriac), peel it before spiralizing. If the outer skin *is* edible and you prefer to eat it, there's no need to peel.

If your produce exceeds 15cm in length, halve it. Some vegetables can be very round, large and heavy, making it tough for them to stay secured to the spiralizer. To combat this, using a sharp knife, trim the edges off to make a rectangular shape no more than 13cm wide. You can use the excess in another recipe or eat it as a snack.

CHOOSE A BLADE

If you're working with a gadget that has multiple blades, you get to decide your noodle shape, depending on which blade you choose to spiralize with. All the brands and models out there produce similar shapes with blades that we'll refer to here as A, B, C and D.

BLADE A: Makes thin, ribbon-like noodles, similar to pappardelle.

BLADE B: Makes thicker-shaped noodles, similar to bucatini or fettuccine.

BLADE C: Makes linguine-shaped noodles.

BLADE D: Makes spaghetti-shaped noodles or, with some models, angel-hair-shaped noodles. If you cannot find a vegetable with a diameter of at least 4cm, always use this blade. If yours is a three-blade tool, use blade C instead.

The Inspiralizer displays these letters on a blade-changing knob. If you're using another brand, check the manual so you know which blade makes which noodle shape. Most have either comb-like teeth or triangular spokes for slicing. The smaller the distance between the teeth or the smaller the spokes, the thinner the noodle it will produce. The blade without any spokes is always blade A. Every recipe in this book indicates which blade you should use to prep your produce.

Since writing *Inspiralized*, I taught myself a new trick to adjust the width of the noodles without necessarily changing the blade. It's especially helpful if you love angel hair spaghetti and don't have a spiralizer with blade D, or if you're creating a thick pasta sauce and simply want a sturdy noodle. It's easy: just apply more or less pressure as you spiralize. To achieve thinner noodles, spiralize slowly and gently using light pressure. To achieve thicker noodles, spiralize more quickly with strong pressure. This technique works with any blade.

Time to spiralize!

You've got your vegetable or fruit and you've got your blade – you're ready to go! Take a peek at the manual that came with your tool. In general, if yours is a worktop model you'll first secure the machine to the work surface. Then load on the vegetable or fruit, first aligning its centre on the central coring blade, and then securing the spokes of the handle into the other end. Start cranking and watch the magic happen!

While you're spiralizing, if you notice that spiralizing makes more half-moon-style noodles instead of full spirals, it is most likely because your vegetable has moved off the centre of the coring blade and isn't slicing evenly. To combat this, simply remove and re-centre the vegetable.

After the blade indication in the ingredients lists, you'll often see 'noodles trimmed'. Just take kitchen shears and roughly cut the noodles so you don't have any that are super long. If you're cooking for kids, this step is especially important, as they may want to play with their noodles if they are too long, and won't easily be able to chew them. You can trim the noodles after the vegetable or fruit is fully spiralized or every couple of seconds as you spiralize.

CLEANING YOUR SPIRALIZER
Once you have the proper brush (see page 21 for details), cleaning your spiralizer is easy. Place the gadget under running water and, using soap, scrub the blades in a circular motion until all the food bits are washed away. Most important is the timing – it's essential to clean your spiralizer right after you use it to avoid staining and discoloration. After washing, place it on a rack and let it air-dry, or carefully pat it dry with kitchen paper.

What can I make with spiralized vegetables?
In the recipes in this book, sometimes the spiralized produce is the hero of the dish, and other times it's the sidekick. No matter how the produce is incorporated, it always adds texture, flavour and nutrients. You probably know by now that the most popular way to incorporate spiralized vegetables is to use them in place of regular pasta and noodles. You won't think twice about eating a big bowl of spaghetti or pad Thai when it's light in calories and carbs, but still bursting with flavour. Some other easy ways to include them are in soups and stews, salads, pasta salads, casseroles, breakfast dishes and baked goods. But it's not *just* about the noodles…

RICE
Ginger-crab Fried Mooli Rice (page 203)? Chicken and Celeriac Rice Soup (page 94)? Why not! Spiralized rice is a great replacement for rice in any traditional use. To make it, first spiralize your vegetable with blade C or D. Pack the noodles into a food processor and pulse in 3-second intervals until they become rice-like. Take care not to overpulse, or you'll end up with shredded vegetables or mush. If there are any pieces that don't break down properly, pick them out and pulse them again separately.

Some vegetable rices require their excess moisture to be squeezed out before use in recipes. If you're using mooli, turnip or courgette, place the rice in a piece of kitchen paper and wring it out over the sink before cooking with it.

The Best Veggies for Ricing

- **Beetroot**
- **Butternut squash**
- **Carrots**
- **Celeriac**
- **Courgettes**
- **Kohlrabi**
- **Mooli**
- **Parsnips**
- **Swede**
- **Sweet potatoes**
- **Turnip**

NOODLE BUNS
Spiralized noodles can also be enjoyed in the form of a bun, which can be used as the base for sandwiches, as burger buns, as miniature pizzas or simply on their own. I bet you didn't think you could spiralize avocado toast (page 167)! To make buns, spiralize your vegetable with blade C or D. You can use any spiralizable produce, but starchy vegetables are best – parsnip, swede, sweet potato and potato.

Season the noodles with salt and pepper and cook them in some heated olive oil in a non-stick frying pan until tender. You can also substitute cooking spray for the olive oil and cover the pan to let the noodles steam. Once they're cooked, transfer the noodles to a bowl, add one beaten egg per medium vegetable, and toss to coat. Pack the noodles into a ramekin or a similar vessel and place foil, baking or greaseproof paper directly on top, pressing down with your hands or a weighted can. Leave the noodles to set for at least 15 minutes in the fridge. Heat 1 tablespoon olive oil in a large frying pan over a medium-high heat. When the oil is shimmering, invert the moulded noodles into the pan. Sear until the buns are firm and browned on both sides, about 5–7 minutes total.

THE INSPIRALIZED KITCHEN

You've got your gadget all set up, but what about the rest of the kitchen? It's absolutely crucial for a healthy home cook to be well-equipped in terms of storecupboard items and cookware. If not, cooking can be frustrating and disappointing, and you'll probably end up ordering in pizza. As the saying goes, failure to prepare is preparing to fail. So let's prepare!

The storecupboard

I've included an updated list of must-have items for a healthy Inspiralized storecupboard. In addition to the initial set-up, it's important to occasionally (every month, if you cook regularly) survey what you're running low on and what you aren't using. Perhaps the foods you aren't using as much will inspire you to make something new! If you have the essentials on hand, you won't end up halfway through a recipe saying, 'Oh no! I'm out of crushed tomatoes!' I've been there and it's *non bene*. Many of the storecupboard items listed here are great for cooking whether or not your meal is Inspiralized. Some of these ingredients are new to this book, so definitely take a moment to assess what you have!

Extra-virgin olive oil: A heart-healthy fat, and my favourite to cook with. If you're going to have one oil in your storecupboard, make it extra-virgin olive. Investing in a quality olive oil is essential (and totally worth it), as it cooks well and has a gentler, less processed flavour.

Extra-virgin coconut oil: The flavour of this oil makes it ideal for stir-fries; plus, it's packed with healthy fatty acids. As a bonus, it can be used in your beauty routine for facial masks, moisturizing and more. It is solid at cold temperatures and often melted before use, either in the microwave or directly in a frying pan on the hob.

Assorted canned beans (black, kidney, white, chickpeas): If your storecupbaord is stocked with beans, you can always easily whip up a quick protein-packed meal. Always buy 'no salt added', and be sure to rinse and drain your beans to remove about 40 per cent of the sodium.

Low-sodium chicken, beef and vegetable stock: Whether you're making soup, braising meat or cooking sauce, you'll need stock. Stocks also add flavour when used for simmering legumes.

Sesame oil: This is a must for many Asian dishes. All you need is a teaspoon or two to add significant flavour – it's potent!

Nuts (pistachios, almonds, walnuts, pecans, cashews, pine nuts): Whether used as a garnish or eaten as a snack, nuts are a versatile part of any storecupboard, and are packed with healthy fats, protein and antioxidants.

Seeds (hemp, chia, sunflower): These superfoods can be used as a nutritional garnish or more completely, like in pudding, salad dressing or

baked goods. I love the pleasantly nutty taste of hemp hearts, which are called for in a few of these recipes. They are an excellent source of protein, omega-3 fatty acids, magnesium and dietary fibre.

Low-sodium soy sauce: Not only is soy sauce an essential part of Asian dishes like stir-fries and soups, but it's also great to have on hand to add salty umami flavour to pretty much anything. Soy sauce does typically contain gluten, so if your diet is gluten-free, look for a brand that works for you, or try alternatives like tamari and coconut aminos.

Flours (tapioca, almond flour, coconut flour): Whether you're gluten-free or just want to infuse more nutrients into your meals, these less-processed wheat-free flours are the ones to have. They have a low glycaemic index, so they won't give you that sugar-level rollercoaster feeling.

Vinegars (red wine, rice, balsamic, apple cider): Having a variety of vinegars on hand allows you to make all different kinds of dressings in a pinch, or even to create marinades, glazes and sauces for veggies and proteins.

Dried herbs and spices (chilli powder, parsley, rosemary, thyme, basil, curry powder, coriander, oregano, paprika, cumin, garlic powder, chilli flakes, bay leaves, onion powder): These are the seasonings I use every week and consider must-haves to add healthy, low-calorie flavour to anything.

Sea salt and peppercorns (with a grinder): When using freshly ground pepper and salt, you don't need as much because of its freshness. They're also less processed!

Dried fruits (apricots, raisins, cranberries): Dried fruit jazzes up even the most lacklustre salad, but it can also be tossed with nuts for a snack that's just sweet enough.

Bottled sauces (tomato-basil, teriyaki): When there's just no time to make a sauce from scratch, having healthy canned and jarred options on hand can take a lot of pressure off dinner plans – just make sure there are no additives or other processed ingredients such as dairy, xanthan gum or sugar in the sauce.

Worcestershire sauce: For making robust stews and grilled and barbecued dishes in the summertime, this sauce is crucial.

Canned coconut milk: I like to cook with full-fat coconut milk, but if you're watching your calories and fat count, the light stuff works great, too. Use it to marinate chicken, stir into curries and soups, flavour sauces or even add into porridge. Coconut cream is an excellent substitute for cream in many sauces. It infuses a dish with healthy fatty acids and naturally hydrating electrolytes. To get coconut cream, as it will be called for in some ingredient lists here, chill a can of full-fat coconut milk for at least 24 hours without disturbing it. When you open the can, carefully scoop out the white solids from the top – that's the coconut cream (discard the liquid left in the can or reserve it for another use). One 400g can typically makes about 240ml of the coconut cream.

Tahini: This condiment, usually sold in paste form, is made from ground sesame seeds. It's my favourite finish on bowl meals – I'll roast some spiralized veggies, throw in some quinoa and drizzle over some tahini and lemon juice for a quick, easy, flavourful meal.

Nut butter: When making nut butter-based sauces (like a Thai peanut sauce), it's important to have a healthy, smooth nut butter with no added sugars. I like almond butter best, but peanut and cashew are great, too. Stock your cupboard with what you like!

Curry paste (red and green): Curry pastes are essential to, well, curries, but they also work well as a marinade for veggies and stirred into yogurt-based sauces or even meatball mixes.

Nutritional yeast flakes: This versatile vegan ingredient enables you to make dishes taste cheesy without the cheese. These flakes can be puréed into sauces like Alfredo (page 55) or simply sprinkled like a grated cheese on top of salads.

Healthy grains (quinoa, lentils, farro, barley): These grains are sustainable sources of protein and nutrients, making them ideal to keep you feeling full and nourished.

Maple syrup and honey: I keep these sweeteners on hand for baked goods and dressings.

Dijon mustard: A quality grainy Dijon mustard can be used in many different ways; for tart dressings and vinaigrettes, for crusting fish and meat or obviously as a spread. It's low in calories and adds a strong bite of flavour!

Canned tomatoes (whole peeled, diced, chopped) and tomato purée: A storecupboard is not complete without canned tomatoes, which are used in sauces, soups and stews, braises and so many others. These are especially helpful in the wintertime, when fresh tomatoes aren't available. Opt for 'no salt added' when possible.

Olive oil cooking spray: I try to avoid using rapeseed oil in my cooking because many are genetically modified and partially hydrogenated, so I always buy olive oil cooking spray. Certain spiralized veggies (like courgettes) just need a few spritzes of spray in a heated pan.

Water-packed tuna (chunk light): An easy-to-use lean protein, water-packed tuna is low in calories and packed with essential omega-3s. Try tossing it together with courgette noodles, lemon juice and chilli flakes for a quick dish.

Other storecupboard items
There are some storecupboard items that aren't crucial, but as you grow your storecupboard and start cooking more, you may want to include them as well.

Ground flaxseed: Sprinkled over salads and breakfast bowls, flaxseed adds a nutty, textural topping that's high in antioxidants and omega-3s.

Gluten-free oats: Not only for breakfast and cookies, oats are also great to fold into meatball mix as a binding alternative to bread crumbs.

Other spices: Nutmeg, cinnamon, ground ginger, turmeric, herbes de Provence, garam masala, Chinese five-spice.

Tools

This probably won't shock you, but I'm kind of a gadget nut. I own everything from a 4-minute pizza maker to a strawberry huller. Those may not be essential to an Inspiralized kitchen, but there are certain kitchen tool must-haves that I use regularly and couldn't cook healthfully without.

Wok: If you're cooking more than two large spiralized vegetables, you will need to do so in batches or use a larger vessel, such as a wok. I use my wok when I'm making dinners for more than two people, since it's large enough to hold all the noodles before they wilt and cook down.

Food processor: Some of the recipes here require a food processor, a tool that allows you to make your own healthy sauces and dressings. Sometimes you can get around it by chopping ingredients super small and stirring them together, but I promise this tool is worth the investment. Most important, you can't make spiralized rice without it!

Tongs: Once you start spiralizing, you'll be doing a lot of tossing, which requires a pair of delicate but sturdy tongs. I prefer stainless steel with a rubber grip, which are strong but gentle enough to handle the daintiest of vegetable noodles.

Vegetable peeler: Many vegetables need to be peeled before they're spiralized (if their flesh is unpleasant or inedible). Certain veggies have tough, knobby exteriors that are difficult to peel. Look for a solid peeler that has a rubber grip for leverage and a stainless-steel blade.

Round palm brush: In my kitchen, I keep a separate brush for the spiralizer – one that has tough bristles and a palm grip. Don't try to use a regular sponge to clean the blades of your spiralizer – the tool will eat it right up. See page 16 for more details on how to clean the spiralizer.

Quality chef's knife: One of the first things I did when I started Inspiralized was invest in a sharp, good-quality chef's knife. My world changed – preparing food for cooking is infinitely better with a great knife, and you don't know until you know.

Non-stick frying pans: Vegetable noodles can be fragile, so non-stick frying pans are all I ever use when cooking them to avoid breakage. When purchasing a set of non-stick frying pans, look for PFOA-free ones.

HOW TO USE THIS COOKBOOK

When I brought the spiralizer home for the first time, I was eager to get started. I'm sure you're feeling excited and ready to start making these recipes. But before you dig in, I have just a few more notes. My goal with this cookbook is not only to inform you of every nuance of spiralizing, but also to prepare you for it. I want you to have a seamless experience when following along, so I've designed it to be as user-friendly as possible. The recipes here are divided by vegetable or fruit, rather than by type of dish as they were in *Inspiralized*. The Apple section, for example, features recipes using spiralized apples. This way, you can cook with what's in season, what's fresh at the market or what you already have on hand. In fact, I encourage you to cook your way down the whole produce aisle!

Each recipe also includes a section called Also Works Well With. Here, I'll list other vegetables that would spiralize well in that recipe. For example, the Broccoli Raab and Sausage Parsnip Pasta (page 172) calls for parsnips, but it would also work well with spiralized butternut squash. This flexibility is one of the things I love most about spiralizing – it truly transforms the way you think about produce and encourages you to eat something you may never have considered before. With an easy swap, a simple tomato-basil courgette pasta can also become a celeriac pasta or a sweet potato pasta. Although Courgette is on page 100 in this book, it's a great place to start. Once you're acquainted with this veggie, you'll understand the full potential of spiralizing and realize that the possibilities are truly endless.

The spiralized ingredient in each recipe will be written in this format:

1 medium courgette, spiralized with BLADE C**, noodles trimmed**

To translate, the vegetable should be spiralized prior to beginning the recipe, along with all the other ingredient preparation like slicing and dicing. Whichever blade is specified is the one you should use to spiralize. If we're making rice, it will say that, too. If you see the star vegetable listed, but it *doesn't* indicate which blade to use, you will find those instructions in the recipe steps, as that specific preparation needs to happen at a specific time. This will come up for making noodle buns, or for making macaroni-style noodles or crisps, like with Grams's Tuna and Macaroni Salad (page 48). It will also come up when a recipe requires a longer cooking method; instead of setting up a full *mise en place*, the spiralizing can happen while another part of the recipe is cooking in order to save time. But in general, when tackling the recipes in this book or otherwise, I strongly encourage you to read the whole recipe first, and to fully prepare the ingredients as listed. This way, you won't have to turn off the hob mid-simmer with an 'Oops, I forgot to finely chop the garlic!' Your whole cooking experience will be more harmonious.

Indicators

Each recipe includes a bunch of indicators to give you an at-a-glance overview.

DIFFICULTY LEVEL

The number of spirals signifies how difficult the recipe is to make.

- **One spiral:** Very easy, no or not much cooking required, basic spiralizing

- **Two spirals:** Medium difficulty, more preparation or cooking required

- **Three spirals:** Most difficult, many steps required and more handling of the spiralized vegetables

But don't let a three-spiral recipe intimidate you – it mainly means that the recipe will take you more time, on account of the extra steps involved. Each recipe also indicates how long it will take to prep and cook so that you can prepare – mentally and logistically.

Diet and feature classification

If you follow a certain dietary lifestyle, I've included indicators to classify the recipes by diet:

Vegan

Vegetarian

Gluten-free

Paleo

Dairy-free: This dietary feature is new to this book, indicating that the recipe contains no dairy.

Dairy-free (opt.): This indication means that the dairy listed in the ingredients is not integral to the dish and can be omitted without sacrificing much flavour.

I've also included some non-dietary cooking features to give you a bit more background information on each dish.

Low-cal: Under 300 calories per serving.

No Cook: Doesn't require any heated cooking, so it is mostly assembly-based.

Saves Well: Works well as leftovers (so you may want to make extra!).

One Pot: Cooked in one pan or pot for the easiest washing up.

All recipes include the following nutritional information: calories, carbohydrates, protein, fat, fibre and sugar. This information was calculated primarily using data from the USDA National Nutrient Database for Standard Reference.

A note about salt

In my opinion, salt should always be added according to your taste preferences, but sparingly – at least to start! You can always add more, but it's impossible to take out. And if you're cooking for other people, remember that everyone's taste buds are different. Aside from a couple of baked goods, you won't find many recipes in this book that necessitate a specific amount of salt. I will, however, indicate when you should salt 'generously'. Almost always, I instruct to 'taste and adjust the seasoning to your preference'. Seasoning is crucial, so don't skip it! Stick a spoon into the dressing or sauce, give it a taste and then adjust accordingly. Just be mindful of how much salt you add, as too much can cause issues like high blood pressure, which can lead to scarier issues like heart failure and obesity.

Now you know all of my spiralized secrets! If you're a new cook, you're about to surprise yourself with how easily you can whip up nutritious and flavoursome meals. If you're a seasoned cook, you'll enliven your repertoire with this new technique. I've made a point to offer recipes that are foolproof, filling meals that you'll want to come back to all the time and will soon become a part of your weekly dinner rotation. Ready? Time to *Inspiralize Everything*!

Apple

Before Inspiralized, apples were really only for baking into pies, making fruit salads, snacking on or to pick as a totally Instagrammable autumn activity. They come in so many varieties with beautiful colours and unique flavour profiles; there's definitely an apple out there for everyone! If you like tart, opt for a Granny Smith, but if you like sweet, grab a Fuji. Try them all and see what tickles your taste buds.

Once Inspiralized, apples take on a new life — they're integral to bountiful salads, stirred into yogurt for a sweet crunch and served up as toppings to starters and meats. They're even useful as an edible garnish, like in the Creamy Roasted Butternut Squash Soup with Apple Noodles on page 28. By spiralizing apples, you'll uncover their true potential.

NUTRITIONAL BENEFITS: Apples are loaded with vitamin C, which is where the old saying 'An apple a day keeps the doctor away' comes from. They also contain high amounts of fibre and have been proven to reduce levels of LDL, the 'bad' cholesterol.

PREPARATION AND STORAGE: Remove the stem prior to spiralizing. I don't recommend saving spiralized apples due to browning, but if you must, seal spiralized apple in an airtight container covered with water and a bit of lemon juice for up to 2 days.

BEST BLADES TO USE
- Blade C
- Blade D

BEST COOKING METHODS
- Raw
- Sauté in a frying pan over a medium heat for 5 minutes

Crabless Crab Cakes
with Green Apple Guacamole

Vegetarian
Gluten-free
Dairy-free

TIME TO PREP 30 minutes
TIME TO COOK 15 minutes
SERVES 4–6

NUTRITIONAL INFORMATION
(for 1 of 6 servings)
Calories: 311
Fat: 21 g
Sodium: 725 mg
Carbohydrate: 30 g
Fibre: 6 g
Sugar: 8 g
Protein: 5 g

Yes, these crab cakes are crabless! It seems like an oxymoron, but once you make them, you'll get it – and smell it. Thanks to Old Bay seasoning, Dijon mustard and hearts of palm, these cakes are fit for a steakhouse. The proverbial cherry on top is definitely the green apple guacamole. Its tart sweetness ties all the flavours together, offering a refreshing balance to the potent Old Bay. The spiralizer creates the perfect apple noodle to give each forkful a crunch!

For the cakes
Kernels from 4 medium ears of sweetcorn (about 280g)
30g onion, finely chopped
30g green pepper, finely chopped
60ml mayonnaise (I prefer homemade or vegan – see Tip)
425g canned whole hearts of palm or artichoke hearts, drained, diced and lightly smashed
2 teaspoons Old Bay seasoning (find online or use cajun seasoning)
2 tablespoons chopped fresh flat-leaf parsley
2 teaspoons Dijon mustard
40g gluten-free breadcrumbs, plus extra as needed, or 50g ground almonds
Salt and pepper

For the guacamole
3 avocados, cubed
2 large garlic cloves, finely chopped
Juice of 2 limes
Salt and pepper
2 jalapeño chillies, deseeded and finely chopped
1 small red onion, diced
2 vine tomatoes, deseeded and diced
10g fresh coriander, chopped
1 large green apple, spiralized with BLADE C

2 tablespoons extra-virgin olive oil

1 Heat a large frying pan over a medium-high heat. When water flicked onto the pan sizzles, add the corn, onion and pepper and cook for 3–5 minutes until tender. Transfer 225g of the mixture to a food processor and pulse until coarse-smooth. Transfer to a medium bowl and add the mayonnaise, hearts of palm, Old Bay, parsley, mustard and breadcrumbs. Season with salt and pepper and stir well.

2 Line a baking sheet with baking paper. Using your hands, form the mixture into twelve cakes, 5cm in diameter, and transfer to the prepared baking sheet. Chill for 10–15 minutes to bind.

3 Make the guacamole. Place all the guacamole ingredients in a medium bowl and stir together until combined but some chunks of avocado still remain. Taste and adjust the seasoning to your preferences, adding more salt, coriander, lime or jalapeño as needed. Chill until ready to serve.

4 Heat 1 tablespoon of the olive oil in a large frying pan over a medium-high heat. When the oil is shimmering, add six cakes and cook for 2 minutes on each side or until golden brown. Transfer to a platter. Wipe down the pan, add another tablespoon of the oil, and cook the remaining cakes.

5 Serve two or three cakes and about 125ml of guacamole on each plate.

I prefer to make my own mayonnaise to ensure that the ingredients are wholesome. Or I'll use a vegan brand. To make your own, in a food processor or by hand, blend together 1 egg yolk and 1½ teaspoons fresh lemon juice. While whisking rapidly to emulsify, slowly stream in 125ml avocado oil, 1 teaspoon at a time. Season with salt and pepper.

Creamy Roasted Butternut Squash Soup
with Apple Noodles

Vegan
Vegetarian
Gluten-free
Paleo
Dairy-free

TIME TO PREP 10 minutes
TIME TO COOK 1 hour
SERVES 4

NUTRITIONAL INFORMATION
Calories: 370
Fat: 13 g
Sodium: 396 mg
Carbohydrate: 57 g
Fibre: 12 g
Sugar: 30 g
Protein: 4 g

ALSO WORKS WELL WITH
Pear

Spiralized vegetables and fruits don't always have to be the main attraction of a dish – they work exquisitely as garnishes, too. Actually, that was their original purpose. They artistically topped dishes in restaurants, where the highlight of a meal is frequently its inventive presentation. While they're a nice finishing touch in this cosy dish, they also offer a sweet zing and cold crunch that elevates this classic autumnal soup.

1 large butternut squash (about 1.3kg), halved lengthways and deseeded

1 tablespoon coconut oil, melted

Salt and pepper

2 teaspoons extra-virgin olive oil

1 small shallot, finely chopped

2 garlic cloves, finely chopped

$\frac{1}{8}$ teaspoon ground nutmeg (just a pinch)

1 teaspoon chilli powder

475ml reduced-salt vegetable or chicken stock

425ml canned light coconut milk

2 sweet red apples (I like Gala)

1 tablespoon roasted and salted shelled pumpkin seeds

If your taste buds prefer a sweeter soup, stir in a teaspoon or two of maple syrup.

1 Preheat the oven to 220°C/425°F. Line a baking sheet with baking paper. Put the butternut squash cut-side up on the prepared baking sheet and drizzle the inside of the squash with the coconut oil. Rub it in with your fingertips or a brush. Season with salt and pepper. Flip over the squash and bake for 45 minutes or until the flesh is easily pierced with a fork. Leave to cool for 5–10 minutes or until cool enough to handle. Use a spoon to scoop out the flesh and transfer it to a bowl, discarding the skin.

2 While the squash cooks, heat the olive oil in a medium frying pan over a medium heat. When the oil is shimmering, add the shallot and cook for 3 minutes or until softened. Add the garlic and cook for 30 seconds or until fragrant.

3 Transfer the shallot and garlic to a high-speed blender. Add the squash, nutmeg, chilli powder, stock, coconut milk and salt and pepper to taste and pulse for about 1 minute until creamy. Taste and adjust the seasoning to your preferences.

4 When the soup is blended, spiralize the apples with **BLADE D**. Divide the soup among four bowls and add apple noodles, pumpkin seeds and more pepper.

Apple-walnut Muffins

When I was in school, my mother used to buy giant, grapefruit-sized muffins and freeze them. After school, she'd take one out, toast it and slice it – then we'd all devour it in a matter of seconds. My favourite flavours were always the ones with nuts or fruit. These muffins are my healthy version, using real, whole ingredients like mashed bananas, cinnamon and coconut oil, which give them an extra nutrient and flavour boost. They are best served with strong coffee and a sunny disposition.

Vegetarian
Gluten-free
Paleo
Low-cal
Saves Well

TIME TO PREP 20 minutes
TIME TO COOK 30 minutes

MAKES 6 large or
12 mini muffins

NUTRITIONAL INFORMATION
(for 1 of 6 servings)
Calories: 226
Fat: 7 g
Sodium: 230 mg
Carbohydrate: 21 g
Fibre: 5 g
Sugar: 11 g
Protein: 6 g

ALSO WORKS WELL WITH
Pear

Cooking spray

55g coconut flour

¾ teaspoon bicarbonate of soda

½ teaspoon salt

2 teaspoons ground cinnamon

½ teaspoon ground nutmeg

3 large eggs

3 tablespoons maple syrup

2 teaspoons vanilla extract

2 tablespoons plain unsweetened almond milk

1 tablespoon coconut oil, melted and cooled to room temperature

1 ripe banana, mashed

1 Honeycrisp apple, spiralized with BLADE B, *noodles trimmed*

55g chopped walnuts

1 Preheat the oven to 180°C/350°F. Coat a large muffin tin with cooking spray and line the wells with strips of baking paper or paper cases.

2 In a medium bowl, combine the coconut flour, bicarbonate of soda, salt, cinnamon and nutmeg. In a separate medium bowl, combine the eggs, maple syrup, vanilla, almond milk, coconut oil and banana. Add the dry ingredients to the wet. Add the apple and stir until the batter is smooth. Fold in the walnuts.

3 Pour the batter into the prepared muffin tin and bake for 30 minutes or until a toothpick inserted into the centre of a muffin comes out clean.

To move these muffins from breakfast to dessert, add some dark chocolate chunks or a tablespoon of unsweetened raw cacao powder to the batter.

Curried Apple Egg Salad Wrap

Vegetarian
Gluten-free
Low-cal
No Cook

TIME TO PREP 20 minutes
SERVES 2–4

NUTRITIONAL INFORMATION
(for 1 of 2 servings)
Calories: 199
Fat: 4 g
Sodium: 135 mg
Carbohydrate: 28 g
Fibre: 4 g
Sugar: 18 g
Protein: 15 g

If you asked me what kind of photos consistently receive the most 'likes' on the Inspiralized Instagram account, the answer would undoubtedly be my spring green wraps. I love creating this bulging burrito-style lunch using spring greens and spiralized veggies. This egg salad version is rich with flavour from the curry powder in my classic fayonnaise, made with Greek yogurt for a lighter choice that's higher in protein and lower in fat. Its creamy texture gets a surprisingly crunchy bite thanks to the celery and apple noodles. The egg salad can be prepped ahead of time and kept in the fridge for up to three days, making it ideal for work lunches. If you can't find spring greens, then use round lettuce or romaine instead.

For the curried fayonnaise
150ml plus 2 tablespoons natural 0% Greek yogurt

1 tablespoon wholegrain or Dijon mustard

½ teaspoon garlic powder

1 tablespoon fresh lemon juice

½ teaspoon curry powder

Salt and pepper

⅛ teaspoon cayenne pepper

For the apple mixture and wrap
1 apple

2 tablespoons raisins

50g celery, diced

1 hard-boiled egg, peeled and chopped

2 large or 4 small spring green leaves, stems trimmed

40g alfalfa sprouts

1 Make the fayonnaise: Combine all the fayonnaise ingredients in a large bowl and whisk until combined. Set aside.

2 Make the apple mixture: Slice the apple halfway through lengthways to create a slit, being careful not to pierce through its centre. Spiralize using **BLADE B**. Add the apple, raisins, celery and egg to the bowl with the fayonnaise. Toss to combine thoroughly.

3 Pack the egg salad into the middle of the spring green leaves, dividing it evenly. Top with sprouts and roll like a burrito, tucking in the ends. Secure both ends with a toothpick and halve before serving.

Not a fan of the curry flavour? Omit it from the fayonnaise and make this a regular egg salad sandwich.

Ginger Pear and Apple Sangria

Vegetarian
Dairy-free
No Cook

TIME TO COOK 4 hours
SERVES 6

NUTRITIONAL INFORMATION
Calories: 312
Fat: 0 g
Sodium: 10 mg
Carbohydrate: 44 g
Fibre: 1 g
Sugar: 38 g
Protein: 0 g

My university room-mate Stacey used to make the best cocktails. On Friday mornings, she would prepare a batch of sangria and leave it in the fridge, and then we'd enjoy it later that night, once classes were finished. Stacey's sangria was fun and festive and always signified the best part of the week: the start of the weekend. What I loved most was that she always used a lot of fresh fruit – and the chunks of alcohol-soaked fruit were fun to eat! This spiralized version looks even prettier than the original with its elegant and colourful spirals. While Stacey always made red sangria, I've updated my version to use white wine and a hint of ginger beer. Bring on summer!

1 (750-ml) bottle Sauvignon Blanc (or other dry white wine)

125ml white rum

60ml brandy

1 (350ml) bottle ginger beer

1 tablespoon honey

1 Gala apple, spiralized with BLADE C

1 William pear, spiralized with BLADE C

1 In a large serving jug, combine the wine, rum, brandy, ginger beer and honey. Stir until the honey has dissolved. Add the apple and pear noodles and stir.

2 Enjoy immediately, or for best results, chill for at least 4 hours and up to 8 hours before serving.

Beetroot

Beetroots are my jam! They're sweet and earthy all at once. They are always in season, are readily available in supermarkets and tend to be the ideal size for spiralizing. Beetroot come in several different varieties, although red ones tend to hog the spotlight. Some of my other favourites are the golden beetroot and the Chioggia beetroot, which resembles a peppermint cane with its stripes. They're common in Mediterranean cooking, but they work well in all different cuisines, as you'll see here.

While beetroot have a lot going for them, the red ones get messy no matter how you prepare them – whether roasted in foil or spiralized raw, they'll bleed. To avoid staining your hands, wear gloves when handling them. I have reusable kitchen gloves just for this purpose! To avoid staining your spiralizer, wash it immediately after use. If need be, scrub your hands or spiralizer with warm water and sea salt to help remove discoloration.

NUTRITIONAL BENEFITS: Beetroot significantly help lower blood pressure thanks to their naturally occurring nitrates. Their concentration of betaine helps fight inflammation. In addition to immune-boosting vitamin C, beetroot contain powerful phytonutrients that may help ward off cancers. In fact, beetroot extract is a popular ingredient in natural cancer-fighting supplements.

PREPARATION AND STORAGE: Peel the beetroot completely, then slice off the ends to make flat, even surfaces. Store in an airtight container in the fridge for up to 5 days. Beetroot noodles can also be frozen for up to 8 months for future use.

BEST BLADES TO USE
- Blade C
- Blade D

BEST COOKING METHODS
- Raw
- Boil for 2–3 minutes
- Sauté over a medium-high heat for 7 minutes
- Roast at 220°C/425°F for 5–10 minutes

Spiced Lamb Skewers
with Beetroot Noodles

Gluten-free

TIME TO PREP 20 minutes
TIME TO COOK 20 minutes
SERVES 4

NUTRITIONAL INFORMATION
Calories: 443
Fat: 34 g
Sodium: 112 mg
Carbohydrate: 10 g
Fibre: 2 g
Sugar: 2 g
Protein: 25g

ALSO WORKS WELL WITH
Sweet Potato, Butternut
Squash, Broccoli, Swede

Since launching Inspiralized, I feel like I've circled the globe by way of food. I'm always looking to healthfully re-imagine my and my readers' favourite meals found while travelling. After one of my readers came back from her honeymoon in Turkey, she wondered if I could re-create the lamb skewers she'd enjoyed there. Challenge accepted. Here we have beetroot noodles that enhance the flavours in the meat and pair well with the yogurt sauce. I'm humbled to be able to bring back someone else's happy memory – and to make a new one for myself.

For the beetroot noodles

2 large red beetroots, peeled, spiralized with BLADE C **and noodles trimmed**

Salt and pepper

For the skewers

450g lamb mince

1 teaspoon ground cumin

2 teaspoons ground coriander

¼ teaspoon paprika

2 garlic cloves, very finely chopped

1 tablespoon finely chopped fresh mint

Salt and pepper

1 tablespoon extra-virgin olive oil

For the yogurt sauce

125ml natural 0% Greek yogurt

1 tablespoon finely chopped shallot

2 teaspoons finely chopped fresh coriander

2 teaspoons fresh lemon juice

¼ teaspoon paprika

Salt and pepper

40g chopped roasted pistachios, to garnish

Mint leaves, to garnish

1 Make the beetroot noodles. Preheat the oven to 220°C/425°F. Line a baking sheet with baking paper and arrange the beetroot noodles on it, spacing them apart. Season with salt and pepper. Roast for 10–15 minutes or until al dente.

2 Meanwhile, make the skewers. In a large bowl, stir together all the ingredients for the skewers except the olive oil. Form the mixture into eight balls, then thread them onto four metal or soaked wooden skewers.

3 Heat the olive oil in a large griddle pan or frying pan over a medium-high heat. When the oil is shimmering, add the skewers and cook for 5 minutes on each side, flattening the meat mixture slightly with a spatula.

4 Meanwhile, make the yogurt sauce. Whisk together all the ingredients for the yogurt sauce in a small bowl.

5 Divide the beetroot noodles among four plates and top with one skewer each. Drizzle with the yogurt sauce and garnish with pistachios and mint leaves.

If lamb isn't your thing, try turkey mince. If you don't eat meat, the vegetarian meatballs on page 95 work well instead.

Tahini Beetroot Noodle Bowl with Falafel

Vegetarian
Gluten-free
Dairy-free
Low-cal

TIME TO PREP 25 minutes
TIME TO COOK 1 hour
SERVES 4

NUTRITIONAL INFORMATION
Calories: 266
Fat: 15 g
Sodium: 359 mg
Carbohydrate: 30 g
Fibre: 10 g
Sugar: 7 g
Protein: 10 g

ALSO WORKS WELL WITH
Butternut Squash, Sweet Potato

Somewhere along the way on my Inspiralized journey, I fell in love with tahini. Tahini sauces complement almost every single meat, grain and vegetable out there. Maple-tahini, lemon-tahini, garlic-tahini, avocado-tahini – I've tried them all. Made from ground sesame seeds, this paste has a nutty flavour that just seems to go with everything. Here, the falafel, beetroot and tomatoes are full of robust Mediterranean flavour – a perfect match for my beloved tahini. This homemade falafel is a lighter version, baked instead of fried. Trust me – this dish will transport you to your favourite falafel spot.

3 tablespoons chopped fresh parsley

2 garlic cloves, finely chopped

1 teaspoon lemon zest

Juice of 1 large lemon

1¼ teaspoons ground cumin

1 teaspoon ground coriander

¼ teaspoon chilli powder

Salt and pepper

425g canned chickpeas, rinsed, drained and patted dry

25g almond flour

30g red onion, diced

2 large beetroots, peeled, spiralized with BLADE D and noodles trimmed

1 tablespoon chopped fresh coriander

85g cherry tomatoes, quartered and deseeded

75g cucumber, diced

1 teaspoon extra-virgin olive oil

For the tahini dressing

2 tablespoons tahini

1 tablespoon fresh lemon juice

1 teaspoon honey

⅓ teaspoon garlic powder

1 tablespoon extra-virgin olive oil

Salt and pepper

1 Preheat the oven to 190°C/375°F. Line a baking sheet with baking paper.

2 Make the falafel. In a food processor, combine the parsley, garlic, lemon zest, lemon juice, cumin, coriander, chilli powder and salt and pepper to taste. Pulse for about 30 seconds to completely combine. Add the chickpeas and pulse until incorporated but still chunky.

3 Transfer the mixture to a medium bowl and add the almond flour and onion. Mix again to form a dough. Using your hands, form the mixture into eight balls and place them on the prepared baking sheet. Press down with a spatula to flatten them into patties, cupping to keep them compact. Chill for 15 minutes to firm up.

4 Transfer the baking sheet to the oven and bake for 35–40 minutes or until the patties are firm and browned, flipping once halfway through.

5 Spread the beetroots on the second prepared baking sheet, spacing them apart, and roast with the falafel for 15 minutes or until al dente.

6 Meanwhile, in a small bowl, combine the coriander, tomatoes, cucumbers and olive oil. Season with salt and pepper and set aside.

7 Make the tahini dressing. Place all the ingredients for the dressing in a food processor and pulse until creamy. Slowly add 1–2 tablespoons water as needed to thin. Taste and adjust the seasoning to your preferences. Set aside.

8 Divide the beetroot noodles among four bowls and top each with two falafel patties and a spoonful of the tomato mixture. Drizzle with the tahini dressing to finish, and serve immediately.

For a crispier, more traditional falafel, heat 2 tablespoons olive oil in a frying pan and sear the patties for 2 minutes on each side before transferring to the oven.

Chicken Tagine
with Apricot Golden Beetroot Rice

Gluten-free

TIME TO PREP 15 minutes
TIME TO COOK 45 minutes
SERVES 4

NUTRITIONAL INFORMATION
Calories: 403
Fat: 22 g
Sodium: 517 mg
Carbohydrate: 21 g
Fibre: 4 g
Sugar: 10 g
Protein: 28 g

ALSO WORKS WELL WITH
Turnip, Butternut Squash,
Carrot, Kohlrabi, Celeriac,
Sweet Potato

My inspiration for this chicken dish came from Daniel Boulud's Mediterranean French restaurant Boulud Sud in New York City. I saw the recipe featured in the *New York Times*, made it and loved it. In fact, I loved it so much that I decided to Inspiralize it. Although the spiralized version is not nearly as elaborate as the original, this traditional North African stew boasts robust, deeply spiced flavours. It is typically served over a starch like couscous, but here we use golden beetroot rice instead, which adds beautiful colour, as well as nutrients such as fibre and calcium.

1 tablespoon extra-virgin olive oil

675g chicken legs and thighs

Salt and pepper

½ yellow onion, diced

2 carrots, diced

2 garlic cloves, fincly chopped

1 (1cm) piece fresh ginger, peeled and finely chopped

½ teaspoon ground coriander

½ teaspoon ground cumin

¼ teaspoon ground cinnamon

350ml reduced-salt chicken stock

20g flaked blanched almonds

40g dried apricots, chopped

140g canned chickpeas, rinsed and drained

2 large golden beetroots, peeled, spiralized with BLADE D, *then riced (see page 16)*

1 tablespoon fresh coriander, to garnish (optional)

1 Heat the olive oil in a large casserole or pot with a lid over a medium-high heat. Season the chicken with salt and pepper. When the oil is shimmering, add the chicken to the pan without crowding, working in batches if necessary. Sear the chicken for about 7 minutes, flipping once, until both sides are golden brown. Set aside on a plate.

2 Immediately add the onion and carrots to the pan, season with salt and pepper and cook for 5–7 minutes until softening.

3 Add the garlic to the pan and cook until fragrant, about 30 seconds. Add the ginger, coriander, cumin and cinnamon and cook, stirring, until fragrant, about 1 minute. Add 125ml of the chicken stock and scrape up any browned bits from the bottom of the pan.

recipe continues

4 Return the chicken to the pan, fitting the pieces into a single layer as best as possible. Pour over the remaining 225ml chicken stock. Increase the heat to high and bring the liquid to the boil. Reduce the heat to low, cover the pan and simmer for 25–30 minutes or until the chicken is no longer pink in the centre and its juices run clear.

5 Reserving the vegetables in the pot, transfer the chicken to a plate and cover with foil to keep warm. Add the almonds, apricots, chickpeas and beetroot rice to the pot. Increase the heat to medium-high and bring to a steady simmer. Reduce the heat to low, cover and cook for a further 5 minutes or until the beetroot rice softens.

6 Transfer the rice mixture to a serving platter and top with the chicken. Garnish with coriander, if you like, and serve immediately.

To minimize prep and for a different variety of sweetness, try tossing in sultanas in place of the apricots.

Green Curry Golden Beetroot Noodle Bowl

Vegan
Vegetarian
Gluten-free
Paleo

TIME TO PREP 15 minutes
TIME TO COOK 15 minutes
SERVES 4

NUTRITIONAL INFORMATION
Calories: 343
Fat: 24 g
Sodium: 316 mg
Carbohydrate: 25 g
Fibre: 9 g
Sugar: 11 g
Protein: 7 g

ALSO WORKS WELL WITH
Turnip, Radish, Courgette,
Cabbage, Carrot, Kohlrabi

This basic bowl is the perfect introduction to coconut curry. In fact, once you've mastered this recipe, I bet you'll be inspired to create your own version. You may want to try a red paste instead of green, or add protein – lentils, chicken and even a strong fish like salmon would work well on top. Maybe you want to include snap peas, broccoli or beansprouts in addition to or instead of the green beans that are called for here. Spiralized curry bowls are comforting, filling, easy and clearly customizable! Have fun with it.

1 tablespoon coconut oil

2 garlic cloves, finely chopped

2 teaspoons finely chopped fresh ginger

½ *small yellow onion, peeled, spiralized with* BLADE A, *noodles trimmed*

4 spring onions, diced, dark green parts kept separate

1½–2 tablespoons Thai green curry paste

425ml canned coconut milk

700ml reduced-salt vegetable stock

4 *small golden beetroots, peeled, spiralized with* BLADE A, *noodles trimmed*

115g green beans, ends trimmed

Salt

60g cashews

1 red bird's eye chilli, thinly sliced

Handful of fresh Thai basil or coriander leaves

1 Heat the coconut oil in a large pot over a medium-high heat. When the oil has melted, add the garlic, ginger, half of the onion noodles and the white and light green parts of the spring onions. Cook for 30 seconds or until fragrant, then carefully add the curry paste, watching out for splatter.

2 Add the coconut milk and stock to the frying pan and cook, stirring to combine, for 30 seconds. Add the beetroot noodles and green beans and season with salt. Reduce the heat to medium-low, add the cashews and simmer for 5–7 minutes or until the noodles are softened.

3 Divide the curry among four bowls and garnish with the dark green parts of the spring onions, chilli slices and Thai basil leaves.

Oven-fried Goat's Cheese with Figs, Bitter Greens and Beetroot Noodles

Vegetarian
Gluten-free

TIME TO PREP 10 minutes
TIME TO COOK 15 minutes
SERVES 4

NUTRITIONAL INFORMATION
Calories: 446
Fat: 31 g
Sodium: 381 mg
Carbohydrate: 18 g
Fibre: 8 g
Sugar: 9 g
Protein: 16 g

ALSO WORKS WELL WITH
Butternut Squash, Sweet Potato

The only thing better than cheese is warm cheese. Baked Brie and *queso* are a thing for a reason! This Inspiralized cheese plate offers the best of everything – savoury oven-fried cheese, nutritious greens, elegant fruit and crunchy vegetables. Take it up a notch with some sliced salami. This dish will add style to any party – try it with a light wine and good company.

40g flaked almonds, roughly chopped

1 (225g) log goat's cheese, chilled and sliced into 8 rounds

2 medium red beetroots, peeled, spiralized with BLADE D, noodles trimmed

Salt and pepper

For the dressing

3 tablespoons extra-virgin olive oil

2 tablespoons apple cider vinegar

1 teaspoon Dijon mustard

1 teaspoon finely chopped shallot

1 teaspoon fresh lemon juice

1 teaspoon honey

Salt and pepper

200g chicory

75g endives, chopped

4 fresh figs, quartered lengthways

To chop the almonds, place them in a food processor and pulse until no large pieces remain. Just make sure to stop before they're ground into a powder.

1 Preheat the oven to 180°C/350°F. Line two baking sheets with baking paper.

2 Spread the almonds over a small plate. Dip each goat's cheese round in the almonds and turn to coat all over, pressing the nuts to adhere. Place the coated goat's cheese rounds on one of the prepared baking sheets.

3 On the other baking sheet, lay out the beetroot noodles, spacing them apart, and season with salt and pepper.

4 Bake the goat's cheese and beetroot together for 10 minutes or until the cheese is warmed through and the beetroot noodles are al dente. Remove the beetroot noodles and leave to cool for 2 minutes. Turn the oven to the grill setting and bake the goat's cheese for a further 2 minutes or until the almond crust is golden brown, watching carefully to ensure the nuts don't burn.

5 Meanwhile, whisk together all the ingredients for the dressing in a large bowl.

6 Add the beetroot noodles, chicory and endives to the bowl with the dressing and toss to combine.

7 Divide the beetroot and greens mixture among four plates and top with with two baked goat's cheese rounds and figs.

Broccoli

Yes – broccoli! Most people are surprised when they hear that broccoli can be spiralized. Doing so is a great way to use the stem in addition to the florets to minimize waste and maximize your vegetable intake. You've probably seen broccoli slaw around, which uses julienned broccoli stems. Broccoli slaw is *okay*, but imagine using noodles that elevate the texture and turn that dish into a fully-fledged pasta alternative. Now imagine what else you can make!

Broccoli noodles are sturdy and therefore resilient, so they can be cooked pretty much any way. I most enjoy them boiled, as they fill up with water and take on the consistency of wholewheat pasta, similar to what happens with spiralized carrots. Just be sure to pick out broccoli stems that are large enough. At the very least, stems should be 4–5cm in width and 7.5–10cm in length for best results. Trick of the trade: Ask your local farmers to save more of the stem the next time they harvest the broccoli. They'll be flattered you asked!

NUTRITIONAL BENEFITS: Broccoli is a good source of lutein, a powerful antioxidant that also supports eye health. It's also packed with phytochemicals, which help the body detoxify, and fibre, which aids digestion.

PREPARATION AND STORAGE: Slice the stem off the broccoli head, preserving as much of it as possible. Trim the sides of the broccoli stem as much as you can without compromising its width, removing any thick pieces that stick out. Slice the ends off to leave flat, even surfaces. Store in an airtight container in the fridge for up to 5 days. Broccoli noodles can also be frozen for up to 8 months for future use.

BEST BLADES TO USE
- Blade D (if you're using a 3-blade spiralizer, use blade C)

BEST COOKING METHODS
- Boil for 2–3 minutes
- Sauté over a medium-high heat for 5–7 minutes
- Bake at 220°C/425°F for 10 minutes

Grams's Tuna and Macaroni Salad

〰〰 | Gluten-free
〰〰 | Dairy-free
      | Low-cal

TIME TO PREP 10 minutes
TIME TO COOK 10 minutes
plus 1 hour to chill
SERVES 2–4

NUTRITIONAL INFORMATION
Calories: 154
Fat: 1 g
Sodium: 289 mg
Carbohydrate: 12 g
Fibre: 3 g
Sugar: 5 g
Protein: 26 g

ALSO WORKS WELL WITH
Courgette, Kohlrabi

Any time my parents have the family over for a summer barbecue, my Grams brings her tuna and macaroni salad, and it's always a welcome treat. It might be the ratio of tuna to noodle or the exact amount of salt she uses – all I know is that it's addictive. Family recipes like this one are tough to re-create without the magic touch of a loving grandmother, but I've tried my hardest. I swapped in avocado fayonnaise for the mayonnaise in the tuna, and instead of macaroni pasta, I used boiled broccoli noodles for a lower-calorie and -carb option. While I still love the original, this spiralized one is second best. Maybe my grandkids will try to re-create it one day!

For the salad
Salt

2 broccoli stems, spiralized with** BLADE D, **noodles trimmed

2 (85g) cans tuna in water, drained

50g celery, diced

For the fayonnaise
½ large ripe avocado, mashed

1 teaspoon Dijon mustard

Salt and white pepper

1 teaspoon fresh lemon juice

¼ teaspoon garlic powder

1 Bring a medium pan filled halfway with salted water to the boil over a high heat. When the water is boiling, add the broccoli noodles and cook for 3 minutes or until al dente. Drain and pat dry thoroughly.

2 Meanwhile, whisk together all the ingredients for the fayonnaise in a large bowl until combined.

3 Add the cooked broccoli noodles, tuna and celery to the bowl with the fayonnaise. Season generously with salt and toss to combine thoroughly. For the best flavour, chill for at least 1 hour before serving.

〰〰〰〰〰〰〰〰

Grams doesn't do this, but you may want to add in a teaspoon of chopped dill into the fayonnaise for extra flavour.

〰〰〰〰〰〰〰〰

Sun-dried Tomato, Chicken and Broccoli Pasta

∼∼ Gluten-free
∼∼ Dairy-free (opt.)
Low-cal
Saves Well

TIME TO PREP 10 minutes
TIME TO COOK 15 minutes
SERVES 4

NUTRITIONAL INFORMATION
Calories: 240
Fat: 8 g
Sodium: 172 mg
Carbohydrate: 11 g
Fibre: 3 g
Sugar: 4 g
Protein: 32 g

ALSO WORKS WELL WITH
Courgette, Butternut
Squash, Sweet Potato,
Turnip, Pepper

At my first job out of university, I spent most of my lunch breaks at the local supermarket salad bar, packing as much as I could fit into their provided containers. This particular salad bar prepared a chilled sun-dried tomato and broccoli bow-tie pasta that was smothered in a garlicky Parmesan sauce. I still remember looking forward to my lunches just for that pasta! Now I've made an Inspiralized version, using broccoli noodles in place of those bow ties. While I haven't looked back since starting Inspiralized, I do sometimes think about those salad-bar lunches...

Salt and pepper

120g broccoli florets

2 broccoli stems, spiralized with BLADE D, noodles trimmed

1 tablespoon extra-virgin olive oil

450g skinless, boneless chicken breast, cut into 2.5cm pieces

1 teaspoon garlic powder

2 garlic cloves, finely chopped

1 tablespoon finely chopped shallot

30g sun-dried tomatoes (dried, not packed in oil), chopped

¼ teaspoon chilli flakes

20g grated Parmesan cheese

To make this dish vegetarian, replace the chicken with a 400g can of chickpeas, rinsed and drained.

1 Bring a medium pot filled halfway with salted water to the boil over a high heat. When the water is boiling, add the broccoli florets and broccoli noodles and cook for 3 minutes or until al dente. Drain and pat dry thoroughly.

2 Meanwhile, heat the olive oil in a large frying pan over a medium heat. Season the chicken with the garlic powder, salt and black pepper. When the oil is shimmering, add the chicken and cook for 3–5 minutes on each side or until browned on the outside and no longer pink inside. Transfer to a plate.

3 To the same pan, add the garlic, shallot, sun-dried tomatoes and chilli flakes. Cook for 1 minute or until the shallot is translucent. Stir in the broccoli florets, broccoli noodles and chicken and cook for 1 minute, tossing continuously to coat the florets in the oil.

4 Remove the frying pan from the heat, add the Parmesan and toss to combine. Divide among four bowls and serve.

Prawn Tom Kha
with Broccoli Noodles

Tom kha is a spicy and sour hot soup made with coconut milk that's most popular in Thailand and Laos. Luckily, you don't need to be in Southeast Asia to enjoy its enticing flavours. The broccoli noodles in their spiralized form are durable enough to stand up to the thick coconut milk, becoming infused with the flavours of the lemongrass and chilli. Each chopstick-full is more delightful than the last!

Gluten-free
Dairy-free
One Pot

TIME TO PREP 15 minutes
TIME TO COOK 20 minutes
SERVES 4

NUTRITIONAL INFORMATION
Calories: 317
Fat: 17 g
Sodium: 951 mg
Carbohydrate: 13 g
Fibre: 2 g
Sugar: 6 g
Protein: 28 g

ALSO WORKS WELL WITH
**Courgette, Kohlrabi,
Turnip, Mooli**

1 litre reduced-salt chicken stock

1 (2.5cm) piece fresh ginger or galangal, peeled and sliced

Zest of ½ lime

425ml canned full-fat coconut milk

120g broccoli florets

2 broccoli stems, spiralized with BLADE C, noodles trimmed

1 fresh lemongrass stalk, roughly cut into 5cm pieces

350g mushrooms (chestnut or button), stemmed and sliced

280g prawns, peeled and deveined

1½ tablespoons fish sauce

1½ tablespoons fresh lime juice

4 hot red chillies, thinly sliced

25g fresh coriander leaves, to garnish

1 Combine the stock, ginger and lime zest in a medium saucepan and bring to a simmer over a medium heat. Reduce the heat to low and simmer for 10 minutes.

2 Add the coconut milk, broccoli florets, broccoli noodles, lemongrass and mushrooms and return the heat to medium. Cook for 5 minutes or until the mushrooms are softened. Add the prawns and cook until pink, opaque and completely cooked through, 3–5 minutes.

3 Stir in the fish sauce and lime juice. Remove the pan from the heat, discard the lemongrass and divide the soup among four bowls. Garnish with the red chilli slices and coriander.

Galangal is a common ingredient in Thai food that's similar in look to ginger but extra fiery in taste. If you can't find it or prefer your Tom Kha with less heat, ginger will work just fine.

Butternut Squash

Taking one look at butternut squash, you'd think it would be a nightmare to spiralize – it's large, heavy and tough, and has an awkward, bulbous bottom. And it's a pain to cut up with a knife! But butternut squash is one of the easiest vegetables to spiralize and makes a plentiful amount of noodles. Just one of these medium veggies can feed up to four people, depending on the dish! Its delicate sweetness makes it one of my favourites to eat in the winter.

When you're picking yours out, ripeness matters – a squash that isn't ripe enough will be too tough to slice, even with the spiralizer, and it won't taste as great, either. A ripe squash should be a dull orange colour with no shiny skin or major blemishes. Choose one that has a longer neck, since that's the part that makes noodles. As for the round bottom, I like to slice it into chunks, roast them and save them in the fridge to toss into salads and pasta dishes, or even to snack on!

NUTRITIONAL BENEFITS: This squash contains a high amount of dietary fibre, making it heart-healthy. It's packed with potassium, which contributes to bone health, and vitamin B, which boosts your immune system and metabolism.

PREPARATION AND STORAGE: Peel the squash using a vegetable peeler. Slice off the bulbous end, maintaining as much of the long neck as possible. Slice the other end off to leave a flat, even surface. If the squash is longer than 15cm, halve it crossways for better leverage. Store in an airtight container in the fridge for up to 5 days. Butternut squash noodles can also be frozen for up to 8 months for future use.

BEST BLADES TO USE
- Blade A
- Blade B
- Blade C
- Blade D

BEST COOKING METHODS
- Roast at 200°C/400°F for 8–10 minutes

Butternut Squash Rice and Beans

≈≈ Vegan
≈≈ Vegetarian
Gluten-free
Dairy-free
Low-cal
Saves Well

TIME TO PREP 15 minutes
TIME TO COOK 40 minutes
SERVES 6

NUTRITIONAL INFORMATION
Calories: 259
Fat: 5 g
Sodium: 1012 mg
Carbohydrate: 52 g
Fibre: 18 g
Sugar: 8 g
Protein: 15 g

ALSO WORKS WELL WITH
Sweet Potato

I'll never forget the first time I went to Puerto Rico with Lu to visit his family. It was Thanksgiving, and I had no idea what to expect. I already knew his relatives were loving, warm and kind people. But I didn't know what Thanksgiving dinner would be like, which was the important matter at hand. Would there be cranberry sauce? Sweet potatoes? Stuffing? Nope! We had a true Puerto Rican holiday — and it was delicious. Most memorably, there was a huge vat of rice and beans, which I devoured (along with about four slices of flan). Every Latin culture prepares its rice and beans differently, but this spiralized version is how Lu and I do it in our house.

1 tablespoon extra-virgin olive oil

1 medium yellow onion, finely diced

½ green pepper, finely diced

2 celery sticks, finely diced

2 large garlic cloves, finely chopped

Salt and pepper

3 (400g) cans red kidney beans, rinsed and drained

1 (400g) can chopped tomatoes

1 tablespoon tomato purée

1 teaspoon dried thyme

1 teaspoon dried oregano

1 teaspoon smoked paprika

½ teaspoon chilli powder

60ml reduced-salt vegetable stock, plus extra as needed

1 large butternut squash, peeled, spiralized with BLADE D, then riced (see page 16)

2 tablespoons chopped fresh coriander

6 lime wedges, to serve

1 Heat the olive oil in a large frying pan with a lid over a medium heat. When the oil is shimmering, add the onion, pepper, celery and garlic. Season with salt and pepper and cook for about 7 minutes until softened.

2 Meanwhile, combine half the beans and half the tomatoes in a food processor and pulse until just about puréed.

3 Add the tomato purée to the vegetables in the pan and stir to coat. Add the blended bean mixture, the remaining beans and canned tomatoes with their juices, tomato purée the thyme, oregano, paprika and chilli powder. Reduce the heat to low, cover and cook for 30 minutes, stirring every 5 minutes. If the liquid reduces too much and the mixture dries out, add stock, 1 tablespoon at a time, to keep the beans moist.

4 Add the butternut squash rice and the stock, cover and cook for a further 5–7 minutes or until the rice softens.

5 Stir in the coriander and serve with lime wedges.

Pumpkin-rosemary Alfredo
with Crispy Prosciutto

Gluten-free
Paleo
Dairy-free
Saves Well

TIME TO PREP 25 minutes
TIME TO COOK 20 minutes
SERVES 4

NUTRITIONAL INFORMATION
Calories: 451
Fat: 29 g
Sodium: 1185 mg
Carbohydrate: 32 g
Fibre: 6 g
Sugar: 9 g
Protein: 22 g

ALSO WORKS WELL WITH
Sweet Potato, Beetroot,
Swede, Carrot

The beginning of autumn is like the end of Cinderella's ball – everything turns into pumpkins: pumpkin ravioli, pumpkin lattes and carved pumpkins in window displays. While you could certainly roast your own pumpkin and make this sauce from scratch, there's no need – canned purée is perfect. Just make sure you don't buy pumpkin *pie filling*. The flavour of the prosciutto in combination with the rosemary and nutmeg in this dish are perfectly autumnal over the butternut squash noodles. The coconut milk ensures a bold sauce that's much lighter on the calories and fat than your typical Alfredo.

1 large or 2 medium butternut squashes, peeled, spiralized with BLADE D, *noodles trimmed*

Salt and pepper

8 thin slices of prosciutto or Parma ham

1 tablespoon finely chopped shallot

2 small garlic cloves, finely chopped

Pinch of chilli flakes

425g canned pumpkin purée

1½ teaspoons fresh rosemary, chopped

240ml coconut cream (see page 19)

½ teaspoon ground nutmeg

1 tablespoon chopped fresh parsley, to garnish

1 Preheat the oven to 200°C/400°F. Line a baking sheet with baking paper and lay out the butternut squash noodles, spacing them apart. Season with salt and black pepper and bake for 8–10 minutes or until al dente.

2 Place the prosciutto in a large frying pan in a single layer, then cook over a medium heat for 5–7 minutes or until crispy, flipping once. Transfer to a kitchen-paper-lined plate to drain.

3 Leave the pan to cool for about 2 minutes, then add the shallot, garlic and chilli flakes and cook, stirring frequently, for 30 seconds or until fragrant, taking care not to burn them. Add the pumpkin purée and rosemary and season with salt and black pepper. Cook for 2–3 minutes or until warmed through. Add the coconut cream and nutmeg. Stir to combine and cook the sauce for a further 5 minutes to allow the flavours to meld.

4 Divide the butternut squash pasta among four bowls and top with the sauce and two slices of prosciutto each. Garnish with the parsley.

Butternut Squash Ravioli
with Sage and Toasted Pine Nuts

〰〰 | Vegetarian
〰〰 | Gluten-free
〰〰 | Low-cal

TIME TO PREP 10 minutes
TIME TO COOK 25 minutes
SERVES 4 (3 ravioli per serving)

NUTRITIONAL INFORMATION
Calories: 83
Fat: 7 g
Sodium: 28 mg
Carbohydrate: 4 g
Fibre: 1 g
Sugar: 1 g
Protein: 3 g

ALSO WORKS WELL WITH
Sweet Potato, Courgette

While no one can mess with my grandfather's ravioli with tomato sauce, this savoury and slightly sweet spiralized version is stunning. A simple ricotta-Parmesan filling seasoned with nutmeg lets the butternut squash do the talking. The light sage sauce flows over the ravioli, and the toasted pine nuts add a nutty, classic crunch. This dish will impress any guest – it certainly makes for a creative dinner!

For the filling
½ teaspoon fresh lemon juice
¼ teaspoon ground nutmeg
175g ricotta cheese
2 tablespoons grated Parmesan cheese
Salt and pepper

For the ravioli
1 medium butternut squash, peeled and prepped
2 tablespoons extra-virgin olive oil
8 fresh sage leaves
35g pine nuts

Want to change it up? Replace the ricotta and Parmesan with goat's cheese for a different, slightly richer flavour.

1 Make the filling. In a medium bowl, combine all the filling ingredients and mix well. Set aside.

2 Make the ravioli. Slice the squash lengthways to create a slit, taking care not to pierce any further than its centre. Spiralize using **BLADE A**. Select 24 slices of squash, saving any extra for another use.

3 Heat 1 tablespoon of the olive oil in a large frying pan over a medium heat. When the oil is shimmering, add the sage and fry for about 5 minutes, then transfer to a kitchen-paper-lined plate to drain. Add the butternut squash slices in a single layer, working in batches if necessary, and cook for 5 minutes in each side or until fork-tender. Transfer to a large piece of foil or baking paper and set aside.

4 Carefully wipe the pan clean and add the remaining 1 tablespoon olive oil over a medium heat. When the oil is shimmering, crumble in the fried sage, then transfer the sauce to a small bowl. Immediately add the pine nuts to the pan and toast, stirring, for 3–5 minutes until golden brown. Add to the bowl with the sauce.

5 To serve, lay out three butternut squash slices on each plate. Using a knife or the back of a spoon, spread 2 tablespoons of the cheese mixture over each slice and then top with another slice. Drizzle the sage-pine nut sauce on top to finish.

Butternut Squash Noodles
with Almond Ricotta and Coconut Bacon

∞ Vegan
∞ Vegetarian
∞ Gluten-free
Paleo
Dairy-free

TIME TO PREP 20 minutes plus 16 hours for the almond ricotta
TIME TO COOK 20 minutes
SERVES 6

NUTRITIONAL INFORMATION
Calories: 317
Fat: 25 g
Sodium: 192 mg
Carbohydrate: 21 g
Fibre: 7 g
Sugar: 5 g
Protein: 9 g

ALSO WORKS WELL WITH
Sweet Potato, Beetroot

I try out all the food trends – every single one of them, from matcha lattes to bone broth. This is partly because I'm a food blogger, but also because curiosity gets the best of me! Some trends are better left as trends (*ahem*, cricket powder), but others make their way into my kitchen as staples. Almond ricotta and coconut bacon are fantastic vegan alternatives that I found this way. The consistency and flavour of both are shockingly comparable to the originals, making for delicious butternut squash pasta without the processed components. I bet you'll end up adopting them, too! Note that making almond ricotta takes some time: you need to soak the almonds overnight, then purée and strain the mixture for 8 hours. Make it ahead of time and store it in an airtight container in the fridge for up to 5 days. Of course, you could also treat yourself and use real, whole milk ricotta.

For the almond ricotta
260g raw blanched almonds, soaked in filtered water overnight, rinsed and drained

225ml filtered water

Salt and pepper

½ teaspoon herbes de Provence

For the coconut bacon
½ tablespoon maple syrup

1 tablespoon liquid smoke (I like the hickory flavour, but use whatever you prefer)

1 tablespoon tamari or reduced-sodium soy sauce

50g unsweetened flaked coconut

Salt

For the butternut squash
1 large butternut squash, peeled, spiralized with BLADE C

1 tablespoon olive oil

Salt and pepper

1 Make the almond ricotta. In a high-speed blender or food processor, combine the soaked almonds and water. Purée until mostly smooth, with some texture but no large chunks remaining. Place a fine-mesh sieve or colander over a bowl and line with muslin. Add the almond mixture and drain for 8 hours. Discard any liquid that collects in the bowl. Transfer the ricotta to it and season with salt, pepper and the herbes de Provence.

2 Make the coconut bacon. Preheat the oven to 180°C/350°F. Line two baking sheets with baking paper.

3 In a medium bowl, whisk together the maple syrup, liquid smoke and tamari. Add the coconut flakes and stir to coat. Season with salt, then spread the coconut flakes over a prepared baking sheet, spacing them apart. Bake for about 10 minutes.

recipe continues

4 Meanwhile, make the butternut squash. Lay out the butternut squash noodles on the other prepared baking sheet, spacing them apart. Drizzle over the olive oil and massage it into the noodles with your fingers. Season with salt and pepper.

5 After the coconut has roasted for 10 minutes, remove it and flip the pieces. Return it to the oven, place the butternut squash noodles in the oven and bake both for a further 10 minutes or until the bacon is crispy and the squash is al dente.

6 Divide the noodles among six plates. Top each serving with almond ricotta and sprinkle with the coconut bacon.

While this dish itself is special, it features two foods that are super versatile: vegan bacon and vegan ricotta. Long story short: double those parts of this recipe, then creatively re-purpose them! I love a smear of the almond ricotta on toast with the coconut bacon sprinkled on top.

Pear, Pomegranate and Roast Turkey Salad
with Butternut Squash and Maple-sesame Vinaigrette

~~~ | Dairy-free (opt.)
~~~ | Saves Well

TIME TO PREP 25 minutes
TIME TO COOK 10 minutes
SERVES 4

NUTRITIONAL INFORMATION
Calories: 477
Fat: 25 g
Sodium: 836 mg
Carbohydrate: 33 g
Fibre: 8 g
Sugar: 13 g
Protein: 34 g

ALSO WORKS WELL WITH
Sweet Potato

In the days after a Christmas feast, there's nothing better than leftovers. But turkey and cranberry sauce sandwiches can get boring pretty fast – and can quickly pack on the holiday kilos. This spiralized butternut squash and pear salad with a sweet vinaigrette is a novel break from the traditional. It's even hearty enough for the Christmas table itself – and works great whenever you're craving the flavours of autumn!

For the salad

1 medium butternut squash, peeled, spiralized with BLADE B, noodles trimmed

Cooking spray

Salt and pepper

1 large Asian pear

140g baby spinach

115g pomegranate seeds

75g roughly chopped pecans

60g goat's cheese, crumbled

450g roasted turkey, carved

For the vinaigrette

1 tablespoon maple syrup

1 tablespoon extra-virgin olive oil

1 tablespoon sesame oil

2 tablespoons apple cider vinegar

1 teaspoon white sesame seeds

1 tablespoon soy sauce

Pepper to taste

1 garlic clove, finely chopped

1 Preheat the oven to 200°C/400°F. Line a baking sheet with baking paper. Spread out the butternut squash noodles on the baking sheet, spacing them apart. Coat lightly with cooking spray and season with salt and pepper. Roast for 10–12 minutes or until al dente.

2 Meanwhile, make the vinaigrette. Whisk together all the ingredients for the vinaigrette in a small bowl.

3 Spiralize the pear with **BLADE D** and place it in a large bowl. Add the spinach, pomegranate seeds, pecans and goat's cheese. Add the roasted squash noodles, drizzle with the vinaigrette and toss to coat. Top with the turkey pieces. Divide the salad among four plates and serve immediately.

No leftover Christmas turkey? No problem. Buy a rotisserie chicken and shred the meat using forks or tongs.

Winter Lasagne
with Brussels Sprouts and Chicken Sausage

〰 | Gluten-free
〰 | Saves Well
〰

TIME TO PREP 20 minutes
TIME TO COOK 60 minutes
SERVES 4–6

NUTRITIONAL INFORMATION
(for 1 of 6 servings)
Calories: 365
Fat: 22 g
Sodium: 505 mg
Carbohydrate: 23 g
Fibre: 5 g
Sugar: 5 g
Protein: 23 g

ALSO WORKS WELL WITH
Sweet Potato, Swede

At school, I played two sports: lacrosse and football. One of my favourite parts of being on both teams was the pasta dinners. The night before a game, we'd all gather at one of the players' parents' home to carb-load and store energy for the next day. Needless to say, I ate my fair share of penne bakes, stuffed shells and, of course, lasagne. After all, lasagne is the best way to feed a hungry crowd! In this dish, I replaced the pasta's refined carbohydrates for complex ones by using butternut squash. As it roasts in the oven, the vegetable's natural sugars release, resulting in subtly sweet layers and gorgeous orange pops of colour. This squash will please everyone – from picky spouses to a team of growing teenagers.

1 medium butternut squash, peeled and prepped

1½ teaspoons extra-virgin olive oil

6 fresh sage leaves

4 chicken sausage links, casings removed

600g Brussels sprouts

3 garlic cloves, finely chopped

¼ teaspoon chilli flakes

1 large shallot, finely chopped

Salt and pepper

340g ricotta cheese

25g Parmesan cheese, grated

1 large egg, beaten

115g Gruyère cheese, grated

1 Preheat the oven to 220°C/425°F.

2 Slice the squash lengthways to create a slit, taking care not to pierce any further than its centre. Spiralize using **BLADE A**.

3 Heat the olive oil in a large frying pan over a medium heat. When the oil is shimmering, add the sage leaves and cook until crispy, about 5 minutes. Transfer to a kitchen-paper-lined plate to drain. Immediately add the sausage to the same pan and cook for 5–7 minutes, breaking up the meat with a wooden spoon as it cooks, until browned.

4 Meanwhile, in a food processor, pulse the Brussels sprouts until mostly shredded. When the sausage is browned, add the Brussels sprouts, garlic, chilli flakes and shallot and season with salt and black pepper. Cook for 2–3 minutes or until the Brussels sprouts are wilted. Remove the pan from the heat.

recipe continues

5 In a medium bowl, whisk together the ricotta, Parmesan and egg.

6 Arrange a layer of butternut squash slices in the bottom of a 4.7-litre casserole dish, overlapping them as needed to create a complete layer. Add a layer of the Brussels sprout and sausage mixture, then add a layer of the ricotta-Parmesan mixture. Repeat these three layers, then top with the remaining butternut squash slices. Finish with the Gruyère.

7 Cover the lasagne with foil and bake for 40–45 minutes or until the squash is easily pierced with a fork and the cheese has melted.

8 Remove the lasagne from the oven, remove the foil and immediately crumble over the sage. Set aside to rest for 5 minutes, then carefully slice and serve.

This recipe is ideal for meal planning, as it freezes well. To reheat, bake at 220°C/425°F for 20 minutes or until warmed through, then slice into portions.

Teriyaki Mini Meatballs
over Roasted Spring Onions and Butternut Squash Noodles

Dairy-free
Saves Well

TIME TO PREP 30 minutes
TIME TO COOK 25 minutes
SERVES 4

NUTRITIONAL INFORMATION
Calories: 352
Fat: 21 g
Sodium: 429 mg
Carbohydrate: 22 g
Fibre: 3 g
Sugar: 9 g
Protein: 21 g

ALSO WORKS WELL WITH
Courgette, Kohlrabi,
Turnip, Sweet Potato,
Mooli

When I'm stumped on what to make for dinner, I usually defer to some adaptation of spiralized spaghetti and meatballs. I love creating and trying out new flavour combinations, and this teriyaki version has fast become a favourite. The Asian tastes are a nice change from traditional Italian style, and the butternut squash noodles' sweetness complements the salty soy and warm sesame in the sauce. And when they're mini, they're just cuter!

For the teriyaki sauce

60ml soy sauce

1 tablespoon rice vinegar

1½ teaspoons grated fresh ginger

1 garlic clove, crushed and finely chopped

1 tablespoon sesame oil

1 tablespoon honey

1 teaspoon hot sauce, or a pinch of chilli flakes

For the meatballs

450g lean turkey mince

1 tablespoon finely chopped shallot

1 teaspoon very finely chopped garlic

2 tablespoons soy sauce

1 tablespoon sesame oil

1 teaspoon white sesame seeds

8 spring onions

Salt and pepper

1 large butternut squash, peeled, spiralized with BLADE D, noodles trimmed

1 Preheat the oven to 230°C/450°F. Line two baking sheets with baking paper.

2 Make the teriyaki sauce: Whisk together all the ingredients for the teriyaki sauce in a small bowl.

3 In a large bowl, combine the turkey, shallot, garlic and 1 tablespoon of the soy sauce. Form the mixture into twelve 2.5cm meatballs and place them on a prepared baking sheet. Brush them with about half of the teriyaki sauce, reserving the remainder.

4 In a shallow dish, mix together the sesame oil, remaining 1 tablespoon soy sauce and the white sesame seeds. Dunk the spring onions into the mixture, turning to coat, and place them on the baking sheet with the meatballs. Bake for 10 minutes. Lay out the squash noodles on the other baking sheet, spacing them apart. Add salt and pepper.

5 Remove the meatballs and spring onions from the oven, flip them over and brush with teriyaki sauce. Return to the oven and add the squash noodles. Roast together for 10 minutes or until the meatballs are cooked through and the noodles are wilted and al dente.

6 Divide the noodles among four plates and top each with three meatballs and two roasted spring onions.

Oven-fried Avocado Tacos
with Chipotle Cream

Vegetarian
Gluten-free
Paleo
Dairy-free
Low-cal

TIME TO PREP 30 minutes
TIME TO COOK 15 minutes
SERVES 4 (3 tacos per serving)

NUTRITIONAL INFORMATION
Calories: 120
Fat: 8 g
Sodium: 24 mg
Carbohydrate: 9 g
Fibre: 3 g
Sugar: 2 g
Protein: 3 g

ALSO WORKS WELL WITH
Courgette

If you've never had fried avocado, allow me the honour of introducing you – I think you'll be fast friends. Fried avocado is my weakness (along with butter-milk pancakes and soft-baked chocolate chip cookies), but here I've created a gluten-free, oven-fried version that is just as tasty on the tongue, but lighter on the hips. Seasoned butternut squash noodles and chipotle cream tie these vegetarian tacos together, making for an irresistible, spiralized taco night.

For the chipotle cream

2 chipotle peppers in adobo sauce with

1 teaspoon sauce

120ml coconut cream (see page 19)

2 tablespoons fresh lime juice

For the oven-fried avocado

45g almond flour

1 teaspoon garlic powder

1 teaspoon onion powder

1 teaspoon sweet paprika

2 large eggs, beaten

90g unsweetened shredded coconut

2 ripe avocados

For the noodles

1 medium butternut squash, peeled, spiralized with BLADE C, noodles trimmed

1 tablespoon extra-virgin olive oil

1 teaspoon ground cumin

1 teaspoon smoked paprika

Salt and pepper

12 large round lettuce leaves

20g fresh coriander leaves, to garnish

12 thinly sliced lime wedges, to serve

1 Preheat the oven to 200°C/400°F. Line two baking sheets with baking paper.

2 Make the chipotle cream. In a food processor, combine all the ingredients for the chipotle cream and pulse until creamy. Taste and add salt to taste.

3 Make the oven-fried avocado. Set up your dredging station. In a small bowl, combine the almond flour and the garlic powder, onion powder and paprika. In a second small bowl, beat the eggs. In a third small bowl, add the shredded coconut. Place the bowls side by side.

4 Halve the avocados and carefully remove the stones. Cut each half into three slices crossways, then halve the slices horizontally to make 24 slices.

5 Dip the avocado slices in the almond flour mixture, shaking off any excess. Then dip them in the egg mixture, allowing any excess to drip off. Finally, dip them in the coconut mixture, turning to coat well and pressing to adhere. Place on one of the prepared baking sheets, spacing them apart. Transfer to the oven.

recipe continues

6 Make the noodles. As soon as the avocado goes into the oven, lay out the butternut squash noodles on the second baking sheet and toss with oil and season with cumin, smoked paprika, salt and pepper. Toss to coat, then space apart. Place in the oven and bake together with the avocado for about 8 minutes. Flip the avocado and continue baking together for a further 2–4 minutes, or until the noodles are al dente and the avocado is lightly golden.

7 Assemble the tacos. Place 12 whole round lettuce leaves on a clean, dry surface and top each with a small handful of butternut squash noodles, dividing them evenly. Add two pieces of avocado each, drizzle with the chipotle cream and garnish with the coriander. Serve with lime wedges.

Make it a taco bowl! Chop up the lettuce and mix it in with the butternut squash noodles as a base. Then add the other ingredients on top.

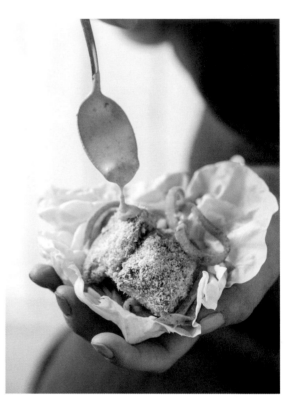

Butternut Squash Noodles
with Butter Beans and Sun-dried Tomato Cream Sauce

≈ Vegan
≈ Vegetarian
  Gluten-free
  Dairy-free
  Low-Cal

TIME TO PREP 20 minutes
TIME TO COOK 20 minutes
SERVES 4

NUTRITIONAL INFORMATION
Calories: 184
Fat: 4 g
Sodium: 260 mg
Carbohydrate: 28 g
Fibre: 6 g
Sugar: 5 g
Protein: 5 g

ALSO WORKS WELL WITH
Swede, Sweet Potato, Turnip, Broccoli, Celeriac

It can be tough for me to plan my meals ahead because I often get recipe ideas and become so consumed with excitement that I have to try them out immediately – I'm like a crazy professor scribbling on the chalkboard. But there is one thing I do always make ahead and keep on hand: pasta sauces! Especially with the more time-consuming ones, prepping in advance makes eating healthy weeknight meals much more realistic and manageable, since I can just throw a sauce on any spiralized vegetable. This sun-dried tomato cream sauce is one of my favourites. It's freezer-friendly, too. In fact, you may want to double it when you make this recipe – you're going to want to keep some extra on hand for your future spiralized creations!

1 large butternut squash, peeled, spiralized with BLADE C

Cooking spray

Salt and pepper

1 teaspoon olive oil

2 garlic cloves, finely chopped

2 teaspoons finely chopped shallot

55g sun-dried tomatoes, drained and chopped

120ml coconut cream (see page 19)

¼ teaspoon chilli flakes

¼ teaspoon dried basil

¼ teaspoon dried oregano

125ml reduced-salt vegetable stock

140g canned butter beans, rinsed and drained

2 tablespoons chopped fresh parsley

1 Preheat the oven to 200°C/400°F. Line a baking sheet with baking paper and lay out the butternut squash noodles, spacing them apart. Spray with cooking spray and season with salt and black pepper. Bake for 8–10 minutes or until al dente.

2 Meanwhile, heat the olive oil in a large frying pan over a medium-high heat. When the oil is shimmering, add the garlic and shallot and cook for 1 minute or until fragrant. Add the sun-dried tomatoes, coconut cream, chilli flakes, basil and oregano and season with salt and black pepper. Increase the heat to high and bring to the boil, then reduce the heat to medium-low and simmer for 2 minutes to develop the flavours.

3 Transfer the sauce to a food processor or high-speed blender. Add the stock and pulse until creamy. Taste and adjust the seasoning to your preference.

4 Return the pan to a medium-high heat and add the sauce, beans and parsley. Cook, stirring, for 1–2 minutes to heat through. Divide the pasta among four bowls and top with the sauce and beans.

Cabbage

Spiralizing a cabbage makes days (maybe even weeks!) worth of cabbage, so it's ideal for Sunday-night meal planning. Spiralizing won't make noodles like you're used to seeing, but rather, it's an easier, quicker and more enjoyable way to shred cabbage. No more laborious knife slicing — just load it onto the spiralizer and spin.

If you think you're underwhelmed by cabbage, hold on. This veggie is super underrated; I love its texture and versatility. I promise that once you try the recipes here, you'll think it's worthy of a chapter in this book and a place on your plate.

NUTRITIONAL BENEFITS: Cabbage contains high amounts of sulphur, which is essential for your body to produce keratin, a protein substance necessary for healthy nails, hair and skin. Cabbage is also a solid source of vitamins C and K, which boost your immune system and help mental function, respectively.

PREPARATION AND STORAGE: Pluck off any loose outer leaves. If necessary, slice off the ends to leave flat, even surfaces. Store in an airtight container in the fridgefor up to 1 week. Spiralized cabbage can also be frozen for up to 8 months for future use.

BEST BLADES TO USE
- Blade A

BEST COOKING METHODS
- Raw
- Blanch
- Steam or boil for 3 minutes
- Sauté over a medium-high heat for 5 minutes

Crunchy Bok Choy and Cabbage Salad

Vegetarian
Gluten-free
Paleo
Dairy-free
Low-cal
No Cook
Saves Well

TIME TO PREP 20 minutes
TIME TO COOK 5 minutes
SERVES 4

NUTRITIONAL INFORMATION
Calories: 236
Fat: 19 g
Sodium: 430 mg
Carbohydrate: 14 g
Fibre: 3 g
Sugar: 6 g
Protein: 6 g

In my opinion, there's no better salad bar than the one at Whole Foods. The sheer volume of creative and delicious options is impressive. Their chefs are constantly inventing new pasta salads that instantly become favourites. In the summer of 2015, it was their Paleo Crunchy Cabbage Salad. It's meant to be a filling side, but you can easily top it with your favourite protein, like baked tofu or grilled chicken, and turn it into a complete meal. This spiralized re-creation is both refreshing and profoundly flavourful. It's the dish that got me so excited over cabbage in the first place!

For the dressing
3 tablespoons sesame oil
2 tablespoons rice vinegar
1 teaspoon honey
Juice of ½ lemon
Salt

For the salad
350g bok choy or pak choi, chopped
1 Chinese cabbage, spiralized with BLADE A
20g spring onions, sliced
40g sliced raw almonds
½ teaspoon white sesame seeds
½ teaspoon black sesame seeds

1 Make the dressing. In a large bowl, whisk together all the ingredients for the dressing.

2 Make the salad. Add all the ingredients for the salad to the bowl with the dressing. Toss to combine thoroughly and place in the fridge to marinate for at least 20 minutes or until the cabbage has softened.

Spanish Cabbage Stew
with Cod and Saffron

∾∾ Gluten-free
∾∾ Paleo
Dairy-free
Low-cal

TIME TO PREP 25 minutes
TIME TO COOK 40 minutes
SERVES 2

NUTRITIONAL INFORMATION
Calories: 242
Fat: 8 g
Sodium: 752 mg
Carbohydrate: 18 g
Fibre: 4 g
Sugar: 9 g
Protein: 23 g

Inspired by Spanish cuisine's use of saffron and light tomato sauces, this dish is definitely one for date night. It plates beautifully and fills the kitchen with an inviting, exotic fragrance. The cabbage soaks up the sauce and meshes well with the simple, flaky cod. Plus, all the vegetables used here are spiralized, so preparation is quick, allowing you to feel more relaxed in the kitchen. This stew satisfies, but is light enough to leave room for dessert, another glass of wine, dancing – or all of the above!

125ml reduced-salt vegetable stock

Pinch of saffron (about 20 small threads)

1 tablespoon extra-virgin olive oil

½ *small white onion, peeled, spiralized with* BLADE A, *noodles trimmed*

1 large garlic clove, finely chopped

1 red pepper, spiralized with BLADE A, *noodles trimmed*

½ *small green cabbage, spiralized* (BLADE A)

¼ teaspoon chilli flakes

1 (400g) can chopped tomatoes, with juices

¼ teaspoon ground cumin

1 teaspoon ground paprika

Salt and pepper

2 (85–115g) skinless pieces of cod

1 tablespoon finely chopped fresh parsley, to garnish

~~~~~~~~~~~~~~~~~~~~~~~~~~~~~~

For an extra kick of flavour, swap in smoked paprika instead of regular, and add a pinch of cayenne pepper.

~~~~~~~~~~~~~~~~~~~~~~~~~~~~~~

1 Bring the stock to a simmer in a small pot over a high heat. Add the saffron and transfer to a small cup or bowl. Leave for 10 minutes to allow the flavour to infuse.

2 Heat the olive oil in a large frying pan with a lid over a medium heat. When the oil is shimmering, add the onion noodles and cook for 5 minutes until tender. Add the garlic and pepper noodles and cook for 2 minutes or until slightly softened. Add the cabbage and cook for a further 5 minutes until slightly softened. Add the saffron-infused stock, chilli flakes, tomatoes and their juices, cumin, paprika and salt and black pepper to taste.

3 Increase the heat slightly and simmer, stirring often, until the tomatoes have cooked down slightly and the mixture is fragrant, about 10 minutes. Reduce the heat to low, cover the pan and simmer for a further 10 minutes.

4 Season the cod with salt and black pepper and place the pieces on top of the stew, nestling them in. Cover and cook for about 7 minutes or until the fish is opaque and cooked through.

5 Divide the cod between two bowls. Portion out the cabbage stew, pouring it on top of the cod. Garnish with the parsley.

Spicy Cabbage and Carrot Detox Soup

Gluten-free
Paleo
Dairy-free
One Pot
Low-cal
Saves Well

TIME TO PREP 20 minutes
TIME TO COOK 35 minutes
SERVES 4

NUTRITIONAL INFORMATION
Calories: 98
Fat: 4 g
Sodium: 713 mg
Carbohydrate: 14 g
Fibre: 4 g
Sugar: 7 g
Protein: 4 g

We've all been there. Whether it's a party with one too many biscuits or that extra slice of birthday cake in the office, you're left feeling sluggish and sloth-like. While it's important to live life to its fullest, it's just as important to balance that out. Enter detox soup. While most detox soups are flavourless and dull, this spicy cabbage and carrot version will leave your taste buds satisfied and your body on its way to a full recovery.

1 tablespoon extra-virgin olive oil

1 white or yellow onion, peeled, spiralized with BLADE A, *noodles trimmed*

1 large carrot, peeled, spiralized with BLADE D, *noodles trimmed*

1 large garlic clove, finely chopped

1½ teaspoons finely chopped Serrano chilli

⅛ teaspoon ground cumin

⅛ teaspoon ground turmeric

⅛ teaspoon ground ginger

1 small Savoy or green cabbage, spiralized with BLADE A

425g canned whole peeled tomatoes, crushed with your hands

1 litre reduced-salt chicken stock

Salt and pepper

1 Heat the olive oil in a stockpot over a medium heat. When the oil is shimmering, add the onion and carrot noodles, the garlic, Serrano, cumin, turmeric and ginger. Cook, stirring, for about 7 minutes until the onion is softened.

2 Add the cabbage, tomatoes and their juices and stock. Season with salt and black pepper and stir well. Bring to the boil, then reduce the heat to low and cover the pot. Simmer for 20–25 minutes or until the cabbage is cooked through and softened. Serve hot.

To make this soup vegan, use vegetable stock instead of chicken stock.

Cabbage Buddha Bowl

with Chickpea-avocado Mash and BBQ Tahini

Vegan
Vegetarian
Gluten-free
Dairy-free
No Cook

TIME TO PREP 15 minutes
TIME TO COOK 5 minutes
SERVES 2

NUTRITIONAL INFORMATION
Calories: 450
Fat: 31 g
Sodium: 523 mg
Carbohydrate: 42 g
Fibre: 17 g
Sugar: 8 g
Protein: 12 g

Buddha bowls are the most efficient way to cram as many superfoods and nourishing ingredients into a meal as you can – plus, they're fun to build. All you have to do is think of everything you'd like to eat at that moment, throw it all in a bowl, then tie the whole thing together with a complementary sauce or dressing. In this cabbage bowl, every bite is chock-full of flavours and textures. It's an enjoyable way to eat up all these healthy ingredients!

For the dressing
1½ tablespoons tahini
3 tablespoons apple cider vinegar
1 tablespoon barbecue sauce
1 tablespoon extra-virgin olive oil
Salt and pepper

For the Buddha bowl
150g canned chickpeas, rinsed and drained
1 very ripe avocado
¼ teaspoon paprika
1 tablespoon fresh lemon juice
Salt and pepper
1 small red cabbage, spiralized with BLADE A
100g kale leaves, shredded

1 Make the dressing. Place all the ingredients for the dressing and 1 tablespoon water in a food processor and pulse until creamy. Add more water if needed to achieve the desired consistency. Taste and adjust the seasoning to your preferences.

2 In a medium bowl, combine the chickpeas and avocado and roughly mash with a potato masher or the back of a fork until mostly smooth but with some chunks remaining. Season with the paprika, lemon juice, salt and pepper.

3 Assemble the Buddha bowls. Divide the cabbage and kale between two bowls and top with equal dollops of the chickpea-avocado mash. Drizzle the dressing over the top and serve.

Carrot

Traditionally, carrots have been served as mundane crudités, or prettily but simply roasted whole, or just julienned and tossed into salads. Why not make them into noodles and rice?

Carrots are beautiful and colourful, with a sweet, earthy flavour. They're my favourite noodle to boil, as they fluff up, absorbing liquid, and are sturdy enough to hold up to thick sauces like a Bolognese or a slow-cooker vegetable stew. Carrot noodles work famously in soups, infusing their healthy flavours into broths.

It can be tough to find a carrot thick enough for spiralizing – many are thin and long. For the best experience, look for those that are at least 4cm in diameter. Be careful, though: many large carrots can be GMOs, so check with your supermarket or farmer to make sure the vegetable is organic or simply non-GMO.

NUTRITIONAL BENEFITS: Carrots are rich in beta-carotene, which helps with vision – it's even been shown to protect against macular degeneration and cataracts. Carrots are also high in vitamin A, which has anti-aging properties to help you glow from the inside out.

PREPARATION AND STORAGE: Peel the carrot and slice off both ends to leave flat, even surfaces. Before loading the carrot onto the spiralizer, be sure neither end is thinner than 2.5cm. Store in an airtight container in the fridge for up to 1 week. Spiralized carrots can also be frozen for up to 8 months for future use.

BEST BLADES TO USE
- Blade D

BEST COOKING METHODS
- Raw
- Boil or steam for 2–3 minutes
- Sauté over a medium-high heat for 5–7 minutes
- Roast at 220°C/425°F for 6–10 minutes

Roasted Carrot Noodles
with Smoked Salmon, Avocado and Creamy Herb Dressing

〰〰 | Gluten-free
〰〰 | Paleo
       | Dairy-free

TIME TO PREP 15 minutes
TIME TO COOK 15 minutes
SERVES 4

NUTRITIONAL INFORMATION
Calories: 402
Fat: 34 g
Sodium: 441 mg
Carbohydrate: 13 g
Fibre: 6 g
Sugar: 4 g
Protein: 14 g

ALSO WORKS WELL WITH
White Potato, Golden Beetroot, Broccoli

This protein-packed dish showcases the saltiness of the smoked salmon and the sweetness that emerges as the carrots roast, enhancing the simplicity of the herb dressing. Tiny yet powerful hemp hearts make for a crunchy, nutty bite that's nutritionally dense. Delicate but robust, this dish checks off all the flavour and nutrition boxes.

3 large carrots, peeled, spiralized with BLADE D, noodles trimmed

4 teaspoons extra-virgin olive oil

Salt and pepper

2 ripe avocados

225g smoked salmon, sliced

1 tablespoon hemp hearts, to garnish

For the dressing
1 large pasteurized egg yolk

¼ teaspoon garlic powder

1 garlic clove, finely chopped

1 tablespoon fresh lemon juice

2 tablespoons red wine vinegar or sherry vinegar

60ml olive oil

10g fresh dill

10g fresh parsley

2 tablespoons chopped fresh chives

Salt and pepper

1 Preheat the oven to 190°C/375°F. Line a baking sheet with baking paper and lay out the carrot noodles, spacing them apart. Drizzle with the olive oil and season with salt and pepper. Roast for 15 minutes or until al dente.

2 Meanwhile, make the dressing. In a food processor, combine the egg yolk, garlic powder, fresh garlic, lemon juice and vinegar and pulse until smooth. Add the olive oil, dill, parsley and chives and process again, adding water if necessary, 1 tablespoon at a time, until the dressing has the consistency of double cream. Season with salt and pepper.

3 Peel and stone the avocados. Cut each half into four slices.

4 Divide the carrot noodles among four plates. Top with smoked salmon, then avocado. Drizzle the dressing over the top and garnish with the hemp hearts.

〰〰〰〰〰〰〰〰

If you're not a fan of smoked salmon, try poached instead.

〰〰〰〰〰〰〰〰

Garlic-miso Soup
with Carrot Noodles, Seaweed and Tofu

When I was at school, I worked at a Japanese restaurant on Friday and Saturday nights. As hostess, part of my role was to help prepare takeaway orders, which more often than not included miso soup with seaweed and tiny precious squares of tofu floating in it. I spent so many hours ladling the delightfully simple soup into takeaway containers that every time I smell seaweed and miso together, I'm transported back there. This recipe is my version of that memory. I added carrot noodles to pull it together into a full meal, plus garlic for added health benefits.

Vegan
Vegetarian
Gluten-free
Dairy-free
Low-cal

TIME TO PREP 10 minutes
TIME TO COOK 25 minutes
SERVES 4

NUTRITIONAL INFORMATION
Calories: 121
Fat: 3 g
Sodium: 888 mg
Carbohydrate: 14 g
Fibre: 3 g
Sugar: 6 g
Protein: 9 g

ALSO WORKS WELL WITH
Courgette, Radish, Turnip

1 teaspoon olive oil

2 teaspoons finely chopped garlic

1.4 litres reduced-salt vegetable stock

1 tablespoon miso paste

40g dried wakame seaweed

350g extra-firm tofu, drained (see Tip) and cubed

1 tablespoon reduced-sodium soy sauce or tamari

2 carrots, peeled, spiralized with BLADE D, noodles trimmed

Cracked pepper

1 Heat the olive oil in a large stockpot over a medium-high heat. When the oil is shimmering, add the garlic and cook for 30 seconds or until fragrant. Add the stock and 1 litre water. Increase the heat to high and bring to the boil.

2 Transfer 125ml of the boiling mixture to a small bowl. Add the miso paste and whisk rapidly to dissolve. Return the miso mixture to the pot. Reduce the heat to medium-low.

3 Add the seaweed, tofu, soy sauce and carrot noodles to the pot. Season with pepper and simmer for a further 5–7 minutes or until the carrot noodles are al dente. Serve immediately.

To drain tofu, halve the block crossways, then sandwich both rectangles between kitchen paper on a plate. Place another plate or heavy object on top and set aside for at least 5 minutes.

Mum's Matzo Ball Soup
with Carrot Noodles

Vegetarian
Dairy-free
Low-cal

TIME TO PREP 15 minutes
TIME TO COOK 45 minutes
SERVES 4

NUTRITIONAL INFORMATION
Calories: 234
Fat: 12 g
Sodium: 73 mg
Carbohydrate: 26 g
Fibre: 1 g
Sugar: 5 g
Protein: 6 g

I know, I know – this recipe calls for a boxed matzo ball mix. Well, that's why it's called Mum's Matzo Ball Soup – because she used the mix! This soup was one of my favourite dinners, and I always requested it when I felt sick. Even though I grew up in an Italian household, it was the ultimate comfort food. What was so special, if it just comes from a mix? Mum made the soup from scratch and always added extra carrots to fill us up. My recipe tweaks the original just slightly, using carrot noodles instead of diced carrots.

For the matzo balls
2 large eggs, beaten
2 tablespoons vegetable oil
1 (140g) packet matzo ball mix (you can buy this online or in speciality shops)

For the soup
1 large yellow onion, quartered
½ head garlic, cloves peeled
2 large carrots, plus 1 large carrot, peeled, spiralized with BLADE D, noodles trimmed
3 celery sticks
4 sprigs of flat-leaf parsley
1½ teaspoons whole black peppercorns
¼ teaspoon salt, plus extra as needed
1 tablespoon chopped fresh dill
Salt and pepper

This recipe is a great base for any vegetable-based soup. Use it and reuse it!

1 Make the matzo balls. In a medium bowl, whisk together the eggs and oil. Add the matzo ball mix and stir to fully combine. Chill for 15 minutes.

2 Meanwhile, bring a large pot of salted water with a lid to the boil over a high heat.

3 Form the chilled matzo ball mixture into eight 2cm balls. Drop them into the boiling water, cover and reduce the heat to low. Simmer for 20–25 minutes or until the balls are fluffed up and firm. Remove with a slotted spoon and set aside.

4 Meanwhile, make the soup. In a separate large pot with a lid, combine the onion, garlic, carrots, celery, parsley, peppercorns and salt. Add enough water to cover the ingredients by 2.5cm. Bring to the boil over a high heat, then reduce the heat to medium-low, cover and simmer for 30 minutes.

5 After 15 minutes, remove the vegetable solids from the soup with a slotted spoon and discard. Increase the heat to medium-high and return to a simmer. Add the carrot noodles and cook for 5 minutes or until al dente.

6 To serve, ladle the carrot noodle soup into four bowls and top each with two matzo balls. Sprinkle the soup with dill. Season with salt and pepper and serve immediately.

Za'atar Chickpeas
over Radicchio and Carrot

∽∽ | Vegetarian
Gluten-free
Dairy-free (opt.)
Low-cal

TIME TO PREP 20 minutes
SERVES 4

NUTRITIONAL INFORMATION
Calories: 300
Fat: 19 g
Sodium: 498 mg
Carbohydrate: 26 g
Fibre: 9 g
Sugar: 2 g
Protein: 9 g

If the atmosphere and vibe of a restaurant or bar is captivating, I think the food tastes slightly better. Whenever I walk into a space that has been gorgeously designed, I'm already in awe and excited for my dining experience. I found this to be true with Barbounia, one of my favourite Mediterranean restaurants in New York City. For my first meal there (of many), I ordered a classic Greek salad that was sprinkled with za'atar, an ancient Middle Eastern seasoning that serves up woodsy and nutty notes and notably includes the spice sumac. Whether it was the décor or the za'atar, that meal left an impression. If you're anything like me, you'll want to sprinkle it on everything – grilled naan bread, meats or fish, or on a spiralized veggie salad!

For the salad
425g canned chickpeas, rinsed and drained
1 tablespoon za'atar
2 teaspoons extra-virgin olive oil
160g radicchio, sliced
1 large carrot, peeled, spiralized with BLADE C, *noodles trimmed*
1½ tablespoons crumbled feta cheese

For the dressing
60ml extra-virgin olive oil
1 teaspoon finely chopped shallot
2 tablespoons fresh lemon juice
2 teaspoons finely chopped fresh parsley
Salt and pepper

1 Preheat the oven to 200°C/400°F. Line a baking sheet with baking paper.

2 In a small bowl, combine the chickpeas, za'atar and olive oil. Toss to combine and spread out the mixture on the prepared baking sheet. Bake for 30–35 minutes or until the chickpeas are crisp, shaking the pan halfway through.

3 When the chickpeas are done, make the dressing. In a large bowl, whisk together all the ingredients for the dressing.

4 Add the radicchio and carrot noodles to the dressing and toss to combine. Divide the salad among four plates and top with the chickpeas and feta.

Za'atar isn't hard to find, but you can make your own version at home if you like. Combine 1 teaspoon each of fresh oregano, sumac, ground cumin and sesame seeds and season with salt.

Slow-cooker Spiced Lentils and Cauliflower
over Carrot Rice

~~~ Vegetarian
~~~ Gluten-free
Paleo
Dairy-free
Low-cal
Saves Well

TIME TO PREP 30 minutes
TIME TO COOK 4 hours
SERVES 8

NUTRITIONAL INFORMATION
Calories: 273
Fat: 1 g
Sodium: 224 mg
Carbohydrate: 41 g
Fibre: 18 g
Sugar: 8 g
Protein: 14 g

ALSO WORKS WELL WITH
Sweet Potato, Butternut
Squash, Celeriac, Turnip,
Beetroot

One of the things I enjoy most about living in Jersey City is that it's ethnically diverse. There are always interesting cultural events happening around town and, of course, many different types of cuisines. On my first trip to a now-favourite Indian restaurant called Mantra, I asked the waiter to bring me their 'best dish'. He returned with a spiced lentil stew with cauliflower. I was blown away by the depth and variety of flavour in each bite, and loved the texture of the softened lentils and velvety cauliflower. This spiralized version is my way of sharing a little piece of Jersey City with you.

350g brown lentils

1 onion, diced

2 garlic cloves, finely chopped

1½ teaspoons finely chopped fresh ginger

2½–3 tablespoons red curry paste

1½ teaspoons garam masala

2 bay leaves

½ teaspoon ground turmeric

½ teaspoon ground cumin

½ teaspoon salt

¼ teaspoon cayenne pepper (or less, if you don't like spice!)

1 (400g) can chopped tomatoes

1 tablespoon tomato purée

700ml reduced-salt vegetable stock

300g cauliflower florets, chopped

8 large carrots, peeled, spiralized with BLADE D, then riced (see page 16)

60ml coconut cream (see page 19)

Large handful of fresh coriander, to garnish

1 Rinse the lentils and place them in a large slow cooker. Add the onion, garlic, ginger, curry paste, garam masala, bay leaves, turmeric, cumin, salt and cayenne. Stir to combine thoroughly.

2 Add the canned tomatoes, tomato purée, stock and cauliflower. Stir well to combine, making sure the lentils are mostly submerged. Cover and cook on High for 3½ hours.

3 Stir in the carrot rice and cook together until the lentils and carrot rice are soft but not mushy, about 30 minutes.

4 Remove the bay leaves and stir in the coconut cream. Divide the mixture among eight bowls and garnish with coriander.

~~~~~~~~~~

This recipe serves 8 but if you are making it to save for future use and want just a few servings immediately, spiralize only 1 large carrot per desired serving.

~~~~~~~~~~

Celeriac

At first glance, celeriac (also known as celery root) is gnarly looking – it's hairy, knobbly and bulbous. While it may never win a vegetable beauty contest, it has the same wonderful flavours as its cousins carrot, parsley and parsnip.

The root of the celery sticks you're used to seeing, eating and cooking with, celeriac definitely carries hints of that taste. It's herbal and slightly smoky in a way that balances out robust sauces and heavy proteins. It also works well in lighter dishes, offering a refreshing bite. Before I started spiralizing, I had only seen celeriac prepared as a mash, roasted with other root vegetables or tossed raw into salads and slaws. You'll find much more creative interpretations here!

Although it takes a few minutes to peel and prep the vegetable to be spiralized, it makes an abundance of noodles. When you're shopping, opt for a medium celeriac for best results.

NUTRITIONAL BENEFITS: Celeriac is high in dietary fibre, potassium, magnesium and vitamin B. Thus, it has potent anti-inflammatory powers, leaves you feeling fuller longer and keeps your metabolism revved. It's low on the glycaemic index, making it a great pasta alternative that won't spike your blood sugar levels, nourishing and satisfying you instead.

PREPARATION AND STORAGE: Slice off any large hairy knobs and peel entirely. Then slice off each end to leave flat, even surfaces. Store in an airtight container for up to 5 days in the fridge. Spiralized celeriac can also be frozen for up to 8 months for future use.

BEST BLADES TO USE
- Blade A
- Blade B
- Blade C
- Blade D

BEST COOKING METHODS
- Raw
- Sauté over a medium-high heat for 5–7 minutes
- Boil for 3 minutes
- Roast at 220°C/425°F for 10 minutes

Stuffed Cabbage Rolls
with Celeriac Rice and Adzuki Beans

≋ Vegan
≋ Vegetarian
≋ Gluten-free
Dairy-free
Saves Well

TIME TO PREP 25 minutes
TIME TO COOK 1 hour
SERVES 4–6
(2–3 rolls per serving)

NUTRITIONAL INFORMATION
(for 1 of 6 servings)
Calories: 307
Fat: 11 g
Sodium: 515 mg
Carbohydrate: 42 g
Fibre: 14 g
Sugar: 10 g
Protein: 13 g

ALSO WORKS WELL WITH
Butternut Squash, Sweet
Potato, Kohlrabi, Turnip

Halupki **is an Eastern European stuffed cabbage dish. Traditionally, the cabbage is filled with beef and rice, covered with a sweet, thin tomato sauce and baked. This vegetarian version swaps in beans for the beef and spiralized celeriac rice for the regular stuff. This dish makes twelve fluffy, gorgeous cabbage rolls that can be frozen, so make a batch and warm them up for future dinners.**

1 large head green cabbage, cored

1½ tablespoons extra-virgin olive oil

½ yellow onion, diced

3 garlic cloves, finely chopped

½ red pepper, diced

½ green pepper, diced

Salt and pepper

1 large celeriac, peeled, spiralized with BLADE D*, then riced (see page 16)*

425g canned adzuki beans, drained and rinsed

150g coarsely ground walnuts

1 (400g) can tomato sauce

1 teaspoon garlic powder

1 litre reduced-salt vegetable stock

2 tablespoons finely chopped fresh parsley, to garnish

1 Preheat the oven to 190°C/375°F.

2 Fill a large pot halfway with water and bring it to the boil. Add the cabbage and cook for 2–3 minutes, then, using a spoon or tongs, peel away 12 whole large leaves and transfer them to a kitchen paper. Pat dry. Chop the remaining cabbage.

3 Heat 1 tablespoon of the olive oil in a large frying pan over a medium-high heat. When the oil is shimmering, add the onion, garlic and peppers and season with salt and pepper. Cook for 5 minutes or until the onions are softened. Add the celeriac rice, beans and walnuts and stir to combine. Cook for 5 minutes or until the rice is softened. Remove the pan from the heat and set aside.

4 Combine the tomato sauce and garlic powder in a medium pot. Season with salt and pepper. Bring to a simmer over a medium-high heat, then reduce the heat to maintain a simmer and cook for 5 minutes to develop the flavours.

5 Cover the bottom of a 23 x 33cm baking dish with the chopped cabbage. Pour over 225ml of the

tomato sauce. Lay out one whole cabbage leaf on a clean, dry surface and cut out the thick stem in the centre in a V shape, keeping the leaf intact. Place about 75g of the celeriac rice filling in the centre. Fold both sides over the filling and roll up. Place the roll seam-side down in the baking dish. Repeat with the remaining leaves and filling.

6 Pour the stock over the rolls, then pour over the remaining sauce. Bake for 45 minutes or until the celeriac rice is cooked through and softened. Garnish with parsley before serving.

Chicken and Celeriac Rice Soup

Chicken and rice soup comes in a second for Most Comforting Soup of All Time (after chicken noodle, of course). This lighter version uses celeriac rice in place of regular rice, giving you the same consistency without the high glycaemic index and calorie count. The chicken cooks in the stock, infusing it with a salty and deeply savoury flavour. If I'm feeling under the weather or just need a quick pick-me-up, this soup always does the trick.

~~~ Gluten-free
~~~ Paleo
~~~ Dairy-free
Low-cal
Saves Well

TIME TO PREP 15 minutes
TIME TO COOK 45 minutes
SERVES 4

NUTRITIONAL INFORMATION
Calories: 244
Fat: 14 g
Sodium: 1010 mg
Carbohydrate: 12 g
Fibre: 2 g
Sugar: 3 g
Protein: 18 g

ALSO WORKS WELL WITH
Turnip

65g red onion, diced

1 large carrot, finely diced

2 garlic cloves, finely chopped

Small pinch of chilli flakes

Salt and pepper

1 tablespoon fresh thyme, or 1 teaspoon dried

1 tablespoon fresh oregano, or 1 teaspoon dried

4 skin-on, bone-in chicken thighs (about 600g)

2 bay leaves

1.4 litres reduced-salt chicken stock

1 large celeriac

1 tablespoon finely chopped fresh parsley

This recipe freezes well, so make a big batch to keep on hand for the winter.

---

1 In a large stockpot with a lid, combine the onion, carrot, garlic and chilli flakes and season with salt and black pepper. Cook over a medium heat for 3–5 minutes or until the onion is softened and mostly translucent. Add the thyme and oregano and stir until combined, about 30 seconds.

2 Add the chicken thighs and bay leaves. Pour in the stock and 475ml water. Increase the heat to medium-high, cover and bring to the boil. Reduce the heat to medium-low and simmer for 30 minutes.

3 While the chicken cooks, peel the celeriac and spiralize with blade D. Working in batches, if necessary, pulse the noodles in a food processor until rice-like.

4 Remove the chicken from the stock. Remove and discard the skin, then pull off and shred the meat, reserving the bones and any juices. Return the bones to the pot and add the celeriac rice. Simmer, uncovered, for a further 10 minutes or until the rice is softened.

5 Remove and discard the bones and bay leaves. Add the shredded chicken to the soup and season with salt and black pepper. Cook for a further 5 minutes, then stir in the parsley and serve.

Celeriac Spaghetti and Vegetarian Meatballs

Vegetarian
Dairy-free
Saves Well

TIME TO PREP 30 minutes
TIME TO COOK 1 hour
SERVES 4

NUTRITIONAL INFORMATION
Calories: 317
Fat: 13 g
Sodium: 655 mg
Carbohydrate: 40 g
Fibre: 13 g
Sugar: 8 g
Protein: 13 g

When you think of spaghetti and meatballs, do you think of *Lady and the Tramp*? I definitely do, and thanks to the endless noodle possibilities spiralizing presents, that scene can be re-created infinitely. These meatballs were inspired by and adapted from the Veggie Balls from the Meatball Shop in New York City, a restaurant with a build-your-own type of menu. They have plenty of veggie sides to create a more wholesome meal. Perhaps one day, one of them will be spiralized? A girl can dream.

90g dried brown lentils, rinsed

1 bay leaf

225g button mushrooms, trimmed and roughly chopped

2 tablespoons extra-virgin olive oil

¼ teaspoon chilli flakes

2 garlic cloves, finely chopped

125ml reduced-salt vegetable stock

1 tablespoon soy sauce

45g rolled oats

¼ teaspoon dried basil

¼ teaspoon dried oregano

¼ teaspoon dried parsley

¼ teaspoon dried rosemary

Salt and pepper

1 large or 2 medium celeriacs

350ml jarred tomato basil sauce

1½ tablespoons finely chopped fresh parsley

1 Preheat the oven to 180°C/350°F. Line a baking sheet with baking paper.

2 In a small saucepan, combine the lentils, bay leaf and 225ml water. Bring to the boil over a high heat, then reduce the heat to low and simmer for 20–30 minutes, slightly overcooking the lentils. Remove from the heat, drain and leave to cool for about 5 minutes. Remove and discard the bay leaf.

3 Transfer the lentils to a food processor, add the mushrooms and pulse until roughly chopped.

4 Heat 1 tablespoon of the olive oil in a large frying pan over a medium-high heat. When the oil is shimmering, add the chilli flakes and garlic and cook, stirring continuously, for 30 seconds or until fragrant. Stir in the lentil-mushroom mixture and cook for 3–5 minutes or until browned. Stir in the stock, soy sauce, oats, basil, oregano, dried parsley and rosemary. Cook until the liquid has been completely absorbed. Season with salt and black pepper. Remove the pan from the heat and leave to cool for about 5 minutes.

recipe continues

5 Using your hands, form the mixture into about twelve 4cm balls. Place on the prepared baking sheet, spacing them apart. Bake for 40 minutes or until golden brown.

6 While the meatballs cook, peel your celeriac and spiralize with **BLADE D**, then trim the noodles.

7 Wipe clean the frying pan from the meatball mixture and heat the remaining 1 tablespoon olive oil over a medium heat. When the oil is shimmering, add the celeriac noodles and season with salt and pepper. Cook for about 7 minutes, then pour over the tomato sauce and toss to coat the noodles. Cook for a further 2–3 minutes or until the sauce is heated through and the noodles are al dente.

8 Using tongs, divide the celeriac among four bowls and top each with three meatballs. Pour over the remaining sauce from the pan. Garnish with the parsley and serve.

Try using a basil pesto instead of the tomato sauce for a totally new version of this dish.

Buffalo Wings
with Celeriac Slaw

◇◇◇
◇◇◇ | Gluten-free

TIME TO PREP 15 minutes
TIME TO COOK 45 minutes
SERVES 4

NUTRITIONAL INFORMATION
Calories: 358
Fat: 22 g
Sodium: 214 mg
Carbohydrate: 15 g
Fibre: 2 g
Sugar: 5 g
Protein: 28g

For all those people who reach first for the carrots and celery sticks when the Buffalo wings are served, this recipe is for you. Whenever I go out to a bar with Lu to watch a game, he usually orders them, and they always come with ranch slaw. Yummy, but not the healthiest. I've taken matters into my own hands and created a slimmed-down wings recipe. A plentiful side of spiralized slaw that uses a Greek yogurt-based dressing over celeriac noodles invokes the same refreshing bite of celery. Game time ready!

For the wings
450g skin-on, bone-in chicken wings
1 tablespoon extra-virgin olive oil
1½ teaspoons garlic powder
Salt and pepper
2–3 tablespoons hot sauce

For the slaw
225ml natural 0% Greek yogurt
1 teaspoon fresh lemon juice
1 tablespoon red wine vinegar
1 teaspoon Dijon mustard
1 tablespoon chopped fresh parsley
2 teaspoons chopped fresh chives
½ teaspoon garlic powder
½ teaspoon onion powder
Salt and pepper
1 large celeriac, peeled and prepped
1 large carrot, peeled, spiralized with BLADE D

1 Make the wings. Preheat the oven to 200°C/400°F. Place a wire rack on top of a baking sheet.

2 Put the chicken in a medium bowl. Drizzle the olive oil over and rub it into the wings with your fingers. Season generously with garlic powder, salt and pepper. Place the wings on the rack and bake for 45 minutes or until the skin is crispy and the chicken is cooked through. Transfer the wings to a clean medium bowl, add the hot sauce and toss thoroughly to coat.

3 Meanwhile, make the slaw. In a large bowl, stir together all the ingredients for the slaw except the celeriac and carrot. Taste and adjust the seasoning to your preferences. Slice the celeriac halfway through lengthways to create a slit, being careful not to pierce any further than its centre. Spiralize with **BLADE C** and add to the bowl with the dressing. Add the carrots and toss thoroughly to combine. Chill until ready to serve.

4 Serve the celeriac slaw alongside the Buffalo wings.

~~~~~~~~~~

Try this slaw alongside a spicy fish dish or a burger.

~~~~~~~~~~

Courgette

Courgette, like a first love, will always have a special place in my heart – and on my plate. Whenever I introduce people to spiralizing, I always encourage them to start with this vegetable, like I did.

Courgette is the most popular vegetable to spiralize: it requires barely any prep, moves through the gadget effortlessly and has a consistency similar to that of real pasta. The noodles are also resilient, so they won't break up in the pan.

When you cook courgette, it releases quite a bit of moisture. To minimize this effect, there are a few steps you can take:

- Pat the noodles dry to blot out excess moisture as soon as they're spiralized.
- Cook the noodles in their own pan and drain them in a colander before topping them with any sauces or dressings.
- If you're cooking the noodles directly in a sauce, transfer the finished dish to the serving plate using pasta tongs, allowing the excess moisture to drip off into the pan rather than collect on the plate.
- Keep your noodle-to-sauce ratio heavier on the noodles, as their liquid will add to (and thin out) the sauce.

When picking out your courgette, make sure it's firm, bright in colour, at least 4cm in diameter, and no longer than 20cm (any longer and their taste becomes bitter).

NUTRITIONAL BENEFITS: Courgettes are very low-caloric and contain moderate amounts of folates, which helps with cell function. It is also a good source of potassium and vitamin C. Since it is composed of so much water, it also has detoxifying and hydrating benefits. Peeling is not necessary, so keep the skin on, as it carries many nutrients, including dietary fibre.

PREPARATION AND STORAGE: Slice off the ends to leave flat, even surfaces. Seal in an airtight container lined with kitchen paper in the fridge for up to 5 days.

BEST BLADES TO USE
- Blades A, B, C and D

BEST COOKING METHODS
- Raw
- Simmer in soups
- Sauté over a medium-high heat for 2–5 minutes

Thai Steak Salad

Dairy-free
Saves Well

TIME TO PREP 20 minutes
TIME TO COOK 20 minutes
SERVES 4

NUTRITIONAL INFORMATION
Calories: 408
Fat: 27 g
Sodium: 484 mg
Carbohydrate: 15 g
Fibre: 4 g
Sugar: 9 g
Protein: 29 g

ALSO WORKS WELL WITH
Kohlrabi

If I'm going to eat steak, the rest of the plate must be filled with heart-healthy vegetables. Here, the spiralized vegetables expertly complement the heartiness of the meat and add beautiful colour. The slightly sweet, nutty sauce brings life to the raw courgette noodles, and the longer they sit, the more they soften. No matter how you like your steak cooked, it shines in this Thai-inspired dish.

1 tablespoon extra-virgin olive oil

450g sirloin or skirt steak

Salt and pepper

For the dressing
60g almond butter

1½ tablespoons fresh lime juice

1 tablespoon rice vinegar

1 tablespoon soy sauce

1½ teaspoons sesame oil

1½ teaspoons honey

1 teaspoon grated fresh ginger

1 teaspoon hot sauce

2 medium courgettes, peeled, spiralized with BLADE C*, noodles trimmed*

1 large carrot, peeled spiralized with BLADE D*, noodles trimmed*

1 large red pepper, spiralized with BLADE A*, noodles trimmed*

1 spring onion, sliced

2 tablespoons slivered raw almonds

50g fresh coriander

1 Heat the olive oil in a griddle pan or large frying pan over a medium-high heat. Season the steak generously with salt and pepper. When the oil is shimmering, add the steak and sear for 4 minutes each side until medium-rare. Transfer to a chopping board to rest for about 10 minutes. Slice it thinly against the grain, then cut each slice into thirds.

2 While the steak rests, make the dressing. Place all the ingredients for the dressing in a food processor and pulse until creamy. Add water, 1 tablespoon at a time, as needed to reach the desired consistency. Taste and adjust the seasoning to your preferences.

3 In a large bowl, combine the courgette, carrot and pepper noodles and add the spring onion, almonds and coriander. Pour the dressing over the salad and toss thoroughly to combine. If liked, marinate the salad in the fridge for 15 minutes or until the courgette softens.

4 Divide the noodle salad among four plates and top evenly with the sliced steak.

I prefer to serve the steak chilled in this dish, so if you have the time, leave it to sit in the fridge after it rests for about 30 minutes. Hello, cold steak salad leftovers!

Hoisin Salmon
with Courgette Slaw

Many people ask me if I ever eat the same thing twice. Everyone figures I'm always testing new recipes, experimenting and cooking different styles of meals. While that's certainly true, I definitely have my lazy meals – the ones I default to when I'm not feeling inspired. One of those is hoisin salmon, and it may quickly become *your* lazy meal, too! Hoisin sauce is a thick, barbecue sauce-like condiment used in Chinese cooking to flavour dishes – it's both sweet and spicy. The courgette slaw absorbs all the flavours from the hoisin sauce and adds a nice crunch. Consider this lazy meal upgraded!

Dairy-free

TIME TO PREP 25 minutes
TIME TO COOK 25 minutes
SERVES 2

NUTRITIONAL INFORMATION
Calories: 424
Fat: 10 g
Sodium: 2300 mg
Carbohydrate: 45 g
Fibre: 8 g
Sugar: 24 g
Protein: 42 g

ALSO WORKS WELL WITH
Sweet Potato, Butternut Squash, Turnip

For the glaze
Juice of 2 limes

¼ teaspoon chilli flakes

90ml reduced-salt soy sauce

90ml hoisin sauce

1 (4cm) piece fresh ginger, peeled and chopped

2 garlic cloves, crushed

2 (115g) salmon fillets

2 medium courgettes, spiralized with BLADE D, noodles trimmed

3 spring onions, thinly sliced

2 carrots, peeled, spiralized with BLADE D, noodles trimmed

1 red pepper, spiralized with BLADE A, noodles trimmed

2 tablespoons chopped fresh coriander

1 teaspoon white sesame seeds, to garnish

The hoisin sauce is very sticky, so you might want to clean as you cook.

1 Preheat the oven to 200°C/400°F. Line a baking sheet with baking paper.

2 Make the glaze. Place all the ingredients for the glaze in a food processor and pulse until smooth.

3 Place a medium frying pan over a medium-high heat. When water flicked onto the pan sizzles, add the prepared glaze, reserving 60ml in a small bowl. Simmer until it has reduced and thickened into a syrup, about 15 minutes. Remove the pan from heat.

4 Set the salmon fillets on the prepared baking sheet and brush with a thin layer of the reserved glaze.

5 Bake the salmon for 9–12 minutes or until it is opaque and flakes easily.

6 Meanwhile, heat a large frying pan over a medium-high heat. When water flicked onto the pan sizzles, add the courgettes, spring onions, carrots and pepper and cook until al dente, about 3 minutes. Drain the vegetables in a colander, then return them to the pan over a medium-high heat and immediately pour over the reserved glaze. Toss to coat with the glaze for about 1 minute, then stir in the coriander.

7 Divide the slaw between two plates and top each with a salmon fillet. Garnish with sesame seeds.

Green Goddess Courgette Pasta

Vegan
Vegetarian
Gluten-free
Dairy-free (opt.)
No Cook
Saves Well

TIME TO PREP 35 minutes
TIME TO COOK 5 minutes
SERVES 2

NUTRITIONAL INFORMATION
Calories: 413
Fat: 32 g
Sodium: 65 mg
Carbohydrate: 31 g
Fibre: 8 g
Sugar: 6 g
Protein: 10 g

This recipe is for my fellow green goddesses out there – those of us who proudly embrace a healthy lifestyle full of wholesome, nourishing foods, including, of course, lots of greens. You'll feel and shine like your goddess self after eating this bowl of, well, green noodles. With anti-inflammatory avocado, immune-boosting ginger and detoxifying lemon, this dish will truly make you feel like you're glowing from the inside out. Whether it was the second slice of birthday cake at lunch or an emotionally draining week that led to a junk food bender, we've all been there – and this meal will get you back to feeling like the goddess you are!

40g quinoa

For the dressing
1 small garlic clove
½ medium avocado
2 tablespoons finely chopped fresh basil
2 tablespoons finely chopped fresh parsley
2 tablespoons finely chopped fresh chives
3 tablespoons extra-virgin olive oil
1 spring onion (green parts only), sliced
½ teaspoon lemon zest
Juice of 1 small lemon
1 tablespoon red wine vinegar
Salt and pepper

2 medium courgettes, spiralized with BLADE A, *noodles trimmed*
2 tablespoons flaked almonds
50g watercress
2 tablespoons crumbled goat's cheese (optional)

As you spiralize the courgette, apply very soft pressure and crank the handle slowly, making thinner-than-usual ribbons. If you're not sure how to do this, just spiralize with blade D instead.

1 Place the quinoa and 150ml water in a small saucepan. Cover and bring to the boil over a high heat, then uncover, reduce the heat to medium-low and simmer for 15 minutes or until the quinoa fluffs up. Transfer the quinoa to a small bowl and chill for 30 minutes.

2 Meanwhile, make the dressing. Place all the ingredients for the dressing plus 1 tablespoon water in a food processor and pulse until smooth. It should be thick, but add more water, 1 tablespoon at a time, as needed until the desired consistency is reached. Taste and adjust the seasoning to your preference.

3 Put the courgette noodles in a large bowl. Pour the dressing over the noodles and toss to combine. Leave to soften for 5 minutes.

4 Place a small frying pan over a medium-high heat. Toast the almonds in the frying pan, tossing to avoid burning, for about 5 minutes or until fragrant and golden brown. Immediately remove them from the pan.

5 Add the watercress and quinoa to the bowl with the courgettes and toss to combine. Divide the courgette pasta between two plates and top with the toasted almonds and, if you like, goat's cheese.

Dairy-free Clam Chowder

with Courgette Noodles

∾∾ Gluten-free
∾∾ Dairy free
∾∾ Low-cal

TIME TO PREP 15 minutes
TIME TO COOK 30 minutes
SERVES 4

NUTRITIONAL INFORMATION
Calories: 200
Fat: 4 g
Sodium: 476 mg
Carbohydrate: 35 g
Fibre: 9 g
Sugar: 13 g
Protein: 9 g

ALSO WORKS WELL WITH
Kohlrabi

Clam chowder is a summer classic. Traditionally made with milk and flour, it's not the lightest, but it is so universally desirable that I had to create an Inspiralized version. A seasoned cauliflower mash gives this chowder its chunky, thick consistency, just like the original. The moment after you sip your last spoonful of this soup, you'll look down at the bowl and say, 'Was that really dairy-free?!' The addition of courgette noodles lends substance and a slight crunch. If there's a little bit of stock left over, sop it up with some toasted multigrain bread.

1 large head of cauliflower, chopped into florets

1 tablespoon extra-virgin olive oil

1 small onion, diced

2 garlic cloves, finely chopped

1 carrot, diced

1 celery stick, diced

2 bay leaves

350ml reduced-salt chicken stock

375g canned chopped clams in juice

½ teaspoon garlic powder

2 tablespoons nutritional yeast, plus extra if needed

1 teaspoon fresh thyme leaves

Salt and pepper

1 teaspoon chilli powder

2 small courgettes, peeled, spiralized with BLADE D, noodles trimmed

140g frozen organic sweetcorn, thawed

If you'd like to make a thinner soup, use only half the cauliflower florets and add another 125ml chicken stock.

1 Bring a large pot of water to the boil over a high heat. Add the cauliflower and cook until fork-tender, about 10 minutes. Drain and transfer to a food processor.

2 Wipe the pot clean and heat the olive oil over a medium-high heat. When the oil is shimmering, add the onion, garlic, carrot and celery and sauté for 5 minutes or until the vegetables are softened. Add the bay leaves, 225ml of the stock and the clams along with their juice. Reduce the heat to medium and simmer.

3 Add the garlic powder, nutritional yeast, thyme and remaining 125ml stock to the cauliflower and season with salt. Blend until smooth. Taste and adjust the seasoning to your preference with more nutritional yeast, salt or pepper.

4 Add the cauliflower mixture and chilli powder to the simmering clam stock and stir to combine thoroughly. Season with pepper, then season generously with salt. Simmer for 10 minutes to let the flavours develop.

5 Add the courgette noodles and corn to the chowder and cook for 5 minutes until the noodles are al dente. Taste and adjust the seasoning, if needed. Before serving, remove the bay leaves.

Italian-style Chicken Sliders

This probably won't shock you, but my theory is that everything is better with courgette noodles. So why not stir them into your burgers? It's a fun, quick and super-easy way to sneak more vegetables into your meals. This recipe uses chicken mince, keeping the fat content low while incorporating the same great juicy flavours as a traditional burger. Those green swirls are sure to be a conversation starter at a dinner party.

Gluten-free
Paleo
Dairy-free
Low-cal
Saves Well

TIME TO PREP 20 minutes
TIME TO COOK 15 minutes
SERVES 4 (2 sliders per serving)

NUTRITIONAL INFORMATION
Calories: 120
Fat: 9 g
Sodium: 52 mg
Carbohydrate: 4 g
Fibre: 1 g
Sugar: 2 g
Protein: 12 g

1 small courgette, spiralized with BLADE D, *noodles roughly chopped*

450g lean chicken mince

1 large garlic clove, finely chopped

2 teaspoons dried parsley

1 teaspoon dried oregano

1 teaspoon dried basil

½ teaspoon onion powder

¼ teaspoon chilli flakes

Salt and pepper

2 tablespoons extra-virgin olive oil

½ small red onion, peeled, spiralized with BLADE A, *noodles trimmed*

8 leaves Little Gem lettuce

8 Roma (plum) tomato slices (from about 2 tomatoes)

Handful of micro-greens

Ketchup, to serve (optional)

1 In a large bowl, combine the courgette noodles, chicken, garlic, parsley, oregano, basil, onion powder and chilli flakes and season with salt and black pepper. Using your hands, form the mixture into eight small patties (or four large). Chill for about 10 minutes to set.

2 Heat the olive oil in a griddle pan or large frying pan over a medium-high heat. When the oil is shimmering, add the onions to one half of the pan and the patties to the other, working in batches if necessary. Season the onions with salt and pepper and sear, tossing occasionally, until mostly caramelized. Sear the patties for 5 minutes on each side or until browned and cooked through.

3 On a serving platter, lay out the lettuce leaves and place a burger on each (if you made sliders). Top each with a tomato slice, caramelized onion and microgreens. (Top with another piece of lettuce if you made larger burgers.) Serve with ketchup, if liked.

I love packing in even more vegetables by putting burgers on thick roasted slices of sweet potato as the 'bun'. You can also make spiralized buns (see page 16). Give it a try!

Chocolate Chip Courgette Noodle Bread
with Coconut Cream Icing

Gluten-free
Paleo
Dairy-free
Saves Well

TIME TO PREP 20 minutes
TIME TO COOK 50 minutes
SERVES 6–8

NUTRITIONAL INFORMATION
(for 1 of 6 servings)
Calories: 481
Fat: 31 g
Sodium: 238 mg
Carbohydrate: 43 g
Fibre: 7 g
Sugar: 24 g
Protein: 10 g

In gluten-free baking, there are many healthy types of flours to use, like coconut, tapioca and almond. These flours come from vegetables, nuts and fruits, making treats baked with them more nutritiously valuable than if wheat flour were used – plus, they're gluten-free! Spiralizing the courgette here makes this recipe a million times easier than the grating called for in your standard courgette bread recipe; plus, it adds a cool texture and visual appeal. The coconut cream in the sweet, fluffy icing complements the coconut notes of the flour.

For the courgette bread
1 medium courgette
40g tapioca flour
55g coconut flour
¾ teaspoon bicarbonate of soda
¾ teaspoon baking powder
½ teaspoon salt
2 teaspoons ground cinnamon
½ teaspoon ground nutmeg
3 large eggs, beaten
3 tablespoons maple syrup
2 teaspoons vanilla extract
60ml plain unsweetened almond milk
1 tablespoon coconut oil, melted and cooled to room temperature
1 ripe banana, mashed until no large chunks remain
50g chopped walnuts
9og dairy-free chocolate chips

For the frosting
360ml coconut cream (see page 19)
1½ teaspoons vanilla extract
1 tablespoon honey

1 Make the courgette bread. Preheat the oven to 180°C/350°F. Line a 23 x 13cm loaf tin with baking paper, leaving the paper overhanging on two sides.

2 Slice off the ends of the courgette and then slice it halfway through lengthways to create a slit, being careful not to pierce any further than its centre. Spiralize with **BLADE D**. Trim the noodles and pat dry.

3 In a medium bowl, combine the tapioca flour, coconut flour, bicarbonate of soda, baking powder, salt, cinnamon and nutmeg.

4 In a large bowl, stir together the eggs, maple syrup, vanilla, almond milk, coconut oil and banana.

5 Add the dry ingredients to the wet ingredients and stir to combine. Add the courgette noodles and stir until the batter is mostly smooth. Fold in the walnuts and chocolate chips.

recipe continues

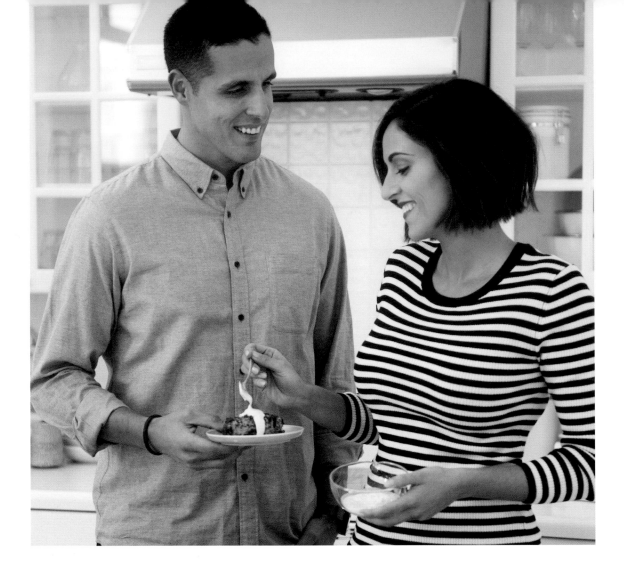

6 Pour the batter into the prepared tin and bake for 40–50 minutes or until a toothpick inserted into the centre of the bread comes out clean and the bread is browned on top. Lift the bread out of the tin using the baking paper. Discard the paper and set the bread on a wire rack to cool for at least 10 minutes.

7 Meanwhile, make the icing. Using a hand-held mixer, beat together the coconut cream, vanilla and honey in a medium bowl for 5 minutes or until whipped. Alternatively, use a stand mixer fitted with the whisk attachment and beat on high, or get in a good bicep workout with a whisk.

8 When the bread has cooled, cut it into thick slices or squares and top each with a generous dollop of the coconut cream.

It's important to let this bread cool completely to let it firm up – and so the icing doesn't melt on top of it. Don't skip that step!

Greek-style Prawn Scampi

Gluten-free
Dairy-free (opt.)
Low-cal

TIME TO PREP 15 minutes
TIME TO COOK 10 minutes
SERVES 4

NUTRITIONAL INFORMATION
Calories: 266
Fat: 10 g
Sodium: 670 mg
Carbohydrate: 13 g
Fibre: 4 g
Sugar: 7 g
Protein: 29 g

ALSO WORKS WELL WITH
Kohlrabi

If you're searching for an easy weeknight dinner, look no further – nothing beats this. Fast-cooked in garlic, olive oil and wine with herbs and traditionally served over pasta, this classic Italian-American dish gets a makeover here, with the addition of tomato and salty feta for a slightly Greek flair. On top of courgette noodles, this zesty dish is suitable for any night. It also *looks* fancy!

2 tablespoons extra-virgin olive oil

1 tablespoon finely chopped garlic

¼ teaspoon chilli flakes

450g large prawns, defrosted, peeled and deveined

Salt and pepper

160g tomato, deseeded and diced

60ml dry white wine

½ teaspoon lemon zest

2 tablespoons fresh lemon juice

3 medium courgettes, spiralized with BLADE D, noodles trimmed

2 tablespoons chopped fresh parsley

40g feta, crumbled, to garnish

1 Heat the olive oil in a large frying pan over a medium heat. When the oil is shimmering, add the garlic and chilli flakes and cook for 30 seconds or until fragrant. Add the prawns, season with salt and black pepper and cook for about 2 minutes on each side or until pink, opaque and cooked through. Using tongs or a slotted spoon, remove the prawns from the pan and set aside.

2 Immediately add the tomato, wine, lemon zest and lemon juice to the pan and scrape up any browned bits from the bottom of the pan with a wooden spoon. Cook for 2 minutes or until reduced slightly. Add the courgette noodles and season generously with pepper. Cook for 2–3 minutes or until al dente.

3 Return the prawns to the pan. Stir in the parsley and divide the pasta among four plates. Sprinkle the feta over the top before serving.

Use chopped lobster tail meat instead of prawns for an amped-up scampi.

Minestrone
with Courgette Noodles

≈ Vegan
≈ Vegetarian
Gluten-free
Dairy-free
One Pot
Saves Well

TIME TO PREP 15 minutes
TIME TO COOK 30 minutes
SERVES 4

NUTRITIONAL INFORMATION
Calories: 373
Fat: 8 g
Sodium: 720 mg
Carbohydrate: 60 g
Fibre: 15 g
Sugar: 16 g
Protein: 18 g

When I was vegan and went to my grandparents' house for Sunday dinner, aside from a few wisecracks here and there, my family was totally supportive of my diet. My grandmother would always prepare a *pasta e fagioli* or a minestrone soup especially for me. Minestrone is an Italian soup made with diced vegetables, beans and pasta. If I had known about spiralizing back then, I definitely would have had her make this version! Even though I'm no longer vegan, whenever I'm in the mood for something comforting and hearty, I always opt for this version with courgette noodles – it does the trick.

2 tablespoons extra-virgin olive oil

2 garlic cloves, finely chopped

½ teaspoon chilli flakes

130g red onion, diced

120g carrots, diced

100g celery, diced

2 bay leaves

2 (400g) cans chopped tomatoes

1.4 litres reduced-salt vegetable stock

1 teaspoon dried oregano

½ teaspoon dried rosemary

1 teaspoon dried thyme

½ teaspoon dried basil

Salt and pepper

2 medium courgettes

2 (400g) cans cannellini beans, rinsed
   and drained

The longer the courgette sits in this soup, the more it releases its water and dilutes the flavour of the soup. It's best to serve it straight away.

1 Heat the olive oil in a medium pot over a medium heat. When the oil is shimmering, add the garlic and chilli flakes. Cook for 30 seconds or until fragrant. Add the onion, carrots and celery. Sauté until softened, about 7 minutes.

2 Add the bay leaves and stir in the tomatoes, stock, oregano, rosemary, thyme and basil and season with salt and pepper. Increase the heat to high and bring the soup to the boil, then reduce the heat to medium-low, cover and simmer for 20 minutes to allow the flavours to develop.

3 While the soup simmers, slice the courgette halfway through lengthways to create a slit, being careful not to pierce any further than their centres. Spiralize with **BLADE D**.

4 Uncover the saucepan and add the beans and courgette noodles. Cook for about 3 minutes or until the courgette noodles soften. Remove the bay leaves and serve immediately.

Gluten-free Chicken Parmesan
over Courgette Noodles

≈≈≈
≈≈≈
≈≈≈   Gluten-free

TIME TO PREP 20 minutes
TIME TO COOK 30 minutes
SERVES 4

NUTRITIONAL INFORMATION
Calories: 461
Fat: 23 g
Sodium: 805 mg
Carbohydrate: 24 g
Fibre: 8 g
Sugar: 13 g
Protein: 44 g

ALSO WORKS WELL WITH
Sweet Potato, Butternut
Squash, Swede

I've always loved chicken Parm, but I rarely order it in restaurants because it's breaded, fried, covered with melted cheese and usually served with a bowl of pasta alongside. This gluten-free version uses a nutrient-dense ground almond blend to coat the chicken, which gets baked in the oven and is then served with a mound of tomato-basil courgette noodles. The ultimate meal, without the heavy calorie or carb count, it's my go-to Friday night dinner – and you're about to find out why.

For the breadcrumbs
90g ground almonds
½ teaspoon garlic powder
Salt and pepper
½ teaspoon dried parsley
½ teaspoon dried oregano
¼ teaspoon onion powder
3 tablespoons grated Parmesan cheese

1 large egg
4 (5mm thick) skinless, boneless chicken breasts
1 tablespoon extra-virgin olive oil
65g onion, diced
2 garlic cloves, finely chopped
½ teaspoon chilli flakes
800g canned chopped tomatoes
1 teaspoon dried oregano
Salt and pepper
1 bunch of fresh basil, chopped
4 (5mm thick) slices mozzarella cheese
4 courgettes, spiralized with BLADE D, noodles trimmed

1 Preheat the oven to 200°C/400°F. Line a baking sheet with baking paper.

2 Set up your dredging station. On a large plate, combine all the ingredients for the breadcrumbs and stir to combine. Beat the egg in a shallow medium bowl. Set the dishes side by side. Working one piece at a time, dip the chicken first in the egg and allow the excess to drip back into the bowl. Then dip it in the breadcrumbs, turning to coat and pressing to adhere. Place on the prepared baking sheet and bake for 15–20 minutes or until cooked through and no longer pink.

3 While the chicken bakes, heat the oil in a large frying pan over a medium heat. When the oil is shimmering, add the onion, garlic and chilli flakes and cook for 2 minutes or until the onion begins to soften. Add the tomatoes with their juices and the oregano, and season with salt and pepper. Crush the tomatoes with the back of a wooden spoon. Reduce the heat to low and simmer for 10 minutes or until the sauce thickens. Stir in the basil. Transfer half the sauce to a medium bowl and set aside, reserving the remainder in the pan over a low heat.

4 Remove the baking sheet from the oven and pour the sauce from the bowl over the chicken. Top each piece with a mozzarella slice and return to the oven to bake for a further 5–10 minutes or until the cheese has melted.

5 Return the frying pan with the remaining sauce to a medium-high heat. Add the courgette noodles and cook for about 5 minutes or until al dente. Divide the noodles among four plates. Top with the chicken.

Seared Scallops
over Courgette Noodles
with Roasted Pepper Sauce

≋ | Gluten-free
≋ | Paleo
≋ | Dairy-free
  | Low-cal

TIME TO PREP 15 minutes
TIME TO COOK 40 minutes
SERVES 2

NUTRITIONAL INFORMATION
Calories: 239
Fat: 13 g
Sodium: 387 mg
Carbohydrate: 19 g
Fibre: 5 g
Sugar: 10 g
Protein: 14 g

ALSO WORKS WELL WITH
Butternut Squash

Some jarred dressings and pasta sauces are so good that if you're crunched for time, there's no need to make your own. But it can be difficult to find a healthy version of some types. In my opinion, red pepper sauce is always better made from scratch, free of any dairy, preservatives or added sugars – like this one! The sauce is light but with a deep, roasted flavour, and coats the courgette noodles beautifully. This dish feels like a gourmet meal!

Cooking spray

2 red peppers

1 tablespoon plus 2 teaspoons olive oil

2 garlic cloves, finely chopped

¼ teaspoon chilli flakes

35g white onion, diced

1 teaspoon dried oregano

90ml reduced-salt chicken stock

2 medium courgettes, spiralized with BLADE C, **noodles trimmed**

6 large scallops, patted dry

Salt and pepper

1 tablespoon chopped fresh parsley, to garnish

Blade B also works well in this recipe. Try it for a change in texture!

1 Preheat the oven to 200°C/400°F. Lightly coat a baking sheet with cooking spray.

2 Slice off the tops and bottoms of the peppers, then halve them lengthways. Keeping the peppers intact, remove and discard the seeds. Place them cut-side up on the prepared baking sheet. Roast for 25 minutes, then transfer the roasted peppers to a food processor and pulse until mostly smooth.

3 Heat 1 tablespoon of the olive oil in a large frying pan over a medium heat. When the oil is shimmering, add the garlic, chilli flakes and onion and sauté for 5 minutes or until the onion is soft. Stir in the roasted pepper purée and the oregano, then add the stock. Cook for 5–7 minutes or until the mixture thickens. Reduce the heat to low and bring to a simmer to allow the flavours to develop.

4 Heat a separate large frying pan over a medium-high heat. When water flicked onto the pan sizzles, add the courgette noodles and cook for 3–5 minutes or until al dente. Drain and set aside in a large bowl.

5 Add the remaining 2 teaspoons olive oil to the frying pan you used for the courgette and heat over a medium-high heat. Season the scallops generously with salt and pepper. When the oil is shimmering, add the scallops and cook for 2–3 minutes on each side or until opaque and cooked through.

6 Pour the pepper sauce over the courgette noodles in the bowl and toss to coat. Divide the noodles between two plates, top each with three scallops and garnish with parsley.

Courgette Ravioli
with Tomato Basil and Cashew Cheese

≈≈≈ | Vegan
≈≈≈ | Vegetarian
≈≈≈ | Gluten-free
      | Paleo
      | Dairy-free
      | Low-cal

TIME TO PREP 30 minutes
plus 2 hours for the cashews
TIME TO COOK 15 minutes
SERVES 4 (3 ravioli per
serving)

NUTRITIONAL INFORMATION
Calories: 59
Fat: 4 g
Sodium: 100 mg
Carbohydrate: 5 g
Fibre: 1 g
Sugar: 2 g
Protein: 2 g

If you aren't already sold on the spiralizer being the most incredible kitchen gadget on the planet, these spiralized ravioli should seal the deal. This version uses cashew cheese, which raw vegans have been making ravioli with for ages. But to me, there's just something about this dish that needs to be warm and velvety smooth. So I've combined the best of both worlds: the courgette slices are warmed up in a pan before the vegan cheese is added, then the dish is topped with a cosy and aromatic tomato-basil sauce.

For the cashew cheese
90g raw, unsalted cashews, soaked in water
    for at least 2 hours (preferably overnight)
    and drained
1 tablespoon nutritional yeast
¼ teaspoon dried oregano
¼ teaspoon dried basil
¼ teaspoon dried parsley
¼ teaspoon garlic powder
1½ tablespoons fresh lemon juice
Salt and pepper

For the ravioli
1 medium courgette
225ml tomato-basil sauce
1 bunch of fresh basil, chopped, to garnish

~~~~~~~~~~~~~~~~~~~~~~~~~~~~~~

The size of your ravioli will depend on the width of your courgette. Opt for a medium courgette (about 4cm in diameter) for optimal results.

~~~~~~~~~~~~~~~~~~~~~~~~~~~~~~

1 In a food processor or high-speed blender, combine the cashews, yeast, herbs, garlic powder and lemon juice. Season with salt and pepper. Pulse a few times to break down the cashews until they have a coarse texture. Add 2 tablespoons water, 1 tablespoon at a time, and pulse until the cashew cheese has the consistency of thick hummus.

2 Make the ravioli. Slice the courgette lengthways to create a slit, taking care not to pierce any further than its centre. Spiralize with **BLADE A**. Select 24 courgette slices, saving any extra for future use.

3 Heat the tomato sauce in a small pot over a medium-high heat. Bring to a simmer, then reduce the heat to low to keep the sauce warm until ready to serve.

4 Heat a large frying pan over a medium heat. When water flicked onto the pan sizzles, add the courgette in a single layer, working in batches if necessary. Cook for 2 minutes or until heated through, then transfer to a piece of foil or baking paper, keeping them separated.

5 Lay out one courgette round on each of four plates. Spoon 1 tablespoon of cashew cheese on top, then add another round, pressing firmly to form a ravioli. Repeat until each plate has three ravioli. Pour 60ml of sauce over each plate and garnish with basil.

Avocado BLT Courgette Pasta

Gluten-free
Paleo
Dairy-free

TIME TO PREP 10 minutes
TIME TO COOK 20 minutes
SERVES 2

NUTRITIONAL INFORMATION
Calories: 330
Fat: 21 g
Sodium: 432 mg
Carbohydrate: 28 g
Fibre: 12 g
Sugar: 9 g
Protein: 20 g

ALSO WORKS WELL WITH
**Butternut Squash,
Parsnip, Broccoli,
Sweet Potato**

When Lu and I go back to restaurants we've visited before, we always try to order something new – especially at our neighbourhood staples. There's one restaurant, however, where Lu refuses to order any other thing on the menu, despite having ordered it dozens of times. That's the BLAT: a bacon, lettuce, avocado and tomato sandwich. He loads it up with a fried egg, chicken and a heaped pile of sweet potato fries alongside. He just can't resist it! This courgette pasta is a healthier, lighter version of Lu's favourite sandwich. It comes together quickly and works well for brunch or dinner.

170g cherry tomatoes

1 tablespoon extra-virgin olive oil

½ teaspoon garlic powder

Salt and pepper

4 bacon rashers

1 garlic clove, finely chopped

¼ teaspoon chilli flakes

2 medium courgette, spiralized with BLADE C, noodles trimmed

100g kale leaves, chopped

½ ripe avocado, cubed

Make this dish vegetarian by using the coconut or shiitake bacon on pages 59 and 154, respectively.

1 Preheat the oven to 200°C/400°F. Line a baking sheet with baking paper.

2 In a medium bowl, toss the tomatoes and olive oil to coat. Add the garlic powder, season generously with salt and black pepper and toss again. Spread the tomatoes on the prepared baking sheet, spacing them apart. Roast for 25 minutes or until the tomatoes collapse and their skins are charred. Remove from the oven, lift the baking paper and pour the tomatoes and their juices from the paper into a medium bowl.

3 Meanwhile, place the bacon in a large frying pan. Cook over a medium-high heat, flipping occasionally, for 8–10 minutes or until crispy. Transfer to a kitchen-paper-lined plate to drain.

4 Discard most of the rendered bacon fat and leave the pan to cool for a few minutes. Return the pan to a medium heat and add the fresh garlic and chilli flakes. Cook until fragrant, about 30 seconds. Add the courgette noodles, kale and avocado. Cook, tossing frequently, for 2–3 minutes or until the noodles are al dente. Add the tomatoes and their juices and crumble the bacon over the top, tossing to combine. Serve immediately.

Lemon Halibut
with Summer Squash Gratin and Tomato Coulis

≈≈ | Gluten-free
≈≈ | Paleo
≈≈ | Dairy-free

TIME TO PREP 30 minutes
TIME TO COOK 15 minutes
SERVES 4

NUTRITIONAL INFORMATION
Calories: 338
Fat: 18 g
Sodium: 168 mg
Carbohydrate: 22 g
Fibre: 4 g
Sugar: 9 g
Protein: 27 g

ALSO WORKS WELL WITH
Potato, Sweet Potato, Swede, Butternut Squash, Golden Beetroot

Because they're typically heavy, gratins are usually reserved for cold winter nights. I happen to love gratins, so I wanted to create a warm-weather version with a light, dairy-free sauce. This recipe not only uses courgette, but also yellow squash, making it a true celebration of summer produce. The halibut sits delicately in a tomato coulis and matches the freshness of the gratin.

For the tomato coulis
675g ripe Roma (plum) tomatoes, deseeded and chopped

1 garlic clove, crushed

2 fresh basil leaves

Salt and pepper

For the cashew cream
120g raw unsalted cashews, soaked in water for at least 2 hours, rinsed and drained

225ml reduced-salt vegetable stock

1 tablespoon fresh lemon juice

1 tablespoon nutritional yeast

Salt and pepper

For the gratin
1 green courgette

1 yellow summer squash

Cooking spray

2 teaspoons extra-virgin olive oil

2 garlic cloves, finely chopped

1 tablespoon finely chopped shallot

2 tablespoons chopped fresh basil

For the halibut
4 (85–115g) skinless halibut fillets

1 lemon, cut into 4 slices

Salt and pepper

2 teaspoons extra-virgin olive oil, plus extra as needed

1 Preheat the oven to 230°C/450°F.

2 Make the tomato coulis. Place all the ingredients for the coulis in a food processor and pulse until smooth. Season, transfer to a medium bowl and set aside. Clean the food processor bowl and blade.

3 Make the cashew cream. Place all the ingredients for the cashew cream in the food processor and pulse until creamy. Taste and adjust the seasoning to your preferences.

4 Make the gratin. Slice the courgette and squash halfway through lengthways to create a slit in each, being careful not to pierce any further than their centres. Spiralize with **BLADE A** and trim the noodles so that the pieces lay flat, rather than in spirals.

5 Coat a medium baking dish with cooking spray and create a layer of alternating courgette and squash slices over the base.

6 Heat the olive oil in a large frying pan over a medium-high heat. When the oil is shimmering, add the garlic and shallot and cook for 30 seconds or until fragrant. Add the cashew cream and basil and stir to combine.

7 Pour 60ml of the cashew cream mixture into the baking dish, then top with another layer of alternating courgette and squash slices. Repeat twice more, ending with the cashew cream. Season the top with salt and pepper. Bake for 15–20 minutes or until easily pierced with a fork.

8 Meanwhile, make the halibut. Coat a separate medium baking dish with cooking spray. Spread the tomato coulis evenly over the base. Place the halibut on top and layer the lemon slices over the fish. Season the halibut with salt and pepper and drizzle each fillet with ½ teaspoon of the olive oil. Transfer to the oven to bake alongside the gratin for 10–12 minutes or until the fish is opaque and cooked through.

9 Remove both dishes from the oven. Spoon the coulis back over the top of the halibut fillets. Serve each fillet with a portion of the gratin.

To enhance the flavour of the gratin, drizzle some of the tomato coulis over the squash slices before topping them with the sauce.

Cauliflower Pizza
with Courgette, Ricotta, Corn and Pesto

Vegetarian
Gluten-free
Low-cal

TIME TO PREP 20 minutes
TIME TO COOK 35 minutes
SERVES 4

NUTRITIONAL INFORMATION
Calories: 270
Fat: 16 g
Sodium: 173 mg
Carbohydrate: 20 g
Fibre: 6 g
Sugar: 7 g
Protein: 16 g

A couple of years back, I read an article that proclaimed, 'Cauliflower is the new kale!' Well, I've seen it everywhere – as a stand-in for chicken (see page 237), as rice, and, like here, as a pizza base. I guess whoever wrote that article was right! While this cauli-base doesn't have the same texture as a regular wheat base (it's not quite as thick or resilient), it dutifully serves its purpose – to hold delicious toppings! After all, without the toppings, a pizza would just be a giant piece of baked dough, right? The ricotta, pesto and sweetcorn showcase delicious summer flavours on top of a fluffy, soft mound of courgette noodles.

1 head cauliflower, cut into florets

1 teaspoon dried oregano

½ teaspoon dried basil

½ teaspoon garlic powder

2 large eggs, beaten

2 tablespoons grated Parmesan cheese

25g almond flour

Salt and pepper

Cooking spray

1 ear of sweetcorn, kernels sliced off

For the pesto

90g fresh basil leaves

1 large garlic clove, finely chopped

2 teaspoons pine nuts

1 tablespoon extra-virgin olive oil, plus extra as needed

1 tablespoon grated Parmesan cheese

Salt and pepper

112g ricotta cheese

1 medium courgette, spiralized with BLADE D, *noodles trimmed*

1½ teaspoons chilli flakes (optional)

recipe continues

1 Preheat the oven to 220°C/425°F. Line a baking sheet or 25cm pizza pan with baking paper.

2 Place the cauliflower florets in a food processor and pulse until rice-like. Transfer to a piece of muslin or a very thin kitchen cloth and wring out all the excess moisture. Transfer to a large bowl and add the oregano, basil, garlic powder, eggs, Parmesan and almond flour. Season with salt and black pepper and mix thoroughly with a fork until dough-like.

3 Spread the dough over the prepared pan, packing it in until it's about 1cm thick all round. Bake for 10–15 minutes or until the crust is firm and lightly golden brown on the edges. Remove from the oven and transfer the pizza base on the baking paper to a wire rack.

4 While the base bakes, place a medium frying pan over a medium-high heat and coat with cooking spray. When water flicked onto the pan sizzles, add the corn and sauté for 5 minutes or until fork-tender.

5 Meanwhile, make the pesto. Place all the ingredients for the pesto in a food processor and pulse until creamy. Taste and adjust the seasoning to your preference.

6 Assemble the pizza. Spread the pesto evenly around the base, leaving a 2cm wide border. Dollop the ricotta on top, spreading it out evenly with the back of a spoon. Season with salt and black pepper. Lay out the courgette noodles and scatter the sweetcorn over the base.

7 Return the pizza, still on the baking paper, to the baking sheet or pizza pan. Bake for a further 10 minutes or until the courgette noodles wilt and the base is browned on the bottom. Remove and sprinkle the chilli flakes, if you like, over the pizza. Leave to rest for 5 minutes, until the base solidifies. Using a pizza wheel or a sharp knife, cut the pizza into slices and serve.

Make sure your pizza base is at least 1cm thick; otherwise, it will crumble too easily. If you're worried, add an extra 2 tablespoons almond flour to help it bind a bit more. Depending on the size of your pan, your base may not fill its whole surface.

Vegetable Ribbon and Barley Salad

with Basil-feta Vinaigrette

Vegetarian
Gluten-free
Low-cal
Saves Well

TIME TO PREP 15 minutes
TIME TO COOK 60 minutes
SERVES 4

NUTRITIONAL INFORMATION
Calories: 172
Fat: 11 g
Sodium: 263 mg
Carbohydrate: 13 g
Fibre: 3 g
Sugar: 5 g
Protein: 5 g

Before there were vegetable noodles, there were vegetable ribbons. Ribbons can be made simply using a vegetable peeler, shaving the vegetables into thin strips – or they can be made using light pressure on your spiralizer with Blade A (see page 15). This salad combines my favourite vegetables with a healthy whole grain and a salty, fresh basil-feta vinaigrette. It's ideal for a summer get-together – it feeds a crowd well and looks beautiful, with those plush, colourful strands of vegetables. Note that you'll still have to rely on the peeler for the asparagus.

110g pearl barley

1 tablespoon olive oil

1 medium courgette, spiralized into ribbons with BLADE A*, noodles trimmed*

1 large carrot, peeled, spiralized into ribbons with BLADE A*, noodles trimmed*

12 large asparagus spears, shaved into ribbons with a peeler

Salt and pepper

For the vinaigrette

3 tablespoons sliced fresh basil

75g feta, crumbled

1 shallot, finely chopped

1 tablespoon fresh lemon juice

Salt and pepper

2 tablespoons olive oil

2 tablespoons red wine vinegar

1 Put the barley and 350ml water in a large pot with a lid and bring to the boil over a high heat. Reduce the heat to medium-low, cover and simmer until tender, about 45 minutes.

2 Make the vinaigrette. Place all the ingredients for the vinaigrette in a food processor and pulse until blended and creamy.

3 Heat the olive oil in a large frying pan over a medium-high heat. When the oil is shimmering, add the courgette, carrots and asparagus. Season with salt and pepper and cook for 3–5 minutes or until the vegetables are lightly softened. Transfer to a large bowl.

4 Add the barley to the vegetables and pour the vinaigrette over the top. Toss thoroughly to combine.

If you're maintaining a grain-free diet, use 100g of cauliflower rice in place of the barley.

Sausage and Peppers
with Courgette Noodles

Gluten-free
Paleo
Dairy-free
Saves Well

TIME TO PREP 15 minutes
TIME TO COOK 30 minutes
SERVES 4–6

NUTRITIONAL INFORMATION
Calories: 399
Fat: 32 g
Sodium: 488 mg
Carbohydrate: 16 g
Fibre: 3 g
Sugar: 10 g
Protein: 15 g

I daresay that, with a loaf of oven-toasted semolina bread alongside for dipping, sausage and peppers is my absolute favourite Italian dish to indulge in during the summertime. From June to September, almost every time I stopped by my grandparents' house, there was sausage and peppers. In an attempt to fill up on fibre-filled vegetables and resist the bread, I've tossed in raw courgette noodles here. They add an al dente, pasta-like crunch and bulk up this dish, making it a fully satisfying meal. And yes, there's a lot of olive oil here, because it wouldn't be the same without it. It's all about balance, right?

5 tablespoons extra-virgin olive oil

2 sweet fennel Italian sausage links

2 spicy Italian sausage links

2 medium yellow onions, peeled, spiralized with BLADE A, *noodles trimmed*

1 red pepper, spiralized with BLADE A, *noodles trimmed*

1 orange pepper, spiralized with BLADE A, *noodles trimmed*

1½ tablespoons tomato purée

¼ teaspoon chilli flakes

4 garlic cloves, finely chopped

½ teaspoon dried oregano

225ml reduced-salt chicken stock

Salt and pepper

2 tablespoons finely chopped fresh curly parsley

2 medium courgettes, spiralized with BLADE D, *noodles trimmed*

If you're serving this dish in the summer, try fresh basil instead of parsley to garnish.

1 Heat 2 tablespoons of the olive oil in a large frying pan with a lid over a medium-high heat. When the oil is shimmering, add the sausages and cover the pan. Cook for about 7 minutes or until just browned on the bottom. Uncover and cook for a further 5 minutes, turning, until browned on the outside but not cooked through. Using tongs, transfer the sausages to a chopping board and slice into 2.5cm pieces. Reserve.

2 Immediately add the remaining 3 tablespoons olive oil, the onion noodles and the pepper noodles to the same pan. Cook for about 5 minutes or until the vegetables soften. Add the tomato purée, and stir to cook the vegetables. Add the chilli flakes and garlic and cook for 30 seconds or until fragrant. Return the sausage to the pan and add the oregano and stock. Season with salt and black pepper. Cover the pan and simmer until the sausage is cooked through, about 10 minutes. Uncover and simmer for a further 5 minutes until the sauce has reduced by one-quarter. Stir in the parsley.

3 Transfer to a large serving platter or bowl and add the courgette noodles. Toss thoroughly until the noodles begin to wilt and are fully incorporated. Serve immediately.

Cucumber

Most of the time, cucumbers are dunked into dips, sliced for a sandwich or diced and tossed into salads. Not a whole lot to them. . . until now! Cucumber noodles can be used as a stand-alone noodle alternative, but they also work as a crunchy addition to trendy bowl meals.

Since cucumbers are composed primarily of water, they're wonderful for hydration, but they start to release that liquid the moment they are spiralized. Be sure to pat them dry thoroughly before using them in a recipe, and avoid cooking them. However you choose to incorporate your cucumber noodles, they're sure to be more exciting than ever before.

NUTRITIONAL BENEFITS: Cucumbers help you stay hydrated, which is essential for your body to run optimally and can help flush out unwanted toxins. They also contain skin-clearing magnesium, potassium and silicon. That's why so many beauty products are cucumber-scented or fortified!

PREPARATION AND STORAGE: Avoid peeling; simply slice off the ends to leave flat, even surfaces. Store in an airtight container over kitchen paper in the fridge for 2–3 days.

BEST BLADES TO USE
- Blade A
- Blade B
- Blade C
- Blade D

BEST COOKING METHODS
- Raw

Turkey, Spinach and Hummus Cucumber Noodle Roll-ups

Gluten-free
Dairy-free
Low-cal
No Cook

TIME TO PREP 15 minutes
TIME TO COOK 5 minutes
SERVES 2 (2 roll-ups per serving)

NUTRITIONAL INFORMATION
Calories: 64
Fat: 2 g
Sodium: 219 mg
Carbohydrate: 4 g
Fibre: 1 g
Sugar: 1 g
Protein: 7 g

ALSO WORKS WELL WITH
Courgette, Apple

I distinctly (and lovingly!) remember my mother making me 'turkey roll-ups' for after-school snacks. I loved dipping them into mustard and munching on them while telling her about my day. Now I've re-created that childhood memory into something a little more grown up. The spinach and crunchy cucumber noodles add texture and vitamins, and the hummus packs in more protein and flavour. Whether you're looking for a snack for your children or something to pack for yourself at the office, these roll-ups are satisfying and, most important, fun to eat.

4 slices of deli turkey

4 tablespoons hummus

2 teaspoons hemp hearts (optional)

50g baby spinach leaves

1 medium seedless cucumber, spiralized with BLADE D, *noodles trimmed and patted dry*

Hot sauce, to serve

1 Lay out the turkey slices on a clean, dry surface. Spread 1 tablespoon of the hummus on each and top evenly with hemp hearts, if you like. On the short side end furthest from you, add about 15g of the spinach leaves to each, then top with the cucumber noodles.

2 Roll it all up like a burrito. Secure with a toothpick if needed and drizzle with or dip into hot sauce.

You'll immediately love these roll-ups and want to make them over and over again. To keep things interesting, try using other types of deli meat and smears. I like them with pastrami and mustard.

California Roll Sushi Bowl
with Ginger-carrot Dressing

∿∿   Dairy-free
∿∿   Low-cal
∿∿

TIME TO PREP 25 minutes
TIME TO COOK 10 minutes
SERVES 4

NUTRITIONAL INFORMATION
Calories: 300
Fat: 16 g
Sodium: 445 mg
Carbohydrate: 22 g
Fibre: 7 g
Sugar: 11 g
Protein: 13 g

ALSO WORKS WELL WITH
Carrot

If you've never tried a sushi bowl, you're in for a treat. They deliver all the same great flavours as your sushi favourites, but they think outside the box – or the roll. What's even better about bowls is that you can create your own bites. Fork up more avocado in one and more kani in the next. The fluffy radish rice and crunchy cucumber noodles make this dish more filling than traditional sushi rolls. I chose the classic California roll here because its ingredients are readily available at most supermarkets, but if you like something else better, deconstruct it into your own spiralized sushi bowl!

For the dressing

2 tablespoons extra-virgin olive oil

2 teaspoons grated fresh ginger

60ml rice vinegar

1 tablespoon reduced-salt soy sauce

1 teaspoon honey

1 carrot (115g), peeled and finely grated

For the sushi bowl

1 large radish, peeled, spiralized with BLADE D, then riced (see page 16) and drained

4 spring onions, sliced

1 teaspoon rice vinegar

1 large cucumber, spiralized with BLADE C, noodles trimmed

1 sheet nori (dried seaweed), cut into thin strips

350g kani (crabmeat), cut into 5mm pieces and halved

1 avocado, sliced

4 teaspoons toasted white sesame seeds

1 Make the dressing. In a food processor, combine all the ingredients for the dressing and pulse until creamy.

2 In a medium bowl, combine the radish rice, spring onions and rice vinegar.

3 Divide the seasoned radish rice among four bowls and top each with equal amounts of the cucumber noodles, nori, kani, avocado and sesame seeds. Drizzle over the dressing and serve.

Lamb-feta Burgers
with Greek Cucumber Noodle Salad

~~~   Gluten-free
~~~

TIME TO PREP 25 minutes
TIME TO COOK 15 minutes
SERVES 4

NUTRITIONAL INFORMATION
Calories: 413
Fat: 30 g
Sodium: 499 mg
Carbohydrate: 15 g
Fibre: 3 g
Sugar: 4 g
Protein: 22 g

ALSO WORKS WELL WITH
Courgette, Beetroot

You probably already know that your first line of defence when ordering healthily at a restaurant is answering 'Salad, please' when asked 'Fries or a side salad?' Sadly, that measly pile of lettuce never quite competes with those crispy, mouthwatering fries. When you're at home, you can change all that. Instead of serving burgers with a predictable salad, change it up with spiralized noodles! These cucumber noodles are hydrating, crunchy and filling, and won't leave your fingertips oil-slicked. This Greek-flavoured lamb burger is lightly stuffed with feta, which complements the tangy cucumber noodles. Plus, since you swapped fries for cucumbers, there's room for a dessert. That's my kind of compromise!

For the burgers
450g lean lamb mince
3 tablespoons chopped fresh parsley
½ teaspoon ground cumin
½ teaspoon dried oregano
½ teaspoon paprika
½ teaspoon garlic powder
75g feta, crumbled
Salt and pepper

For the dressing
1½ teaspoons dried oregano
1 teaspoon garlic powder
Pinch of chilli flakes
1 tablespoon red wine vinegar
1 tablespoon olive oil
Salt and pepper

For the cucumber salad
2 seedless cucumbers, spiralized with BLADE C, *noodles trimmed and patted dry*
65g red onion, diced
170g cherry tomatoes, halved
50g packed baby spinach
60g pitted Kalamata olives, halved
55g red pepper, diced
40g canned chickpeas, drained and rinsed

1 tablespoon extra-virgin olive oil
4 large romaine or cos lettuce leaves, to serve (optional)

recipe continues

1 Make the lamb burgers. In a large bowl, combine all the ingredients for the burgers and, using your hands, mix thoroughly. Form the mixture into four patties and set them on a plate. Chill for 10 minutes.

2 Meanwhile, make the dressing. In a large bowl, whisk together the oregano, garlic powder, chilli flakes, vinegar and olive oil for the dressing. Taste and add salt and black pepper to your preferences.

3 Add all the ingredients for the cucumber salad to the bowl with the dressing and toss to combine.

4 Heat the olive oil in a large frying pan over a medium-high heat. When the oil is shimmering, add the burgers, working in batches if necessary, and cook for 3–4 minutes on each side for medium doneness.

5 Serve each burger on a romaine lettuce leaf, if you like, with a side of the cucumber noodle salad.

The burgers in this recipe can be served on romaine or cos, but if you like, add a bun, or just top the salad with the burger and dig in with a fork!

Chicago-style Carrot Dogs
with Spiralized Pickles

〰   Vegetarian
〰   Vegan
〰   Dairy-free
     Low-cal
     Saves well

TIME TO PREP 20 minutes, plus 2 hours marinating (optional)
TIME TO COOK 45 minutes
SERVES 4

NUTRITIONAL INFORMATION
Calories: 203
Fat: 2 g
Carbohydrates: 39 g
Sodium: 1070 mg
Protein: 6 g
Sugar: 13 g

ALSO WORKS WELL WITH
Courgette

I first visited Chicago to run a half marathon. While I was definitely excited (and totally nervous), I was also thinking about the food. Chicago is famous for its food scene, so I was anticipating some great meals. How would Chicago-style pizza compare to New York's? What about their hot dogs? It's tough for me to admit, but Chicago-style hot dogs are just more impressive – they have crunchy veggie toppings and seem more meal-like, with onions, peppers, tomatoes and other garnishes like relish and pickles. I made them vegan with these carrot dogs, and spiralized the pickle to get more in every bite. After all, a pickle's just a cucumber, right? Now, as for pizza. . . I'll always prefer a New York slice!

4 thick carrots

2 tablespoons liquid smoke (I like the hickory flavour)

2 tablespoons soy sauce

1 tablespoon maple syrup

¼ teaspoon onion powder

¼ teaspoon garlic powder

Pepper

4 hot dog buns (see note below)

2 vine tomatoes, sliced into 8 wedges

8 peperoncinos (Italian chillies)

Yellow mustard

65g small white onion, diced

Sweet relish

2 gherkins, spiralized with BLADE D, noodles trimmed

〰〰〰〰〰〰〰〰〰〰〰〰

When selecting a bun, check the ingredients list for sneaky, processed components like milk or preservatives.

〰〰〰〰〰〰〰〰〰〰〰〰

1 Preheat the oven to 220°C/425°F.

2 Prepare the carrots. Peel them, carefully rounding the edges to create a shape that resembles a hot dog.

3 In a small bowl, whisk together the liquid smoke, soy sauce, maple syrup, onion powder and garlic powder. Place the carrots in a shallow baking dish and pour over the liquid mixture. Toss to coat, massaging the marinade into the carrots. If you have the time, marinate for at least 2 hours.

4 Season the marinated carrots with pepper and place on a baking sheet, reserving the marinade. Transfer to the oven and roast for 45–50 minutes or until fork tender. Every 20 minutes, brush the carrots with the reserved marinade.

5 Place the roasted carrot dogs in hot dog buns. On one side of each, add 2 tomato wedges. On the other side, add the peppers. Squirt yellow mustard on top in a zigzag. Top with about 2 tablespoons of white onion and a dollop of sweet relish. Finish with the spiralized pickles and serve.

Kohlrabi

Kohlrabi is sometimes known as the 'alien turnip', but don't let its odd shape deter you — it's one of the easiest vegetables to spiralize. They are either purple or green on the outside, but both have a similar cream-yellow-coloured flesh with the texture of a radish as well as a hint of cucumber and broccoli. This overall mildness makes them super versatile for spiralized cooking.

The bulb of a kohlrabi sprouts a bundle of greens that also can be cooked along with the flesh. When choosing a kohlrabi for spiralizing, try to find one with unblemished leaves and a bulb that does not appear cracked or overgrown. If you get one in your weekly veg box delivered to your door or buy one from the supermarket, just flip to this chapter and discover what you can do with this delightful vegetable.

NUTRITIONAL BENEFITS: Like most cruciferous vegetables, kohlrabi is a great source of dietary fibre, which helps with digestive health and reduces bloating. Low in calories, it is helpful for weight loss. Kohlrabi is also a great source of potassium and iron, which promote vascular health.

PREPARATION AND STORAGE: Peel the kohlrabi bulb. If it has uneven round ends, slice off the ends to leave flat, even surfaces. Store in an airtight container in the fridge for up to 5 days.

BEST BLADES TO USE
- Blade A
- Blade B
- Blade C
- Blade D

BEST COOKING METHODS
- Raw
- Boil or steam
- Sauté over a medium heat for 5 minutes
- Roast at 200°C/400°F for 15 minutes

Kohlrabi Spaghettini Aglio e Olio

Vegetarian
Dairy-free (opt.)
Gluten-free
Low-cal
Saves Well

TIME TO PREP 20 minutes
TIME TO COOK 10 minutes
SERVES 4

NUTRITIONAL INFORMATION
Calories: 104
Fat: 9 g
Sodium: 51 mg
Carbohydrate: 5 g
Fibre: 3 g
Sugar: 2 g
Protein: 4 g

ALSO WORKS WELL WITH
Courgette

Spaghettini, by definition, is a pasta strand that is thinner than spaghetti but thicker than vermicelli. Since this noodle is so fine, it's best served with a simple olive oil and garlic sauce, like an *aglio e olio* ('garlic and oil' in Italian). When we were studying abroad and visiting friends in Italy, my friends and I often found ourselves out late at night, drunk on wine and laughter, gathered around a massive vat of spaghettini! This easy pasta dish works for every occasion, whether a late-night meal or a quick vegetarian dinner.

2 tablespoons extra-virgin olive oil

2 medium kohlrabies, peeled, spiralized with BLADE D**, noodles trimmed**

Salt and pepper

4 medium garlic cloves, sliced into rounds

¼–½ teaspoon chilli flakes

1 bunch of fresh flat-leaf parsley, chopped

4 tablespoons grated Parmigiano-Reggiano cheese

1 Heat 1 tablespoon of the olive oil in a large non-stick frying pan over a medium-high heat. When the oil is shimmering, add the kohlrabi noodles. Season with salt and pepper and cook for about 5 minutes or until al dente. Transfer to a plate.

2 Turn off the heat and leave the pan to cool for about 2 minutes. Return the heat to medium-high and add the remaining 1 tablespoon olive oil, the garlic and chilli flakes. Cook for about 2 minutes or until the garlic is golden, taking care not to brown or burn it. Remove the pan from heat, add the kohlrabi noodles and parsley, and season generously with salt and pepper. Toss thoroughly to combine.

3 Divide the pasta among four bowls and top each with 1 tablespoon of the cheese.

Grate some lemon zest over the pasta to add a tangy, refreshing accent.

General Tso's Cauliflower
with Kohlrabi Rice

〜〜 | Vegetarian
〜〜 | Dairy-free
〜〜 | Low-cal

TIME TO PREP 15 minutes
TIME TO COOK 45 minutes
SERVES 4

NUTRITIONAL INFORMATION
Calories: 214
Fat: 11 g
Sodium: 134 mg
Carbohydrate: 28 g
Fibre: 7 g
Sugar: 16 g
Protein: 5 g

ALSO WORKS WELL WITH
Butternut Squash, Golden
Beetroot

I definitely believe in moderation when it comes to food, but some dishes are just so nutritionally bad that after embarking on a healthy journey and nourishing yourself, you don't want to do that to your body. General Tso's is one of those foods for me, but with this spiralized, lightened-up version, I can take the classic Chinese dish off that no-no list. Thanks to arrowroot powder – a gluten-free thickening agent commonly used in healthy cooking – and the crunchy, sturdy nature of cauliflower, these General Tso's cauliflower bites have all the flavours of the original without the deep-frying, flour, cornflour or sugar. The kohlrabi rice soaks up all the sauce, making this dish a true takeaway fake-out.

1 small head cauliflower, cut into florets

1 tablespoon extra-virgin olive oil

Salt and white pepper (use black pepper if you don't have white)

3 spring onions, sliced, white and green parts kept separate

2 medium kohlrabies, peeled, spiralized with BLADE D, then riced (see page 16)

1 tablespoon sesame oil

3 tablespoons dark soy sauce

2 teaspoons rice vinegar

2 tablespoons honey

225ml reduced-salt vegetable stock

1 tablespoon coconut oil

2 teaspoons very finely chopped fresh ginger

2 garlic cloves, very finely chopped

5 whole dried red chillies, halved

1 tablespoon arrowroot powder, mixed with 1 tablespoon water

1 tablespoon white sesame seeds

recipe continues

1 Preheat the oven to 230°C/450°F. Line a baking sheet with baking paper. Place the cauliflower on the baking sheet and drizzle with the olive oil. Using your hands, massage the oil into the cauliflower. Space the florets apart, season with salt and white pepper and bake for 20–25 minutes or until golden brown, flipping once halfway through. Remove and set aside.

2 Place a large frying pan over a medium-high heat. When water flicked onto the pan sizzles, add the white parts of the spring onions and cook for 1 minute or until fragrant. Add the kohlrabi rice and season with salt. Cook for 5 minutes or until al dente. Divide the kohlrabi rice among four serving plates and set aside.

3 Meanwhile, in a small bowl, stir together the sesame oil, soy sauce, vinegar, honey and vegetable stock and set aside.

4 In the same pan you used for the kohlrabi rice, heat the coconut oil over a medium heat. When the oil has melted, add the ginger, garlic and chillies and stir. Add the soy sauce mixture, increase the heat to high and bring to the boil. Reduce the heat to low and simmer the sauce for 1 minute. Add the arrowroot powder mixture and whisk constantly until the sauce thickens. Add the cauliflower and spring onion greens and cook, stirring and spooning the sauce over the cauliflower as you stir, for 5 minutes or until the cauliflower is heated through and completely coated in the sauce.

5 Add the cauliflower to the plated kohlrabi rice. Garnish with sesame seeds.

This dish doesn't save well for more than 1 day in the fridge, so if you're making it for only yourself and want leftovers, halve the recipe to make two servings.

Spicy Kohlrabi Tortilla Soup
with Prawns

Gluten-free
Dairy-free
One Pot
Saves Well

TIME TO PREP 15 minutes
TIME TO COOK 20 minutes
SERVES 4–6

NUTRITIONAL INFORMATION
Calories: 384
Fat: 11 g
Sodium: 1155 mg
Carbohydrate: 39 g
Fibre: 15 g
Sugar: 10 g
Protein: 36 g

ALSO WORKS WELL WITH
Courgette

When I'm at a restaurant, I rarely order soup – they tend to be overloaded with sodium and contain hidden processed ingredients like sugar. But whenever I see tortilla soup on the menu, I can't resist – it's always perfectly spicy, crunchy from the tortilla, and packed with vegetables. This spiralized version replaces the tortilla strips with crispy kohlrabi noodles and adds prawns for extra protein and flavour.

1 medium kohlrabi, peeled and prepped

1 tablespoon extra-virgin olive oil

1 small white or yellow onion, diced

1 large garlic clove, finely chopped

1 large jalapeño chilli, deseeded and finely diced

1 teaspoon chilli powder

1 teaspoon dried oregano

½ teaspoon ground cumin

¼ teaspoon smoked paprika

1.4 litres reduced-salt vegetable stock or chicken stock

1 (400g) can chopped tomatoes

1 (400g) can black beans, rinsed and drained

450g frozen medium prawns, thawed, peeled and deveined

1 avocado, sliced

Juice of 2 small limes

50g fresh coriander leaves, roughly chopped

Salt and pepper

1 Slice the kohlrabi halfway through lengthways to create a slit, being careful not to pierce any further than its centre. Spiralize with **BLADE D** and set aside.

2 Heat the olive oil in a large pot over a medium-high heat. When the oil is shimmering, add the onion and cook for 3–5 minutes or until softened. Add the garlic and jalapeño chilli and cook for 30 seconds or until fragrant. Add the chilli powder, oregano, cumin and paprika and stir to combine.

3 Add the stock, tomatoes and beans to the pot. Increase the heat to high and bring to the boil, then reduce the heat to medium-low and add the prawns, avocado and lime juice to the pot. Cook for 5 minutes more or until the prawns are pink, cooked through and opaque.

4 Stir in the coriander and kohlrabi noodles. Season with salt and pepper and simmer for 30 seconds more. Ladle the soup into bowls and serve.

Fried Green Tomatoes
with Avocado Ranch Kohlrabi

≈≈≈ | Vegetarian
≈≈≈ | Gluten-free
≈≈≈ | Paleo
    | Dairy-free

TIME TO PREP 20 minutes
TIME TO COOK 10 minutes
SERVES 4

NUTRITIONAL INFORMATION
Calories: 421
Fat: 31 g
Sodium: 132 mg
Carbohydrate: 30 g
Fibre: 13 g
Sugar: 12 g
Protein: 15 g

ALSO WORKS WELL WITH
Courgette

One of the best parts about dating someone is introducing him or her to something they may have never heard of, done or tried – something you love. On a trip to Napa Valley, California, with Lu a month after our wedding, we sat down at the acclaimed restaurant Farmstead, and one of the daily specials was fried green tomatoes. I have eaten my fair share of fried green tomatoes, but Lu had never tried them. Obviously, I insisted we order them! As we dipped the tomatoes in the decadent aioli that accompanied them, nothing else mattered in the world except for our next bite – they were *that* good! In an effort to make a healthier version, I dusted the tomatoes in almond flour and replaced the dipping sauce with an avocado ranch-dressed kohlrabi salad.

For the dressing
1 ripe avocado
225ml plain unsweetened almond milk
3 tablespoons fresh lemon juice
2 teaspoons red wine vinegar
1 teaspoon garlic powder
1½ teaspoons finely chopped fresh dill
2 teaspoons finely chopped fresh parsley
1 teaspoon onion powder
1 teaspoon paprika
Salt (I use about ¼ teaspoon)
Black pepper

2 medium kohlrabies, peeled and prepped
2 large eggs
90g almond flour
1 teaspoon onion powder
¼ teaspoon paprika
½ teaspoon garlic powder
¼ teaspoon cayenne pepper
Salt and black pepper
2 tablespoons plus 1 teaspoon coconut oil
4 green tomatoes, thinly sliced (about 5mm thick)

1 Make the dressing. In a food processor, combine all the ingredients for the dressing and pulse until creamy. Taste and season to your preference.

2 Slice the kohlrabies halfway through lengthways to create a slit, being careful not to pierce any further than their centres. Spiralize with **BLADE C** and transfer the noodles to a large bowl. Add the dressing and toss to combine. Chill until ready to serve.

3 Set up your dredging station. In a shallow medium bowl, beat the eggs. On a large plate, mix together the almond flour, onion powder, paprika, garlic powder and cayenne. Season with salt and black pepper. Set the dishes side by side.

4 Heat 2 teaspoons of the coconut oil in a large frying pan over a medium-high heat until melted. Dip a few tomato slices in the egg and allow any excess to drip back into the bowl. Transfer to the almond flour mixture, pressing to coat. Place in the pan in a single layer and fry for 3–4 minutes on each side or until golden brown. Repeat with the remaining tomato, using 2 teaspoons of oil per batch.

5 Serve three tomato slices with the avocado-ranch kohlrabi.

For a salty kick, sprinkle the kohlrabi salad with roasted pumpkin seeds or sunflower seeds.

Chicken Mole
with Kohlrabi Rice

I've always appreciated the richness, fragrance and beauty of mole, a sauce used in Mexican cuisine. There are many different types, but this recipe showcases mole poblano, a dark red version served over meat. The story goes that nuns in a convent needed to whip up something quickly for a visiting archbishop, so they rummaged through the kitchen and made a sauce from whatever ingredients they could find – mainly chillies, spices and chocolate. Yes, chocolate! Here we use 70% cacao, which gives the sauce a deep flavour and colour while counteracting the heat of the chillies. The kohlrabi rice is simply prepared, letting the mole-bathed chicken do all the talking.

Gluten-free
Paleo
Dairy-free (opt.)
Saves Well

TIME TO PREP 20 minutes
TIME TO COOK 25 minutes
SERVES 4

NUTRITIONAL INFORMATION
Calories: 460
Fat: 16 g
Sodium: 424 mg
Carbohydrate: 28 g
Fibre: 8 g
Sugar: 17 g
Protein: 54 g

ALSO WORKS WELL WITH
Sweet Potato, Swede

---

1 tablespoon plus 3 teaspoons extra-virgin olive oil

4 skinless, boneless chicken breasts

Salt and pepper

2 garlic cloves, finely chopped

½ yellow onion, diced

1 (175g) can or jar tomato purée

1 large chipotle chile in adobo, finely chopped, plus 1 teaspoon adobo sauce

2 tablespoons sultanas

25g dark chocolate (at least 70% cacao), finely chopped

1 teaspoon ground cinnamon

1 teaspoon ground cumin

½ teaspoon chilli powder

½ teaspoon ground coriander

350ml reduced-salt chicken stock

2 medium kohlrabies, peeled, spiralized with BLADE D, *then riced (see page 16)*

2 tablespoons chopped fresh coriander

1 tablespoon fresh lime juice

2 tablespoons crumbled cotija cheese, to garnish (optional)

1 Heat 1 tablespoon of the olive oil in a medium frying pan over a medium heat. Season the chicken with salt and pepper on both sides. When the oil is shimmering, add the chicken and cook for 3–5 minutes on each side or until golden brown on the outside and cooked through. Transfer to a plate and tent with foil to keep warm.

2 In the same pan, heat 2 teaspoons of the oil over a medium heat. When the oil is shimmering, add the garlic and onion and cook, stirring frequently, for 3–5 minutes or until the onion is softened. Stir in the tomato purée and chipotle chilli and adobo and cook, stirring constantly, for about 1 minute or until combined.

3 Stir in the sultanas, chocolate, cinnamon, cumin, chilli powder, coriander and stock. Season with salt. Increase the heat to medium-high and bring the sauce to a strong simmer. Reduce the heat to low and simmer, stirring occasionally, for 5–7 minutes or until slightly reduced.

4 Return the chicken to the pan, including any collected juices. Simmer for 3–5 minutes or until the chicken is warmed through and coated well with the sauce.

5 Meanwhile, prepare the rice. Heat the remaining 1 teaspoon oil in a large frying pan over a medium heat. When the oil is shimmering, add the kohlrabi rice and season with salt and pepper. Cook for 5 minutes or until al dente. Stir in the coriander and lime juice and stir.

6 To serve, divide the rice among four plates. Add one chicken breast to each and spoon the mole sauce over the top. Garnish with cotija, if liked.

It's important to use a high-quality chocolate bar here to avoid any unwanted bitterness or staleness. Heck, if you're eating chocolate, might as well make it good.

Onion

Before the spiralizer became as popular and widely used as it is today, it was called a 'vegetable slicer', as it easily cuts and shreds most produce. What's one of the most tedious veggies to take a knife to? The onion! Whenever I use the spiralizer at cooking classes or demos, I get the most *ooh*s and *ahh*s when I spiralize an onion. The tool effortlessly slices through the onion, producing bountiful curly cuts in mere seconds. It's quicker and easier than using a knife – and more tear-free.

Onions are used as the base in many types of dishes. If nothing else, I encourage you to ditch the knife and use the spiralizer to slice your onions, whether you're preparing a creative recipe from this book or merely making a salad.

NUTRITIONAL BENEFITS: Onions help promote the flow of vitamin C in the body, which supports immunity. Raw onions also encourage the production of the good cholesterol, HDL.

PREPARATION AND STORAGE: Peel the onion and slice off both ends to leave flat, even surfaces. Store in an airtight container in the fridge for 2–3 days.

BEST BLADES TO USE
- Blade A

BEST COOKING METHODS
- Raw
- Bake at 220°C/425°F for 15–20 minutes

Kale and Quinoa Salad
with Pickled Onions and Caesar Dressing

Vegetarian
Gluten-free
Dairy-free
Low-cal
No Cook

TIME TO PREP 2 hours
TIME TO COOK 15 minutes
SERVES 4

NUTRITIONAL INFORMATION
Calories: 218
Fat: 5 g
Sodium: 461 mg
Carbohydrate: 34 g
Fibre: 5 g
Sugar: 11 g
Protein: 10 g

Quick-pickling onions is an excellent party trick to have in your back pocket. They work well on top of burgers and hot dogs and in tacos, curries and salads. Their tartness and tanginess add dimension and appeal to any dish. Pickling also takes the bite out of sharp red onions – and the longer you let them stand, the more flavourful they become. This seasonal winter kale salad is loaded with vitamin C – packed pomegranate, protein-laden quinoa and a dairy-free Caesar dressing, all topped with ground flaxseed for a crunchy, nutty taste.

For the pickled onions
125ml apple cider vinegar
1 tablespoon honey
1½ teaspoons sea salt
1 red onion, peeled, spiralized with BLADE A, noodles trimmed

75g quinoa

For the dressing
30g raw cashews, soaked for at least 2 hours (preferably overnight) and drained
60ml plain unsweetened almond milk
1 large garlic clove
1½ teaspoons fresh lemon juice
2 teaspoons nutritional yeast
½ teaspoon Dijon mustard
Salt and pepper

270g curly kale leaves, finely chopped
75g pomegranate seeds
2 teaspoons ground flaxseed

1 Make the pickled onions. In a resealable container, whisk together the vinegar, honey and salt. Add the onion and set aside to pickle at room temperature for at least 1 hour, or overnight in the fridge.

2 Make the quinoa. Place the quinoa and 225ml water in a small pot, cover and bring to the boil over a high heat. Uncover, reduce the heat to low and simmer for 10–15 minutes, adding more water as needed until the quinoa fluffs up and is tender. When the water has evaporated and the quinoa is fluffy, transfer to a bowl and chill.

3 Meanwhile, make the dressing. Place all the ingredients for the dressing in a high-speed blender or food processor and pulse until creamy. Taste and adjust the seasoning to your preferences.

4 Put the chilled quinoa, kale and pomegranate seeds in a large bowl. Drizzle the Caesar dressing over the salad and toss to combine thoroughly. Divide the salad among four plates. Top with pickled onions and sprinkle with the flaxseed.

Make the pickled onions and dressing the day before to simplify preparation and increase their flavour.

Wedge Salad
with Caramelized Onions, Mushroom Bacon and Greek Yogurt-balsamic Dressing

Vegetarian
Gluten-free

TIME TO PREP 15 minutes
TIME TO COOK 30 minutes
SERVES 4

NUTRITIONAL INFORMATION
Calories: 362
Fat: 26 g
Sodium: 335 mg
Carbohydrate: 29 g
Fibre: 8 g
Sugar: 16 g
Protein: 10 g

The wedge salad is a steakhouse classic – it is its own institution. Traditionally served with blue cheese dressing and bacon bits, it's definitely one of the tastiest salads, but not the most waistline-friendly. I've transformed the wedge salad into a mostly wholesome version, starring caramelized onions, a Greek yogurt dressing and mushroom bacon. This vegan bacon is made entirely from sliced mushrooms with sweet-smoky seasonings. It crisps up in the oven, making crunchy pieces that truly taste like the real thing.

For the mushroom bacon

2 tablespoons olive oil

2 tablespoons liquid smoke

2 tablespoons sesame oil

¼ teaspoon garlic powder

¼ teaspoon paprika

4 teaspoons maple syrup

Salt and pepper

225g king oyster (also sold as trumpet royale) mushrooms, cut lengthways into 1cm pieces

For the dressing

60ml natural 0% Greek yogurt

3 tablespoons balsamic vinegar

2 teaspoons Dijon mustard

1 tablespoon honey

Salt and pepper

For the salad

2 romaine or cos lettuce heads, rinsed, ends chopped off and halved lengthways

2 tablespoons extra-virgin olive oil

Salt and pepper

1 onion, peeled, spiralized with BLADE A, noodles trimmed

¼ teaspoon garlic powder

170g halved heirloom cherry tomatoes or deseeded and diced Roma (plum) tomatoes

70g blue cheese, crumbled

recipe continues

1 Preheat the oven to 180°C/350°F. Line a baking sheet with baking paper.

2 Make the bacon. In a medium bowl, whisk together all the mushroom bacon ingredients except the mushrooms. Add the mushrooms and stir gently to coat. Spread out the mushrooms on the prepared baking sheet, spacing them apart. Bake for 10 minutes, then flip and bake for a further 10 minutes or until browned, taking care not to burn them. Remove the mushrooms from the oven and place on a kitchen-paper-lined plate to drain. The bacon will crisp up over the next 5–7 minutes.

3 Meanwhile, make the dressing. Place all the ingredients for the dressing in a food processor and blend until creamy. Taste and adjust the seasoning to your preferences.

4 Make the salad. Heat a griddle pan or large frying pan over a medium-high heat. Brush the cut sides of the romaine lettuce with 1 tablespoon of the olive oil. Season lightly with salt and generously with pepper. When the pan is hot, add the romaine, cut-side down, working in batches if necessary. Grill for about 5 minutes or until lightly charred and marks appear, periodically pressing down with a spatula. Transfer each romaine half to a serving plate.

5 Heat the remaining 1 tablespoon oil in the same pan over a medium-high heat. When the oil is shimmering, add the onion noodles and season with the garlic powder, salt and pepper. Cook for 5–7 minutes or until caramelized and lightly browned. Remove the pan from the heat.

6 Scatter the onions, mushroom bacon, tomatoes and blue cheese over the romaine halves and drizzle with the balsamic vinaigrette.

You can find pre-made mushroom bacon in some health food shops and online. Shiitake mushrooms work well here, too, if you can't find oyster mushrooms.

No-cheese French Onion and Lentil Soup

Gluten-free
Dairy-free
One Pot
Saves Well

TIME TO PREP 15 minutes
TIME TO COOK 1 hour
SERVES 4–6

NUTRITIONAL INFORMATION
(for 1 of 6 servings)
Calories: 325
Fat: 8 g
Sodium: 145 mg
Carbohydrate: 44 g
Fibre: 7 g
Sugar: 6 g
Protein: 19 g

Okay, so this technically isn't a French onion soup – it doesn't have the signature cheesy giant croûton top. But this soup *is* all about everything else you find in that classic dish: gentle hints of thyme, caramelized onions and a beef and wine stock that's robust and aromatic. A filling protein, the lentils here add more substance to this soup.

3 tablespoons extra-virgin olive oil

4 red onions, peeled, spiralized with BLADE A, **noodles trimmed**

Salt and pepper

125ml dry red wine

400g lentils, rinsed

2 bay leaves

1.4 litres reduced-salt beef stock

1 teaspoon dried thyme

2 tablespoons chopped fresh parsley

1 Heat the olive oil in a large stockpot over a medium heat. When the oil is shimmering, add the onion noodles and a pinch of salt. Cook, stirring, until the onions are translucent, about 5 minutes. Reduce the heat to medium-low and cook, stirring, until the onions have reduced to half their size and are browned and softened, 20–30 minutes.

2 Add the red wine to the onions, scraping up any browned bits from the base of the pot with a wooden spoon. Add the lentils, bay leaves, stock and thyme. Season with salt and pepper, stir once, cover halfway and simmer for 20 minutes or until the lentils are just cooked through. Taste and adjust the seasoning to your preferences.

3 Stir in the parsley and simmer for 1 minute to finish. Remove the bay leaves before serving.

If you're vegetarian, substitute vegetable stock for the beef stock. While the flavours will be less intense, the swap will still be delicious.

Almond-crusted Lemon Sole

with Tomato, Sweet Onion and Caper-parsley Salad

Gluten-free
Paleo
Dairy-free

TIME TO PREP 15 minutes
TIME TO COOK 15 minutes
SERVES 4

NUTRITIONAL INFORMATION
Calories: 405
Fat: 29 g
Sodium: 386 mg
Carbohydrate: 15 g
Fibre: 4 g
Sugar: 7 g
Protein: 24 g

I've always loved fish – and if you'd ever tasted my mother's breaded lemon sole, you'd have always loved fish, too. The slightly crispy, golden brown breading combined with the tender, flaky, light white fish is magical. I would run to the table whenever I smelled fresh lemon and seafood in the kitchen – and now hopefully your loved ones will, too! This sweet onion and caper salad is my own personal touch, adding a refreshing complement.

For the fish

2 large eggs

50g ground almonds

1 teaspoon garlic powder

Salt and pepper

2 tablespoons extra-virgin olive oil

4 (85g) skinless lemon sole fillets

4 large lemon wedges

For the salad

2 small brown onions, peeled, spiralized with BLADE A, noodles trimmed

4 Roma (plum) tomatoes, cut lengthways into 5mm thick slices

45g capers, drained

15g fresh parsley, chopped

60ml red wine vinegar

60ml fresh lemon juice

2 tablespoons plus 2 teaspoons extra-virgin olive oil

Salt and pepper

1 Make the fish. Set up your dredging station. In a shallow medium bowl, beat the eggs. On a large plate, mix together the ground almonds and garlic powder. Season with salt and pepper. Set the dishes side by side.

2 Heat the olive oil in a medium frying pan over a medium-high heat. Working with one fillet at a time, dip the sole into the egg, turn to coat and allow any excess to drip back into the bowl. Dip the fish into the ground almond mixture, pressing to adhere. When the oil is shimmering, add the fish, working in batches if necessary, and cook for 3 minutes, then flip, squeeze over the lemon juice, and cook for a further 2–3 minutes or until the fish is opaque and the crust is golden brown.

3 Make the salad. Place all the ingredients for the salad in a large bowl and toss to combine.

4 Serve the sole with lemon wedges and the salad alongside.

Stir some finely chopped almonds into the ground almonds before breading the sole for a crunchier texture.

Rosemary, Olive and Onion Frittata
with Rocket Salad and Parmesan Vinaigrette

Vegetarian
Gluten-free
Dairy-free (opt.)
Low-cal

TIME TO PREP 10 minutes
TIME TO COOK 25 minutes
SERVES 4–6

NUTRITIONAL INFORMATION
(for 1 of 6 servings)
Calories: 221
Fat: 16 g
Sodium: 293 mg
Carbohydrate: 5 g
Fibre: 1 g
Sugar: 1 g
Protein: 14 g

On rainy weekends, I've been known to spend an hour lying on my back with my hands extended up in the air, iPhone grasped, doing nothing other than 'sgramming – scrolling through Instagram, that is. Even when the weather is bad, there are somehow always pictures of chic women with perfect hair sitting in stilettos, packed into tiny restaurants in town. Once I get over the fact that I'm at home and in tracksuit bottoms and totally unmotivated to get off the sofa, I notice that they're almost always eating an elegant slice of frittata with the daintiest of salads to keep it company. This frittata is my way of having a little of that sophistication in my life, especially on my cherished relaxing weekends.

For the frittata
1 tablespoon olive oil

1 medium red onion, peeled, spiralized with BLADE A, noodles trimmed

Leaves from 1 sprig of rosemary

¼ teaspoon garlic powder

Salt and pepper

90g pitted large black olives, quartered

9 egg whites plus 3 large eggs, beaten

For the dressing
2 tablespoons extra-virgin olive oil

1 tablespoon red wine vinegar

2 teaspoons grated Parmesan cheese

Salt and pepper

⅛ teaspoon garlic powder

¼ teaspoon dried oregano

1 teaspoon fresh lemon juice

Pinch of chilli flakes

80g baby rocket

1 Preheat the oven to 190°C/375°F.

2 Heat the olive oil in a medium ovenproof frying pan over a medium-high heat. When the oil is shimmering, add the onion and season with the rosemary, garlic powder, salt and pepper. Cook for 5 minutes or until softened. Stir in the olives, then pour over the eggs. Cook for 3 minutes to lightly set the eggs on the bottom, then transfer the pan to the oven and bake for 15 minutes. Pierce the frittata with a knife. If it comes out clean, it's done. If not, cook for a further 3–5 minutes.

3 Meanwhile, make the dressing. Whisk together all the ingredients for the dressing in a medium bowl. Taste and adjust the seasoning to your preferences. Add the rocket and toss to combine.

4 Cut the frittata into slices and plate with some of the salad alongside.

Parsnip

When the temperatures drop and autumn and winter produce starts to appear at farmers' markets and supermarkets, I always get excited for parsnips. I was first introduced to parsnips while staying with a friend's family in Windsor. My friend's mother made a root vegetable bake that included parsnips, and I was surprised by their pleasant, sweet taste. They've been in my diet ever since!

Parsnips are just a little bit sweet, but also pleasantly nutty, with a fibrous texture. The cold weather converts their starches into natural sugar, which introduces their signature flavour. Because their taste is so distinct, they should be used only with complementary flavours.

Sort of like carrots, but in an even more exaggerated way, all parsnips taper to a very thin end that isn't wide enough to be spiralized. To make the most of your produce, try to find one with the widest wide end possible. Be sure to choose a vegetable that's firm and has an ivory colour.

NUTRITIONAL BENEFITS: Parsnips are packed with folate and potassium, both essential for cardiovascular health, and are also a solid source of vitamin C and dietary fibre.

PREPARATION AND STORAGE: Peel the parsnip. Slice off both ends to leave flat, even surfaces. Discard any part of the parsnip that is less than 1cm in diameter, or use it in a non-spiralized recipe. Peeled or spiralized parsnips oxidize when exposed to air, so store them in a container filled with water with a little bit of lemon juice in the fridge for up to 2 days.

BEST BLADES TO USE
- Blade C
- Blade D

BEST COOKING METHODS
- Sauté over a medium heat for 5–7 minutes
- Roast at 220°C/425°F for 10–15 minutes

Parsnip-chive Waffles and Gluten-free Oven-fried Chicken

∾ Gluten-free
∾ Paleo
∾ Dairy-free

TIME TO PREP 15 minutes
TIME TO COOK 50 minutes
SERVES 4

NUTRITIONAL INFORMATION
Calories: 494
Fat: 30 g
Sodium: 170 mg
Carbohydrate: 24 g
Fibre: 7 g
Sugar: 6 g
Protein: 31 g

ALSO WORKS WELL WITH
Sweet Potato, Swede

Chicken and waffles is a commitment. Of course, it's a mind-blowingly delicious commitment – a soul food delicacy. But that deep-fried chicken is greasy, and the waffle is nutritionally empty. This version is not only gluten-free, but it's also made with real, whole ingredients that offer the same richly indulgent flavours, while helping you with another commitment – to a healthy lifestyle!

For the chicken
Cooking spray
2 large eggs
50g ground almonds
¼ teaspoon dried thyme
¼ teaspoon cayenne pepper
¼ teaspoon paprika
¼ teaspoon onion powder
¼ teaspoon garlic powder
Salt and pepper, to taste
675g skin-on, bone-in chicken pieces (a mixture of thighs, breasts and drumsticks), patted dry

For the waffles
Cooking spray
3 large parsnips, peeled, spiralized with BLADE C, noodles trimmed
½ teaspoon garlic powder
Salt and pepper
2 large eggs, beaten
3 tablespoons chopped fresh chives
Maple syrup, to serve

recipe continues

1 Make the chicken. Preheat the oven to 190°C/375°F. Coat a wire rack with cooking spray and set it on a foil-lined baking sheet.

2 Set up your dredging station. Beat the eggs in a large bowl. Combine the ground almonds, thyme, cayenne, paprika, onion powder, garlic powder and salt and pepper on a large plate. Set the dishes side by side.

3 Working with one piece at a time, dip the chicken in the egg, allowing the excess to drip back into the bowl. Dredge the chicken in the seasoned ground almonds, patting it into any crevices and pressing to adhere. As you bread each piece, set them on the prepared baking sheet on top of the rack. Bake until the chicken is cooked through, 20–30 minutes.

4 Meanwhile, make the waffles. Preheat a waffle iron. Wipe the frying pan from the chicken clean and spray generously with cooking spray. Set over a medium heat. When the pan is hot, add the parsnip noodles and season with garlic powder, salt and pepper. Cover and cook for 5 minutes or until the noodles are wilted. Transfer to a medium bowl. Add the eggs and chives to the bowl and toss to combine.

5 Coat the waffle iron with cooking spray and pack the parsnip mixture into four waffle cavities. Cook according to the manufacturer's instructions.

6 When the waffles are done, transfer them to four plates and top each equally with chicken pieces. Drizzle with maple syrup and serve.

These savoury, nutty waffles work well with many different toppings. If you don't eat chicken or don't have the time to make it, try topping the waffle with mashed avocado, fried eggs or some melted cheese. Heck, they're yummy by themselves, too!

Hearty Beef Stew
with Parsnip and Carrot Noodles

≋ Gluten-free
≋ Dairy-free
Low-cal
Saves Well

TIME TO PREP 20 minutes
TIME TO COOK 1½ hours
SERVES 4

NUTRITIONAL INFORMATION
Calories: 213
Fat: 11 g
Sodium: 449 mg
Carbohydrate: 18 g
Fibre: 7 g
Sugar: 5 g
Protein: 15 g

ALSO WORKS WELL WITH
Sweet Potato, Swede,
Celeriac, Turnip, Butternut
Squash

In the dead of winter, I crave everything slow roasted, oven baked and steadily simmered. Temperatures drop and my appetite shifts – all I can think about are slow-cooker soups and hearty stews. This beef stew with spiralized parsnips and carrots is a great addition to anyone's cold-weather cooking repertoire. The nutty parsnips and sweet carrots are roasted to perfection and soak up the deep flavours of the slow-cooked beef. Curl up with a bowl of this and fall in love with the cosiness of winter.

2 tablespoons extra-virgin olive oil

450g beef stewing meat

2 garlic cloves, finely chopped

½ red onion, diced

¼ teaspoon chilli flakes

3 celery sticks, diced

3 tablespoons Worcestershire sauce

1 teaspoon dried thyme

½ teaspoon cayenne pepper

Salt and pepper

1 litre reduced-salt beef stock

1 (400g) can diced tomatoes

2 bay leaves

*3 large carrots, peeled, spiralized with
BLADE D, noodles trimmed*

*3 large parsnips, peeled, spiralized with
BLADE D, noodles trimmed*

Chopped fresh curly parsley, to garnish

The carrot and parsnip noodles can be frozen after they're cooked, so this entire dish can be made in advance and enjoyed all week long.

1 Preheat the oven to 200°C/400°F.

2 Heat 1 tablespoon of the olive oil in a casserole or stockpot over a medium heat. When the oil is shimmering, add the beef and cook until browned, 7–10 minutes. Using tongs, transfer the beef to a bowl, reserving any juices in the pot.

3 Add the garlic to the pot and cook for 30 seconds or until fragrant. Add the onion, chilli flakes and celery and cook for 2 minutes or until the vegetables are sweating. Return the beef to the pot. Stir in the Worcestershire sauce, thyme and cayenne. Season with salt and black pepper and add the stock and tomatoes with their juices. Place the bay leaves on top. Cover, increase the heat to high and bring to the boil. Reduce the heat to medium-low and simmer for 40 minutes. Remove the cover and simmer for a further 35 minutes or until the stew has thickened.

4 Before serving, heat the remaining tablespoon of oil in a large frying pan over a medium heat. When the oil is shimmering, add the carrot and parsnip noodles, season with salt and pepper and cook for 5–7 minutes or until al dente. Discard the bay leaves. Divide the noodles among four bowls and top each with beef stew. Garnish with parsley and serve.

Avocado 'Toast'
with Cherry Tomato Jam

Gluten-free
Paleo
Dairy-free

TIME TO PREP 20 minutes
TIME TO COOK 45 minutes
SERVES 4

NUTRITIONAL INFORMATION
Calories: 352
Fat: 17 g
Sodium: 93 mg
Carbohydrate: 45 g
Fibre: 12 g
Sugar: 21 g
Protein: 8 g

ALSO WORKS WELL WITH
Sweet Potato, Swede

Whoever invented avocado toast is an absolute genius – and should totally get paid royalties! With creamy, chunky fresh avocado mashed and smeared onto a thick, grainy toast, no wonder it's such a wildly popular dish. With so many variations of toppings, it's a different meal every time. This spiralized version is a gluten-free, nutritious take and it has made my home just a little bit trendier.

For the jam

675g cherry tomatoes, halved

2 tablespoons coconut sugar or honey

2 tablespoons apple cider vinegar

Juice of 1 lemon

½ teaspoon ground cinnamon

¼ teaspoon chilli flakes

1 teaspoon salt

Pepper

60–125ml reduced-salt vegetable
  stock (optional)

For the toast

Cooking spray

4 large parsnips, peeled, spiralized with
  BLADE D, *noodles trimmed*

Salt and pepper

3 large eggs, beaten

2 tablespoons olive oil

1 avocado, mashed

Sea salt

Small handful of micro-greens,
  to garnish (optional)

1 Make the jam. In a large saucepan, combine all the ingredients for the jam, except the stock, and bring to the boil over a high heat. Reduce the heat to medium-low and simmer, stirring occasionally, for 45 minutes–1 hour or until the mixture thickens and is syrupy (with some chunks of tomatoes remaining). If the jam needs to cook longer to further break down the cherry tomatoes but most of the liquid has evaporated, add the stock as needed.

2 Meanwhile, make the toast. Place a large non-stick frying pan over a medium heat and coat with cooking spray. When water flicked onto the pan sizzles, add the parsnip noodles and season with salt and pepper. Cook for 5–7 minutes or until softened and lightly browned. Transfer to a medium bowl and leave to cool for 1–2 minutes. Add the eggs and stir to coat.

3 Fill four ramekins halfway with the noodles. Cover each with a piece of foil or greaseproof paper, pressing it down firmly onto the noodles to compress them. Chill for at least 15 minutes to set.

recipe continues

4 In the same pan in which you cooked the parsnips, heat 1 tablespoon of the olive oil over a medium heat. When the oil is shimmering, add the parsnip buns two at a time, flipping each out of its ramekin into the pan and patting the base until the bun falls out.

5 Cook for 3 minutes or until set, being sure to push in any stray noodles. Carefully flip and cook for a further 2–3 minutes or until the buns are completely set and browned on both sides, pressing down with the back of a spatula. Repeat with the remaining buns, using the remaining 1 tablespoon olive oil.

6 Smear the buns with the mashed avocado, dividing it evenly. Season with sea salt and add a dollop of tomato jam. Garnish with micro-greens, if you like.

If you don't have time to make the cherry tomato jam, you can use jarred instead. Just make sure it's no sugar added.

Parsnip Pasta
with Caramelized Leeks and Ham

Gluten-free
Dairy-free (Opt.)
Low-cal
Saves Well

TIME TO PREP 10 minutes
TIME TO COOK 25 minutes
SERVES 4

NUTRITIONAL INFORMATION
Calories: 176
Fat: 3 g
Carbohydrates: 25 g
Sodium: 600 mg
Fibre: 6 g
Protein: 11 g
Sugar: 9 g

Using spiralized veggies as a pasta substitute is not only a less processed, cleaner alternative, it also adds flavour. While courgette is on the low end of the flavour spectrum (it's a very mild-tasting vegetable), parsnips offer a nutty sweetness, placing them higher on that same spectrum. Here, the parsnips bring out the sweetness in ham, and the leeks add balance with their earthiness and offer a smooth, soft texture overall.

75g ham, diced

110g leeks, sliced

2 tablespoon finely chopped shallots

Salt and pepper

3 large parsnips, peeled, spiralized with BLADE D, noodles trimmed

25g Parmesan cheese, grated

1 Heat a large frying pan over a medium-high heat. When water flicked onto the pan sizzles, add the ham. Cook for 7–10 minutes or until the ham starts to brown. Using a slotted spoon, transfer the ham to a plate and set aside.

2 Immediately add the leeks and shallots to the pan and season with salt and pepper. Cook for 5 minutes or until the leeks are wilted and almost caramelized. Set the leeks aside on the plate with the ham and add the parsnip noodles to the same pan. Season with salt and pepper. Cover and cook for 5–7 minutes or until al dente. Uncover and stir in the ham and leeks.

3 Remove the pan from the heat and stir in the Parmesan, tossing to combine. Divide the pasta into plates and serve immediately.

Broccoli Raab and Sausage Parsnip Pasta

≋≋ | Gluten-free
≋≋ | Dairy-free (opt.)
Low-cal
Saves Well

TIME TO PREP 15 minutes
TIME TO COOK 15 minutes
SERVES 4

NUTRITIONAL INFORMATION
Calories: 213
Fat: 11 g
Sodium: 449 mg
Carbohydrate: 18 g
Fibre: 7 g
Sugar: 5 g
Protein: 15 g

ALSO WORKS WELL WITH
Courgette, Butternut
Squash, Celeriac, Swede,
Turnip

If I had a nickel for every time my grandfather served us broccoli raab and sausage, this cookbook would be gold-plated. This combination is classically Italian, thanks to the undeniable spicy power of the sausage and the slightly bitter kick of the broccoli raab. The parsnip noodles become the star of this dish, absorbing the sauce created by the olive oil and sausage juices. The Parmesan cheese ties everything together, bringing in a silky texture, a slightly salty taste, and a savoury aroma. *Salute!*

1 bunch broccoli raab

2 hot Italian sausage links, casings removed

½ teaspoon dried oregano

2 parsnips, peeled, spiralized with BLADE D, noodles trimmed

2 garlic cloves, finely chopped

¼ teaspoon chilli flakes

Salt and pepper

125ml reduced-salt chicken stock

50g Parmesan cheese, grated

1 tablespoon chopped fresh parsley

If you don't like the bitterness of broccoli raab, try parboiling it after trimming. Bring a large pot filled halfway with water to the boil, add the broccoli raab, cook for 3 minutes, then transfer to a bowl of iced water. Otherwise, broccolini or plain broccoli are great choices with similar textures.

1 Rinse the broccoli raab and pat dry. Cut off most of the stems (the thickest parts). Using a vegetable peeler, pull some skin off the stems, and continue to until you hit the leaves. Chop into 2.5cm pieces and set aside.

2 Place a large frying pan over a medium heat. When water flicked onto the pan sizzles, add the sausage and oregano and cook, breaking up the meat with a wooden spoon, for 6–8 minutes or until browned and cooked through. Using tongs or a slotted spoon, transfer the sausage to a plate.

3 Immediately add the broccoli raab, parsnip noodles, garlic and chilli flakes to the pan. Season with salt and black pepper, then add the stock. Cook until the stock has reduced and the parsnip noodles are al dente, about 5 minutes.

4 Return the sausage to the pan and stir to combine. Remove from the heat and toss the ingredients to combine fully.

5 Divide among four plates, garnish with the cheese and parsley and serve.

Pear

When I want a piece of fruit that's slightly less sweet and a bit softer and juicier, I always opt for a pear. The perfect winter fruit, pears have soft, buttery flesh and delicate skin. They come in many varieties, all unique in flavour, shape and size. Some popular types include Bosc, green and red Anjou, Bartlett, Concorde and Forelle. The easiest type of pear to spiralize with the highest noodle yield is the Asian pear, a round, light-brown type similar in shape to an apple. The best part is that it requires no preparation to spiralize, aside from snapping off the stem.

Pears are readily available in supermarkets year-round. When selecting one, make sure it's firm – not squishy, but also not rock hard. Overripe pears will turn into mush on the spiralizers; underripe will work, but they won't taste as flavourful or fresh.

NUTRITIONAL BENEFITS: Pears are touted as one of the highest-fibre fruits, fighting bloat and keeping cholesterol levels down. There's also an antioxidant in their skin that can help lower blood pressure and possibly even fight cancer.

PREPARATION AND STORAGE: Remove the stem prior to spiralizing. Peeled pears and pear noodles oxidize when exposed to air, so store them in a container filled with water with a little bit of lemon juice in the fridge for up to 2 days.

BEST BLADES TO USE
- Blade A
- Blade C
- Blade D

BEST COOKING METHODS
- Raw
- Bake at 180°C/350°F for 15 minutes

Grilled Halloumi, Lentils and Rocket
with Roasted Fennel and Pear Noodles

Vegetarian
Gluten-free

TIME TO PREP 20 minutes
TIME TO COOK 45 minutes
SERVES 4

NUTRITIONAL INFORMATION
Calories: 430
Fat: 29 g
Sodium: 642 mg
Carbohydrate: 28 g
Fibre: 6 g
Sugar: 7 g
Protein: 23 g

ALSO WORKS WELL WITH
Apple

My mother always tells me I make the best salads. A salad, to me, isn't a bunch of greens mixed together in a bowl. In my mind, it's a plate of freshly prepared ingredients that happen to sit atop a bed of greens. This recipe is a prime example – with roasted sweet fennel, crunchy pear noodles, filling lentils and warm halloumi, there's so much to enjoy. After you try this dish, you'll never think of salads the same way again.

1 fennel bulb, chopped into wedges
1 tablespoon extra-virgin olive oil
1 tablespoon balsamic vinegar
½ teaspoon garlic powder
Salt and pepper
200g lentils, rinsed

For the dressing
3 tablespoons extra-virgin olive oil
2 tablespoons fresh lemon juice
1 teaspoon Dijon mustard
1 teaspoon honey

Cooking spray
225g halloumi cheese, cut into 5cm long
    slices, about 5mm thick
1 Bosc pear
100g baby rocket

If you can't find halloumi cheese, feta works well, too.

1 Preheat the oven to 200°C/400°F. Line a baking sheet with baking paper.

2 In a large bowl, toss together the fennel, olive oil, vinegar and garlic powder. Transfer the wedges to the prepared baking sheet, season with salt and pepper and bake for 30 minutes, flipping once halfway through, until the fennel begins to caramelize.

3 Meanwhile, place the lentils in a medium pot and add water to cover by 2.5cm. Bring the water to the boil over a high heat, then reduce the heat to low and simmer for 25 minutes or until tender. Drain, pat dry and set aside.

4 While the lentils simmer, whisk together all the ingredients for the dressing in a large bowl.

5 Heat a griddle pan or large frying pan over a medium-high heat and coat with cooking spray. When water flicked onto the pan sizzles, add the halloumi and cook for 2–3 minutes on each side or until lightly charred and marks appear. Transfer to a plate.

6 When the fennel is finished roasting, spiralize the pear with **BLADE D** and trim the noodles. Add the pear noodles, roasted fennel and rocket to the bowl with the dressing and toss to coat. Divide the salad and lentils among four plates. Top with the grilled halloumi and serve immediately.

Chai-spiced Pear Porridge

I'm imagining you in a gloriously chunky jumper on a cold, gently snowy day, hovering over the warmth of your hob, stirring these spiced pear noodles as you wait patiently for your morning porridge to fluff up. The chai flavours will fill your kitchen with cosiness, and each bite will relax and nourish you. This porridge is like a snug blanket that will warm you even on the chilliest days.

Vegan
Vegetarian
Gluten-free
Dairy-free
Low-cal

TIME TO PREP 5 minutes
TIME TO COOK 20 minutes
SERVES 2

NUTRITIONAL INFORMATION
Calories: 244
Fat: 11 g
Sodium: 121 mg
Carbohydrate: 32 g
Fibre: 6 g
Sugar: 9 g
Protein: 6 g

ALSO WORKS WELL WITH
Apple

65g gluten-free rolled oats

1 teaspoon coconut oil

1 Anjou pear, spiralized with BLADE D, noodles trimmed

350ml plain unsweetened almond milk

¼ teaspoon pure vanilla extract

¼ teaspoon ground cinnamon

⅛ teaspoon ground cardamom

1 teaspoon maple syrup

2 tablespoons walnut halves

Cardamom is a key spice in chai. But if you don't have it in your storecupboard, that's okay – leave it out! This porridge can stand on its own even without it.

1 Bring 475ml water to the boil in a medium saucepan over a high heat. Add the oats and return to the boil, then reduce the heat to low and simmer for about 10 minutes or until all the water has been absorbed and the porridge is fluffy.

2 Meanwhile, heat the coconut oil in a medium frying pan over a medium-high heat. When the oil has melted, add the pear noodles, almond milk, vanilla, cinnamon, cardamom and maple syrup. Stir to combine and simmer until the milk has evaporated and the sauce has thickened, about 15 minutes.

3 Meanwhile, place a small frying pan over a medium-high heat and add the walnuts. Toast, stirring, for 5 minutes or until fragrant. Remove from the pan.

4 Divide the porridge between two bowls and top with the pear mixture and the toasted walnuts.

Pear Noodle Bowl
with Maple-roasted Acorn Squash and Pomegranate Dressing

≈≈ Vegan
≈≈ Vegetarian
Gluten-free
Dairy-free
Low-cal

TIME TO PREP 15 minutes
TIME TO COOK 45 minutes
SERVES 4

NUTRITIONAL INFORMATION
Calories: 259
Fat: 7 g
Sodium: 5 mg
Carbohydrate: 50 g
Fibre: 8 g
Sugar: 21 g
Protein: 6 g

ALSO WORKS WELL WITH
Apple

Every autumn, I look forward to two things: the crispy colourful leaves on the ground and the large cold-weather squashes at the market. I always end up buying too many, because I get so excited when they first show up. They're decorative thanks to their large shape and gorgeous colour, and I love displaying them in a bowl in my kitchen. In an attempt to save them from going bad, I always slice them up and roast them into velvety slivers. Having roasted squash on hand enables you to throw together a healthy and beautiful meal in a pinch, since the squash is full of hearty, filling dietary fibre. With the tastiness of pomegranate and pear added here, you might even think Mother Nature intended these seasonal ingredients to be eaten together.

1 acorn squash, quartered and deseeded

2 teaspoons extra-virgin olive oil

4 teaspoons maple syrup

Salt and pepper

75g dry red quinoa, rinsed

For the dressing

60ml pomegranate juice

60ml extra-virgin olive oil

2 tablespoons apple cider vinegar

75g pomegranate seeds

1 teaspoon maple syrup

2 red Anjou pears, spiralized with BLADE D, noodles trimmed

40g whole almonds, roughly chopped

Other squashes work well here, too. Try butternut or delicata to switch things up.

1 Preheat the oven to 200°C/400°F. Line a baking sheet with baking paper. Halve each squash quarter and lay them out on the baking sheet, spacing them apart. Drizzle with the olive oil and maple syrup, dividing them evenly over each slice. Season with salt and pepper. Roast for 35–40 minutes or until tender when pierced with a fork.

2 While the squash roasts, place the quinoa and 475ml water in a medium pot. Cover and bring to the boil, then uncover, reduce the heat to medium-low and cook for 15 minutes or until the quinoa is fluffy. Transfer to a large bowl.

3 Make the dressing. Whisk together all the ingredients for the dressing in a small bowl.

4 Add the pear noodles and almonds to the bowl with the quinoa. Pour the dressing over the mixture and toss to combine thoroughly. Divide among four bowls and top each with two squash slices.

Cinnamon and Pecan Pear Noodle Pancakes

If you're ever just yearning for a stack of pancakes, my advice is to go for it. Life's too short to second-guess breakfast happiness! And this healthier version is sure to satisfy your hankering. These pancakes have a surprisingly sweet crunch, thanks to the pear noodles and chopped pecans. They're so good and good *for* you, you just may start craving them more often – and that's okay!

Vegetarian
Gluten-free
Paleo
Dairy-free
Low-Cal

TIME TO PREP 15 minutes
TIME TO COOK 20 minutes
SERVES 4

NUTRITIONAL INFORMATION
Calories: 155
Fat: 8 g
Sodium: 113 mg
Carbohydrate: 18 g
Fibre: 2 g
Sugar: 2 g
Protein: 4 g

ALSO WORKS WELL WITH
Apple

120g gluten-free baking flour

1 teaspoon baking powder

½ teaspoon bicarbonate of soda

1 teaspoon ground cinnamon

½ teaspoon sea salt

2 large eggs, beaten

175ml plain unsweetened almond milk

1 teaspoon pure vanilla extract

2 tablespoons coconut oil, melted and cooled to room temperature

1 Anjou or Bosc pear

40g pecans, chopped

Cooking spray

Maple syrup, to serve

If you're short on time, use a gluten-free pancake mix to create the pancakes themselves and simply stir in the rest of the ingredients.

---

1 In a medium bowl, whisk together the flour, baking powder, bicarbonate of soda, cinnamon and salt. In a separate medium bowl, whisk together the eggs, almond milk, vanilla and coconut oil. Fold the wet ingredients into the dry ingredients and stir together until smooth.

2 Spiralize the pear with **BLADE D** and break up the noodles with your hands. Add the pear noodles and pecans to the batter and mix to combine thoroughly.

3 Place a large frying pan over a medium heat and coat with cooking spray. When water flicked onto the pan sizzles, ladle on the pancake batter – about 90ml for 10–12 mini pancakes or 125ml for four large pancakes – spreading it out with the back of the ladle to flatten. Cook for about 3 minutes. When the tops are bubbling and the edges are slightly dry, flip and cook for a further 3 minutes, flattening with a spatula. Transfer the pancakes to serving plates and repeat with the remaining batter.

4 Drizzle maple syrup over the pancakes and serve.

Easy Pork Chops
with Shredded Brussels Sprouts, Kale and Pear Noodle Salad

~~ Gluten-free
~~ Paleo
Dairy-free
Saves Well

TIME TO PREP 20 minutes
TIME TO COOK 15 minutes
SERVES 4

NUTRITIONAL INFORMATION
Calories: 390
Fat: 24 g
Sodium: 79 mg
Carbohydrate: 17 g
Fibre: 4 g
Sugar: 10 g
Protein: 29 g

ALSO WORKS WELL WITH
Apple

Since my tastes can skew more towards the veg side and less towards the carnivore side, learning to cook meat properly was a process. One of Lu's favourites is the pork chop, so that was first on my list. I've found an easy and quick way to cook a pork chop simply but flavourfully. This crunchy, multi-dimensional salad, packed with nutrients from the leafy kale, healthy fats from the almonds and soft, seasonal flavour from the sweet pear noodles and Brussels sprouts, is the perfect complement, and together they make a filling meal.

2 tablespoons plus 2 teaspoons extra-virgin olive oil

4 boneless pork chops

Salt and pepper

1 tablespoon maple syrup

3 tablespoons sliced blanched almonds

For the vinaigrette
2 tablespoons extra-virgin olive oil

1 tablespoon finely chopped shallot

Salt and pepper

1 teaspoon honey

2 tablespoons apple cider vinegar

½ teaspoon Dijon mustard

175g Brussels sprouts, ends trimmed

1 Bosc or Asian pear, spiralized with
   BLADE D

70g curly kale leaves, finely chopped

1 Preheat the oven to 200°C/400°F.

2 Heat 1 teaspoon of olive oil in a large ovenproof frying pan over a medium-high heat. Rub each pork chop with 1 teaspoon of the olive oil, then season generously with salt and pepper. When the oil is shimmering, add the pork chops and sear for about 3 minutes on each side or until golden brown.

3 While the pork chops cook, whisk together the remaining 1 tablespoon oil and the maple syrup. Pour the mixture over the pork chops and transfer the pan to the oven. Roast until cooked through, 7–9 minutes (if using a meat thermometer, the pork chops should register 60°C/140°F at the thickest part). Transfer to a plate and leave to stand, undisturbed, for at least 5 minutes.

4 Place a medium frying pan over a medium-high heat. When water flicked onto the pan sizzles, add the sliced almonds and toast, stirring frequently, until lightly browned and fragrant, about 3 minutes. Remove the almonds and set aside.

5 Make the vinaigrette. Whisk together all the ingredients for the vinaigrette in a large bowl. Taste and adjust the seasoning to your preferences.

6 Pulse the Brussels sprouts in a food processor until shredded and thoroughly chopped. Transfer to the bowl with the dressing and add the toasted almonds, pear noodles and kale. Toss to combine thoroughly.

7 Divide the Brussels sprouts mixture among four plates and add a pork chop. Pour any pan juices over the top.

Pepper

If you've been cooking out of *Inspiralized*, this section may be new to you. Since that book was published, I discovered that you *can* spiralize peppers. Actually, I was putting together a spoof video showing that certain vegetables and fruits can't be spiralized, like ripe avocado and some others. When I went to spiralize the pepper, it worked! I never posted the video, because I quickly got sidetracked by this game-changing discovery and realized that this veggie has its own amazing flavour, texture and purpose. So let me formally introduce you to. . . pepper noodles!

Spiralizing peppers can simply help you make fajitas faster or quicken the prep for stir-fries, but these colourful noodles also have the power to build the base for complete, creative meals. In red, orange, yellow and green, they brighten up pretty much any dish.

NUTRITIONAL BENEFITS: While all peppers are packed with antioxidants and dietary fibre, red have the most vitamin C and contain beta-carotene, which provides anti-inflammatory benefits. All peppers are very low in calories, making them ideal if you're on a diet.

PREPARATION AND STORAGE: Using a small paring knife, carefully slice just around the stem and remove it entirely, pulling out the seeded middle that's attached. Then flip over the pepper and gently tap it against a bowl to release any remaining seeds. (If you just snap the stem off but don't remove the seeded interior, you'll have a mess when you spiralize, but it will still work.) Attach the handle to the widest part of the pepper (the top, where the stem was sliced off). Store the noodles in an airtight container in the fridge for up to 5 days.

BEST BLADE TO USE
- Blade A

BEST COOKING METHODS
- Raw
- Blanch
- Sauté over a medium-high heat for 5–7 minutes
- Roast at 230°C/450°F for 20 minutes

Spiralized Shakshuka

Whenever I see shakshuka on a menu, I think of the first official get-together I had with my bridesmaids. We toasted with mimosas, discussed hen party ideas and laughed over jokes about my long road to finding the perfect husband, all while I dug into the shakshuka. This bright, spicy meal can be served as breakfast, or just as easily as dinner. This spiralized version creates more texture and interest with its noodles and gets bonus points for being super easy to prepare.

Vegetarian
Gluten-free
Paleo
Dairy-free
Low-cal
One Pot

TIME TO PREP 10 minutes
TIME TO COOK 25 minutes
SERVES 6

NUTRITIONAL INFORMATION
Calories: 157
Fat: 8 g
Sodium: 129 mg
Carbohydrate: 14 g
Fibre: 5 g
Sugar: 8 g
Protein: 10 g

ALSO WORKS WELL WITH
Sweet Potato

---

1 tablespoon olive oil

1 small white onion, peeled, spiralized with BLADE A, *noodles trimmed*

1 large garlic clove, finely chopped

1 green pepper, spiralized with BLADE A, *noodles trimmed*

1 red pepper, spiralized with BLADE A, *noodles trimmed*

Salt and pepper

2 tablespoons tomato purée

1 teaspoon chilli powder

1 teaspoon ground cumin

1 teaspoon paprika

⅛ teaspoon cayenne pepper

2 (400g) can no-salt-added chopped tomatoes

6 whole large eggs

1½ teaspoons chopped fresh parsley, to garnish

1 Heat the olive oil in a 25cm frying pan with a lid over a medium-high heat. When the oil is shimmering, add the onion and garlic and cook until the onion is slightly softened, about 5 minutes. Add all the pepper noodles, season with salt and pepper and cook for 5 minutes or until softened.

2 Add the tomato purée and stir to combine. Add the chilli powder, cumin, paprika and cayenne and cook for 2 minutes to allow the flavours to develop. Add the chopped tomatoes and their juices and cook until the liquid begins to reduce and thicken, 5–7 minutes. Taste and adjust the seasoning to your preferences.

3 Create six cavities in the tomato mixture with a spoon. Crack one egg into each cavity, cover the pan and simmer until the eggs are just set, 5–7 minutes.

4 Garnish with the parsley and serve.

For a kick of salty flavour, sprinkle feta over the shakshuka as soon as you pull it out of the oven.

Turkey Picadillo
with Green Pepper Noodles

Gluten-free
Paleo
Dairy-free
Saves Well

TIME TO PREP 15 minutes
TIME TO COOK 20 minutes
SERVES 4

NUTRITIONAL INFORMATION
Calories: 384
Fat: 20 g
Sodium: 629 mg
Carbohydrate: 23 g
Fibre: 7 g
Sugar: 17 g
Protein: 36 g

ALSO WORKS WELL WITH
Courgette, Sweet Potato, Swede

Remember the Bikini Bolognese from *Inspiralized*? Well, imagine it travelled from Italy to Cuba and got a makeover. Here we have picadillo sauce over pepper noodles. The soft, fragrant sauce has raisins for sweetness and olives for saltiness, which meld together in this enticing dish. The green pepper noodles are crisp and refreshing, and enhance the richness of the stew's seasonings. The whole thing can be made ahead, making it ideal for weekly meal planning.

1 tablespoon extra-virgin olive oil

3 green peppers, spiralized with BLADE A

Salt and pepper

100g white onion, chopped

2 garlic cloves, finely chopped

675g 93% lean turkey mince

1 bay leaf

225ml canned tomato sauce

½ teaspoon ground cinnamon

1 teaspoon ground cumin

1 teaspoon chilli powder

½ teaspoon cayenne pepper

1 teaspoon dried oregano

45g sultanas

60g stuffed pimiento olives, chopped, plus 1½ tablespoons olive juice from the jar

1 Heat the olive oil in a large frying pan over a medium-high heat. When the oil is shimmering, add the peppers and season with salt and pepper. Cook for 5 minutes or until al dente. Transfer to a medium bowl and set aside.

2 Immediately add the onion and garlic to the pan and cook for 5 minutes or until the onion is softened. Add the turkey and cook for 10 minutes or until browned, breaking it up with a wooden spoon as it cooks. Add the bay leaf, tomato sauce, cinnamon, cumin, chilli powder, cayenne and oregano. Season with salt and pepper and stir to combine. Reduce the heat to medium-low, cover and simmer for 10 minutes.

3 Uncover the pan and stir in the sultanas, olives and olive juice. Cover again and simmer for a further 5 minutes. Remove and discard the bay leaf.

4 Divide the pepper noodles among four bowls and top with the picadillo sauce.

Replace half the turkey with crumbled Spanish (dry-cured) chorizo for some extra (and authentic) spice!

Quick Steak and Pepper Stir-fry

Dairy-free
Low-cal
Saves Well

TIME TO PREP 20 minutes
TIME TO COOK 20 minutes
SERVES 4

NUTRITIONAL INFORMATION
Calories: 260
Fat: 16 g
Sodium: 516 mg
Carbohydrate: 12 g
Fibre: 1 g
Sugar: 7 g
Protein: 18 g

ALSO WORKS WELL WITH
Courgette

When I was growing up, whenever we ordered Chinese takeaway, my father's go-to was pepper steak with broccoli. I would always steal some bites, enjoying the salty sauce coating the thin, juicy pieces of steak. By using pepper noodles here, you cut down on prep time and create a more substantial meal. And just like classic takeaway, this dish saves well in the fridge and might even be better as leftovers the next day.

Salt and pepper

120g small broccoli florets

1 tablespoon oyster sauce

2 tablespoons reduced-salt soy sauce

1 teaspoon rice vinegar

60ml reduced-salt chicken stock

2 tablespoons coconut oil

225g skirt steak, thinly sliced against the grain

1 tablespoon sesame oil

¼ teaspoon chilli flakes

4 spring onions, diced, white and dark green parts kept separate

3 garlic cloves, thinly sliced

¼ teaspoon grated fresh ginger

2 tablespoons chopped fresh ginger

1 red pepper, spiralized with BLADE A, noodles trimmed

1 orange pepper, spiralized with BLADE A, noodles trimmed

1 jalapeño chilli, thinly sliced

1 Bring a medium pot of lightly salted water to the boil over a high heat. Add the broccoli and cook for 3 minutes, then drain and set aside.

2 Meanwhile, whisk together the oyster sauce, soy sauce, vinegar and stock in a small bowl.

3 Heat the coconut oil in a large frying pan over a medium-high heat. Season the steak with salt and pepper. When the oil has melted, add the steak to the pan in a single layer and cook until browned on both sides and nearly cooked through, 6–7 minutes. Set aside on a plate to rest for 5 minutes.

4 Add the sesame oil to the same pan. When the oil is shimmering, add the chilli flakes, broccoli, spring onion whites, garlic and ginger and cook, stirring, until fragrant, about 1 minute. Add the pepper noodles and chilli and cook for about 5 minutes or until the noodles soften.

5 Return the steak to the pan and pour over the sauce. Cook, tossing occasionally, until the sauce has thickened, 3–5 minutes. Garnish with the dark green parts of the spring onions and serve.

Pepper Taco Pan

∞∞ | Gluten-free
∞∞ | Dairy-free (opt.)
     | Saves Well

TIME TO PREP 25 minutes
TIME TO COOK 35 minutes
SERVES 4

NUTRITIONAL INFORMATION
Calories: 346
Fat: 21 g
Sodium: 143 mg
Carbohydrate: 21 g
Fibre: 7 g
Sugar: 7 g
Protein: 10 g

ALSO WORKS WELL WITH
Sweet Potato

This Mexican-themed meal is sure to become one of your most craved dishes – the melted cheese, savoury beef and seasoned pepper noodles are irresistible. With easy washing-up, too, what's not to love? Whether you're having a margarita party or looking for a fun, fresh dinner idea, this dish comes together quickly and shows off those classic flavours that make Mexican food so desirable. While any kind of pepper will work here, go for varied colours and embrace that fiesta spirit. And you have my permission to eat this straight out of the frying pan!

For the fajita seasoning
¼ teaspoon cayenne pepper

1 teaspoon chilli powder

¼ teaspoon garlic powder

½ teaspoon paprika

½ teaspoon smoked paprika

½ teaspoon onion powder

¼ teaspoon ground cumin

¼ teaspoon salt

¼ teaspoon dried oregano

1 large ear of sweetcorn, husked

Salt and pepper

225g lean beef mince

3 large garlic cloves, finely chopped

½ teaspoon dried oregano

1 tablespoon extra-virgin olive oil

1 small yellow onion, sliced

2 large peppers (I used yellow and red),
cored, spiralized with BLADE A

2 Roma (plum) tomatoes, deseeded and chopped

65g mature Cheddar cheese

1 tablespoon chopped fresh coriander

1 avocado, thinly sliced

1 Mix together all the fajita seasoning ingredients in a small bowl.

2 Place the sweetcorn in a medium pot and add water to cover and a pinch of salt. Bring to the boil, cook for 2–3 minutes until fork-tender, and drain.

3 While the corn cooks, place a 30cm frying pan (cast iron, if you have it) with a lid over a medium heat. When water flicked onto the pan sizzles, add the beef. Season with salt and black pepper. Add the garlic and oregano and cook for 10 minutes or until the meat is browned, breaking it up with the back of a spoon as it cooks. Remove it from the pan and set aside.

4 Add the olive oil to the pan and heat over a medium-high heat. When the oil is shimmering, add the onion and peppers and cook for 5 minutes or until the vegetables begin to soften.

5 Return the beef to the pan and add the tomatoes and 1 tablespoon of the fajita seasoning. Toss together and cook for 2–3 minutes. Using a knife, slice the corn kernels straight off the cob into the pan. Sprinkle the cheese over the top and cover. Cook for 5–7 minutes or until the cheese melts.

6 Uncover the pan and garnish with the coriander. Serve immediately with the avocado slices.

To make this dish vegetarian, replace the meat with about 75g each of black beans and kidney beans.

Roasted Pepper Chicory Salad

with Anchovy-white Bean Dressing and Soft-baked Eggs

Gluten-free
Dairy-free

TIME TO PREP 10 minutes
TIME TO COOK 15 minutes
SERVES 4

NUTRITIONAL INFORMATION
Calories: 340
Fat: 16 g
Sodium: 130 mg
Carbohydrate: 40 g
Fibre: 9 g
Sugar: 8 g
Protein: 17 g

True to my Italian roots, I love roasted peppers – as snacks, in sandwiches, over pastas, as antipastos and, of course, in salads. This seemingly fancy salad comes together easily and really fills you up. The soft-baked eggs melt into the bitter chicory greens for a bright, creamy bite with full-flavoured, garlicky anchovy dressing. If you're not gluten-free, pair it with toasted sourdough bread.

For the salad

2 red peppers, spiralized with BLADE A, noodles trimmed

2 orange peppers, spiralized with BLADE A, noodles trimmed

½ teaspoon garlic powder

Salt and pepper

4 whole large eggs

120g chicory

For the dressing

2 olive oil-packed anchovy fillets, finely chopped

1 garlic clove, finely chopped

2 teaspoons sherry vinegar

3 tablespoons extra-virgin olive oil

1 bunch of fresh flat-leaf parsley, chopped

Juice of ½ lemon

425g canned cannellini beans, rinsed and drained

Salt and pepper

Anchovies – you either love 'em or you hate 'em. If you're part of the latter contingency, simply omit them and add 45g pitted Kalamata olives, sliced, for a similarly salty and rich taste.

1 Preheat the oven to 230°C/450°F. Line a large baking sheet with baking paper. Lay out the red and orange pepper noodles on the baking sheet, spacing them apart, and season with the garlic powder, salt and pepper. Roast for 20 minutes or until wilted, tossing once halfway through.

2 Meanwhile, place the eggs in a small pan and add water to cover by 5mm. Cover the pan and bring the water to the boil over a high heat. As soon as it's boiling, turn off the heat and leave the eggs to sit, covered, for 7 minutes. Drain and rinse with cold water until cool enough to handle, then peel, halve lengthways and set aside.

3 Meanwhile, make the dressing. Whisk together the anchovies, garlic, vinegar, olive oil, parsley and lemon juice in a medium bowl. Add the beans and toss to coat. Season with salt and black pepper.

4 Transfer the pepper noodles to a large bowl, add the chicory and toss. Pour over the dressing and toss to coat.

5 Divide the pepper-chicory mixture among four plates and top each with two egg halves.

Summer Ratatouille

Ratatouille isn't just an animated Disney movie about a rat that can cook – it's also a traditional Provençal dish. Summertime vegetables are stewed to enhance their flavours before they're baked to tasty perfection. Spiralizing the vegetables reduces the prep time and adds a new texture. While traditional ratatouilles call for each vegetable to cook separately, this quick version simplifies those steps for an easy, breezy summer meal.

Vegan
Vegetarian
Gluten-free
Paleo
Dairy-free
Low-cal
One Pot
Saves Well

TIME TO PREP 25 minutes
TIME TO COOK 35 minutes
SERVES 4

NUTRITIONAL INFORMATION
Calories: 172
Fat: 9 g
Sodium: 957 mg
Carbohydrate: 24 g
Fibre: 6 g
Sugar: 16 g
Protein: 5 g

2 tablespoons extra-virgin olive oil

2 large garlic cloves, pressed

¼ teaspoon chilli flakes

1 brown onion, peeled, spiralized with BLADE A, *noodles trimmed*

2 red peppers, spiralized with BLADE A, *noodles trimmed*

1 medium courgette, spiralized with BLADE D, *noodles trimmed*

1 medium yellow squash, spiralized with BLADE D, *noodles trimmed*

85g aubergine, julienned

Salt and pepper

2 (400g) cans whole peeled tomatoes, with juices

1 bay leaf

1 tablespoon fresh oregano leaves

1 bunch of fresh basil, finely chopped

1 Heat the olive oil in a large pan over a medium heat. When the oil is shimmering, add the garlic, chilli flakes and onion and cook until the onion is softened, about 5 minutes.

2 Add the pepper, courgette and squash noodles and the aubergine. Season with salt and pepper and cook until the vegetables are softened, about 10 minutes.

3 Add the tomatoes and their juices to the pan, crushing them with your hands. Stir in the bay leaf and oregano and further break apart the tomatoes using a wooden spoon. Increase the heat to high and bring to the boil, then reduce the heat to low and simmer until the vegetables are tender, 10–15 minutes. Take care not to overcook them, or they'll be mushy.

4 Stir in the basil and heat for 1 minute. Remove the bay leaf before serving.

Foil Pouch Sea Bass

Gluten-free
Paleo
Dairy-free
Low-Cal

TIME TO PREP 20 minutes
TIME TO COOK 15 minutes
SERVES 4

NUTRITIONAL INFORMATION
Calories: 300
Fat: 21 g
Sodium: 263 mg
Carbohydrate: 13 g
Fibre: 4 g
Sugar: 6 g
Protein: 18 g

ALSO WORKS WELL WITH
Courgette, Kohlrabi

Sea bass has such a delicate flavour that it doesn't need to be cooked with much more than fresh herbs and olive oil. The spiralized peppers soften as their flavours develop with the caper, lemon and parsley-infused juices from the fish. With everything layered together in a foil pouch, washing-up couldn't be easier, making this meal a great weeknight dinner.

3 tablespoons extra-virgin olive oil

2 yellow peppers, spiralized with BLADE A, *noodles trimmed*

2 orange peppers, spiralized with BLADE A, *noodles trimmed*

Salt and pepper

4 (85g) sea bass fillets

2 shallots, finely chopped

4 teaspoons finely chopped garlic

Juice of 1 lemon

45g cherry tomatoes, halved

1 tablespoon drained capers

2 tablespoons chopped fresh parsley, to garnish

If you don't use foil in your household, baking paper works well, too. Try brushing egg wash over the edges to seal the parcels closed.

1 Preheat the oven to 220°C/425°F. Tear off four 46cm lengths of foil. Generously brush ½ tablespoon of the olive oil in the centre of each sheet.

2 In a large bowl, toss together the yellow and orange pepper noodles. Mound them in the centre of each foil sheet and season with salt and pepper. Season the sea bass fillets with salt and pepper and place one on top of the pepper noodles on each foil sheet. Sprinkle the shallots and garlic over the fish, dividing them evenly.

3 In a small bowl, combine the lemon juice, cherry tomatoes, capers and remaining 1 tablespoon olive oil to make the sauce. Pull the sides of the foil up around the fish and drizzle over the sauce. Fold in the edges of the foil to make sealed parcels.

4 Arrange the parcels on a baking sheet and bake for 12–15 minutes or until the sea bass is cooked through and opaque. Open the parcels carefully (the steam is very hot), garnish the fish with the parsley and serve directly from the parcels or plated.

Radish

BI – that is, Before Inspiralizing – I exclusively consumed radishes raw in salads or pickled in sandwiches like banh mi. Now I love making radish rice, radish pasta and radish noodle soups. I do still enjoy radishes in salads, but now they're totally different. As you'll quickly realize, or maybe already have, simply changing the shape of a vegetable alters the way it feels on the palate, due to its different surface area and texture. There are many kinds of radishes. Black radishes have a spicy taste, pairing well with meats and hearty seafood and equalizing their flavours. Mooli has a mild taste. I love to spiralize brilliantly pink watermelon radishes, which tend to grow wider, making them perfect for spiralizing! It can be tough to find other radishes that are large enough to spiralize. Your best bet is to stick to mooli, but if you do find a large ruby radish, snag it!

NUTRITIONAL BENEFITS: Mooli is an effective diuretic, which aids digestion and cleanses the body and palate, helping to improve kidney function. Other radish varieties carry similar powers.

PREPARATION AND STORAGE: Peel the radish entirely. Slice the ends off to leave flat, even surfaces. Store in an airtight container in the fridge for 5–7 days.

BEST BLADES TO USE
- Blade A
- Blade C
- Blade D

BEST COOKING METHODS
- Raw
- Simmer or boil in a soup
- Sauté over a medium heat for 5–7 minutes

Hot-and-sour Soup
with Mooli Noodles

Vegetarian
Dairy-free
One Pot
Low-cal
Saves Well

TIME TO PREP 30 minutes
TIME TO COOK 15 minutes
SERVES 4

NUTRITIONAL INFORMATION
Calories: 110
Fat: 5 g
Sodium: 714 mg
Carbohydrate: 12 g
Fibre: 4 g
Sugar: 5 g
Protein: 8 g

ALSO WORKS WELL WITH
Courgette, Turnip, Carrot

When I was growing up, my mother always ordered hot-and-sour soup whenever we got Chinese food. She claimed it cleared her sinuses and led to the eventual curing of any cold. While I'm not sure hot-and-sour soup has such magical medicinal powers, it's definitely one of the more flavourful, robust soups out there. With wispy eggs, salty stock and soft simmered vegetables, this soup satisfies the senses. The mooli noodles transform this takeaway staple into a hearty noodle soup.

1 dried chilli, deseeded and chopped

1 litre reduced-salt chicken stock

1 tablespoon reduced-salt soy sauce or tamari

6 dried shiitake mushrooms, rehydrated in hot water and thinly sliced

1 (175g) can bamboo shoots, drained and cut into matchsticks

90g firm tofu, drained and cut into matchsticks (see page 84)

¼ teaspoon ground white pepper

60ml white vinegar

1 large mooli radish, peeled, spiralized with BLADE D, noodles trimmed

1 large egg, lightly beaten

1 teaspoon sesame oil

Salt

1 spring onion, thinly sliced

1 Combine the chilli, stock and soy sauce in a large stockpot with a lid and bring to the boil over a high heat. Add the mushrooms and bamboo shoots. Reduce the heat to low, cover and simmer for about 3 minutes or until the mushrooms are softened.

2 Add the tofu, white pepper and vinegar, increase the heat to high and return to the boil. Stir in the mooli noodles and cook for 3 minutes more or until al dente.

3 Turn off the heat and add the egg, stirring gently to create wisps. Stir in the sesame oil. Taste and season with salt, if needed.

4 Ladle the soup into four bowls and garnish with the spring onion.

Black Radish and Orange Salad

with Radicchio and Salmon Cakes

Gluten-free

TIME TO PREP 20 minutes
TIME TO COOK 10 minutes
SERVES 2

NUTRITIONAL INFORMATION
Calories: 323
Fat: 15 g
Sodium: 587 mg
Carbohydrate: 19 g
Fibre: 4 g
Sugar: 8 g
Protein: 28 g

ALSO WORKS WELL WITH
Carrot, Potato

This salad is a prime example of how spiralized veggies can be used to tactfully infuse textures and flavours into meals. If you were to add sliced black radishes to this salad, the bitterness would overpower the other flavours, rendering the meal somewhat unpalatable. But by spiralizing it instead, you're able to enhance the sweet orange and savoury, fragrant salmon by adding a tart bite with each twirly strand.

For the salmon cakes
225g salmon fillet, skinless, cut into cubes

2 teaspoons Dijon mustard

1 small garlic clove, sliced

¼ teaspoon grated lemon zest

1 teaspoon fresh lemon juice

1 tablespoon finely chopped fresh parsley

1 shallot, finely chopped

1 tablespoon extra-virgin olive oil

Salt and pepper

For the vinaigrette
2 tablespoons natural 0% Greek yogurt

1 tablespoon extra-virgin olive oil

1 tablespoon red wine vinegar

1 tablespoon jarred small capers, drained

¼ teaspoon garlic powder

2 teaspoons fresh lemon juice

1 teaspoon Dijon mustard

Salt and pepper

For the salad
1 black radish or turnip, peeled, spiralized with BLADE D, *noodles trimmed*

1 navel orange, peeled and chopped

160g radicchio, chopped

1 Make the salmon cakes. Place the salmon, mustard, garlic, lemon zest and juice and parsley in a food processor. Pulse just until the large pieces of salmon break down, taking care not to overpulse. Transfer the mixture to a medium bowl and stir in the shallot. Using your hands, form the mixture into four 5–7.5cm patties.

2 Heat the olive oil in a large frying pan over a medium-high heat. When the oil is shimmering, add the salmon cakes in a single layer, working in batches if necessary. Season the tops with salt and pepper and cook for 2–3 minutes on each side or until browned on the outside and cooked through.

3 Meanwhile, make the vinaigrette. Whisk together all the ingredients for the vinaigrette in a large bowl. Taste and adjust the seasoning to your preference. Add the radish noodles, orange and radicchio. Toss to coat.

4 Divide the salad between two plates and top each with two salmon cakes.

These salmon cakes can be formed into larger patties and work well as burgers, too.

Ginger-crab Fried Mooli Rice

≋ | Dairy-free
≋ | Low-cal
≋

TIME TO PREP 15 minutes
TIME TO COOK 15 minutes
SERVES 4

NUTRITIONAL INFORMATION
Calories: 147
Fat: 9 g
Sodium: 1025 mg
Carbohydrate: 6 g
Fibre: 2 g
Sugar: 3 g
Protein: 12 g

ALSO WORKS WELL WITH
Kohlrabi, Turnip

As a lover of eclectic foods, I was excited to have a chef like Dale Talde open a sister restaurant in my city. Now a go-to of ours, Talde is a popular, casual Asian-American restaurant and every time we're there, we order the Blue Crab Fried Rice, which Lu and I devour together. This spiralized version mimics many of its diverse flavours, so I can enjoy the dish at home in my tracksuit bottoms.

1 tablespoon coconut oil

1 garlic clove, finely chopped

1 (2.5cm) piece fresh ginger, peeled and finely chopped

¼ teaspoon chilli flakes (or extra if you like more spice)

2 medium mooli, peeled, spiralized with BLADE D, then riced and drained

2 large eggs, beaten

1 tablespoon soy sauce

2–3 tablespoons fish sauce

230g canned white crabmeat

30g cashews, roughly chopped

2 spring onions, green parts only, diced

1 bunch of fresh coriander

Hot sauce or chilli oil, to garnish

1 Heat the coconut oil in a large frying pan over a medium heat. When the oil has melted, add the garlic, ginger and chilli flakes and cook for 1 minute or until fragrant. Stir in the mooli rice and cook for 2 minutes or until softened.

2 Push the rice to the edges of the pan, creating a cavity in the centre. Add the eggs to the centre and stir constantly to scramble until cooked. Stir the rice back in, combining all the ingredients. Stir in the soy sauce and fish sauce. Fold in the crab and cook for 2 minutes to heat through.

3 Remove the pan from the heat and stir in the cashews, spring onions and coriander. Garnish with the hot sauce or chilli oil, if you like.

Watermelon Radish Nourish Salad

with Lemon-ginger Vinaigrette and Vegan Parmesan

Vegan
Vegetarian
Gluten-free
Paleo
Dairy-free
No Cook

TIME TO PREP 30 minutes
SERVES 2

NUTRITIONAL INFORMATION
Calories: 390
Fat: 36 g
Sodium: 171 mg
Carbohydrate: 15 g
Fibre: 6 g
Sugar: 6 g
Protein: 6 g

ALSO WORKS WELL WITH
Golden Beetroot,
Kohlrabi

Sometimes you crave a big, heaped bowl of greens. Or is that just me? There's something comforting about making your own salad – adding whatever you want to it and tossing everything together. Usually when I make salads, I use up whatever I have in my fridge and it becomes one of those 'everything but the kitchen sink' meals that I eat out of a big mixing bowl. But there are also times when I want a simple salad with minimal ingredients. I want to sit down and slowly enjoy a nourishing dish, concentrating on chewing, breathing and feeling my body rejuvenate. This dish is just that: a truly enjoyable salad with stunning watermelon radish slices that pop against dark, leafy kale. The vegan Parmesan adds a graceful sprinkling of nutty flavour.

For the vegan Parmesan
40g pine nuts
1 teaspoon roasted unsalted sunflower seeds
1½ teaspoons nutritional yeast

For the dressing
Grated zest of ½ lemon
1 tablespoon fresh lemon juice
1½ teaspoons grated fresh ginger
2½ tablespoons extra-virgin olive oil
1 teaspoon honey
1 tablespoon finely chopped fresh parsley
Salt and pepper

For the salad
1 large watermelon radish or mooli
700g Swiss chard, shredded
½ avocado, thinly sliced

1 Make the vegan Parmesan. Place all the ingredients for the vegan Parmesan in a food processor and pulse until ground.

2 Make the dressing. In a large bowl, whisk together all the ingredients for the dressing. Taste and adjust the seasoning to your preferences.

3 Make the salad. Slice the watermelon radish halfway through lengthways to create a slit, being careful not to pierce any further than its centre. Spiralize with **BLADE A** and trim the noodles. Add the noodles and the chard to the bowl with the dressing and toss to combine. Divide the salad between two places and top each with avocado. Finish with the vegan Parmesan.

This vegan Parmesan cheese can be used on pretty much anything in place of regular Parmesan cheese, so grab a sticky note and bookmark the page!

Grilled Steak
with Mustard Greens and Radish Noodles

I've never really been a steak person. I love a masterfully braised short rib or a sumptuous Bolognese, but a slab of steak doesn't appeal to me. The only way I've ever enjoyed it has been sliced on a salad. There's something about having a green vegetable in every bite that makes the steak more appealing to me. Whatever your reason for liking steak salads, this one is simple and honest, and it has plenty of crunch.

Gluten-free
Paleo
Dairy-free

TIME TO PREP 15 minutes
TIME TO COOK 15 minutes
SERVES 4

NUTRITIONAL INFORMATION
Calories: 413
Fat: 30 g
Sodium: 347 mg
Carbohydrate: 8 g
Fibre: 3 g
Sugar: 5 g
Protein: 27 g

ALSO WORKS WELL WITH
Pear, Potato

450g sirloin steak or your preferred cut

Salt and pepper

1 tablespoon extra-virgin olive oil

For the dressing
60ml extra-virgin olive oil

2 tablespoons balsamic vinegar

1 teaspoon honey

¼ teaspoon garlic powder

1 teaspoon Dijon mustard

Salt and pepper

For the salad
560g mustard greens, chopped

1 large radish, peeled, spiralized with BLADE D, noodles trimmed

50g endive, chopped

1 Season the steak generously with salt and pepper on both sides.

2 Heat a griddle pan or frying pan over a medium-high heat. When the pan is hot, add the olive oil. When the oil is shimmering, add the steak and cook for about 4 minutes on each side for medium-rare or 6 minutes on each side for medium-well. Transfer to a carving or chopping board to rest for 3–5 minutes. Slice the steak thinly (about 5mm thick slices) against the grain.

3 While the steak cooks, make the salad. Whisk together all the ingredients for the dressing in a large bowl. Add the mustard greens, radish noodles and endive and toss to combine.

4 Divide the salad among four plates and top with slices of steak. Pour any juices from the chopping board back over the steak.

Watermelon radish, black radish and mooli all work well in this recipe. If mustard greens aren't your favourite, use spinach or another mild green instead.

Clear Immunity Soup
with Mooli Noodles

In an attempt to bolster our immune systems and avoid falling ill in the winter, many of us drink green juices, have hot water with lemon, make matcha tea lattes and sip bone broth. My favourite way to ward off any sickness is to whip up this clear immunity-boosting soup. The simple healing powers of garlic and ginger will leave you feeling nourished, rejuvenated and ready to conquer the chilly temperatures. It's a great way to protect yourself from the person next to you in line who just sneezed all over your shoulder!

Vegan
Vegetarian
Gluten-free
Paleo
Dairy-free
Low-cal
One Pot

TIME TO PREP 20 minutes
TIME TO COOK 30 minutes
SERVES 4

NUTRITIONAL INFORMATION
Calories: 70
Fat: 3 g
Sodium: 25 mg
Carbohydrate: 8 g
Fibre: 2 g
Sugar: 3 g
Protein: 3 g

ALSO WORKS WELL WITH
Carrot, Courgette, Turnip

---

1 tablespoon extra-virgin olive oil

1 small white onion, peeled, spiralized with BLADE A, noodles trimmed

2 celery sticks, diced

2 spring onions, sliced, white and green parts kept separate

3 garlic cloves, thinly sliced

2 teaspoons finely grated fresh ginger

Salt

¼ teaspoon white pepper

225g button mushrooms, trimmed and thinly sliced

1 medium mooli, peeled, spiralized with BLADE C, noodles trimmed

70g pea shoots

1 Heat the oil in a large stockpot over a medium heat. When the oil is shimmering, add the onion, celery, white parts of the spring onions, garlic and ginger. Season with salt and cook for 3 minutes or until the onion is softened.

2 Add 1.8 litres water and the white pepper. Increase the heat to medium-high and bring the soup to a strong simmer. Cook for 10 minutes, then add the mushrooms and mooli noodles and simmer for a further 5 minutes or until the mooli is al dente.

3 Ladle the soup into bowls. Top with the pea shoots and spring onion greens.

For more flavour, use chicken stock instead of water. Even better if it's homemade!

Swede

Like celeriac, swedes are tough cookies – er, veggies. They have a very waxy exterior and take time to properly peel. They tend to be larger in both size and weight for a vegetable. But don't let all that intimidate you – once you've prepped your swede, it spiralizes easily and makes loads of noodles. Swedes are perhaps the most resilient of spiralized vegetables, able to withstand all types of cooking methods and hold all kinds of sauces.

Raw swede generally carries a mild and slightly bitter taste, as it's in the same family as the turnip. (In fact, swedes are sometimes known as wax turnips and Swedish turnips, or rutabagas.) But once it's cooked, swede steals the show, with a golden colour and a slight sweetness, making them popular mashed, roasted and stirred into stews. They are less starchy and therefore less carbohydrate-heavy than regular potatoes, so they may be a better option for you, depending on your goals.

When picking out a swede at the supermarket, look for one that's not too heavy or large (under 15cm in diameter, preferably). Properly ripened swedes should have a purple-tinged skin without any major blemishes or a shrivelled appearance.

NUTRITIONAL BENEFITS: A solid source of zinc, swedes help support the immune system and metabolism. They are also high in vitamin C and dietary fibre.

PREPARATION AND STORAGE: Peel the swede entirely and slice the ends off to leave flat, even surfaces. If the swede is large, to get better leverage, slice each side off to leave flat, even surfaces until you have a thinner, more rectangular vegetable that's no more than 15–18cm wide. Store in an airtight container in the fridge for up to 6 days. Swede noodles can be frozen for up to 8 months for future use.

BEST BLADES TO USE
- Blade A
- Blade B
- Blade C
- Blade D

BEST COOKING METHODS
- Boil for 5–10 minutes
- Sauté over a medium-high heat for 10–15 minutes
- Roast at 220°C/425°F for 20–30 minutes, depending on which blade was used

Thai Almond and Pork Curry
with Swede Noodles

Gluten-free
Paleo
Dairy-free

TIME TO PREP 15 minutes
TIME TO COOK 30 minutes
SERVES 4

NUTRITIONAL INFORMATION
Calories: 330
Fat: 14 g
Sodium: 992 mg
Carbohydrate: 22 g
Fibre: 3 g
Sugar: 15 g
Protein: 29 g

ALSO WORKS WELL WITH
Courgette, Sweet Potato,
Turnip, Kohlrabi, Carrot

Where do you stand in the almond butter versus peanut butter battle? Nine times out of ten I'm on team almond, simply based on flavour alone. Whichever way you sway, trust me: almond butter is the way to go in this recipe. The swede makes a hearty noodle, similar in texture to chewy soba. The light pork doesn't overpower the curry, and absorbs the Thai flavours well.

---

2 small swedes, peeled, spiralized with
BLADE C, noodles trimmed

Salt and pepper

1 (400ml) can light coconut milk

3 tablespoons fish sauce

3 tablespoons honey

60g smooth almond butter

1 tablespoon coconut oil

675g pork fillet or tenderloin, sliced into
   1cm thick strips

1 garlic clove, sliced

2 spring onions, diced, white and green parts
   separated

3 tablespoons red curry paste

1 teaspoon chilli paste

2 tablespoons chopped fresh coriander,
   to garnish

2 tablespoons roughly crushed and
   chopped almonds, to garnish

Feel free to replace the pork fillet with chicken,
tofu or your preferred protein source. It won't affect the
overall flavours too much.

1 Preheat the oven to 220°C/425°F. Line a baking sheet with baking paper. Lay out the swede noodles on the baking sheet, spacing them apart, and season with salt and pepper. Bake for 15–20 minutes or until al dente.

2 Meanwhile, in a medium bowl, whisk together the coconut milk, fish sauce, honey and almond butter until smooth.

3 Heat the coconut oil in a large frying pan over a medium heat. When the oil has melted, add the pork and cook for 5–7 minutes, turning occasionally to brown on all sides. Transfer the pork to a plate.

4 Immediately add the garlic, white parts of the spring onions, curry paste and chilli paste to the same pan and stir continuously until combined, about 30 seconds. Add the coconut milk mixture and cooked pork and stir to combine. Reduce the heat to medium-low and simmer for 10 minutes or until the sauce has thickened.

5 Divide the cooked swede noodles among four plates and spoon the pork curry over each. Garnish with the coriander, spring onion greens and almonds.

Swede Gratin
with Leeks

Vegan
Vegetarian
Gluten-free
Paleo
Dairy-free

TIME TO PREP 20 minutes
plus 2 hours to soak cashews
TIME TO COOK 50 minutes
SERVES 4–6

NUTRITIONAL INFORMATION
(for 1 of 6 servings)
Calories: 317
Fat: 22 g
Sodium: 269 mg
Carbohydrate: 24 g
Fibre: 4 g
Sugar: 7 g
Protein: 10 g

ALSO WORKS WELL WITH
Sweet Potato, Butternut
Squash, Potato, Parsnip

Casseroles are the best way to feed a crowd, ideal to bring to dinner parties or serve at your own gatherings. And of the casseroles, gratins are king. They tend to lean on the heavier side, often incorporating ingredients like cream and flour, but this recipe is loaded with good ingredients like cashews, garlic, leeks and, of course, swede. With simple components and big flavour, this shareable vegan dish is sure to become your go-to potluck recipe.

Cooking spray

For the sauce
475ml reduced-salt vegetable stock
240g raw cashews, soaked overnight (or for at least 2 hours) and drained
1 tablespoon nutritional yeast
2 teaspoons fresh lemon juice
2 large garlic cloves, roughly chopped
Salt and pepper

For the gratin
1 tablespoon extra-virgin olive oil
1 small yellow onion, diced
110g leeks, thinly sliced
2 garlic cloves, finely chopped
1½ tablespoons fresh thyme
Salt and pepper
1 medium swede, peeled, spiralized with BLADE A, *noodles trimmed*

1 Preheat the oven to 200°C/400°F. Coat a medium casserole dish with cooking spray.

2 Make the sauce. Place all the ingredients for the sauce in a high-speed blender or food processor and pulse until creamy. Add salt and pepper to taste.

3 Make the gratin. Heat the olive oil in a large frying pan over a medium-high heat. When the oil is shimmering, add the onion and leeks and cook for 5 minutes or until softened. Add the garlic and cook until fragrant, about 30 seconds. Add the sauce and the thyme. Season with salt and pepper. Stir to combine thoroughly, then remove the pan from the heat.

4 Spread about 60ml of the leek mixture over the bottom of the prepared casserole dish. Add a layer of the swede noodles on top. Continue these layers with the remaining ingredients, finishing with the remaining leeks. Season with pepper.

5 Cover with foil and bake for 30 minutes or until the swede is fork-tender. Turn the oven to the grill setting, remove the foil and return the gratin to the oven for 2 minutes or until the top is browned. Cut into portions and serve.

Mussels
over Swede Pasta

≋≋ | Gluten-free
≋≋ | Dairy-free
      | Low-cal

TIME TO PREP 15 minutes
TIME TO COOK 30 minutes
SERVES 4

NUTRITIONAL INFORMATION
Calories: 228
Fat: 6 g
Sodium: 515 mg
Carbohydrate: 21 g
Fibre: 4 g
Sugar: 8 g
Protein: 16 g

ALSO WORKS WELL WITH
Courgette, Turnip,
Kohlrabi

In the wintertime, sweet potatoes and swede compete for my attention. Luckily, there's plenty of veggie love to go around, but if I *had* to pick, it would be swede. This news may be surprising, since sweet potatoes, touted as a superfood, usually steal the spotlight. But these mild, buttery noodles coated in a simple light tomato and white wine sauce with garlic and fresh parsley shine underneath fresh mussels. They look so much like spaghetti that you'll have guests searching your recycling bin for an empty box! If you're looking for a dish to warm up your winter blues, this is the one.

2 small swedes, peeled, spiralized with
   BLADE D, **noodles trimmed**

1 teaspoon garlic powder

Salt and pepper

4 garlic cloves, finely chopped

1 shallot, finely chopped

125ml dry white wine

900g mussels, rinsed, scrubbed and
   debearded

1 (400g) can chopped tomatoes

1 tablespoon extra-virgin olive oil

¼ teaspoon chilli flakes

¼ teaspoon dried oregano

¼ teaspoon dried basil

1 bunch of fresh curly parsley, chopped

1 tablespoon finely grated lemon zest

1 Preheat the oven to 220°C/425°F. Line a baking sheet with baking paper. Lay out the swede noodles on the baking sheet, spacing them apart, and season with the garlic powder, salt and black pepper. Bake for 15–20 minutes or until al dente.

2 Meanwhile, place a casserole dish or large, wide frying pan with a lid over a high heat. When water flicked onto the pan sizzles, add three-quarters of the garlic, the shallot and the wine. Bring to the boil, then add the mussels. Cover and cook, shaking the pan occasionally, for about 3 minutes, but no more than 5 minutes, until the mussels open up. Transfer to a large bowl, discarding any unopened mussels.

3 While the mussels cook, place the tomatoes in a food processor and pulse a few times until coarsely ground – not completely smooth, but with no large chunks remaining.

4 When the mussels are cool enough to handle, remove half of them from their shells. Taste-test one; if it's sandy, rinse them all in a colander.

5 Wipe clean the casserole or frying pan in which you cooked the mussels and heat the olive oil over a medium heat. When the oil is shimmering, add the remaining garlic and chilli flakes and cook until fragrant, about 30 seconds. Add the puréed tomatoes, oregano and basil. Increase the heat to medium-high, and bring to a strong simmer. Cook, stirring often, for 5–10 minutes or until the tomatoes have reduced slightly. Add all the cooked mussels to the pan, cover, reduce the heat to low and cook for a further 5 minutes to allow the flavours to develop.

6 Transfer the swede to a large serving bowl or platter. Uncover the pan with the mussels and fold in the parsley. Garnish with the lemon zest and pour the mussels over the swede. Serve family-style.

Chicken Cacciatore
over Swede Noodles

Gluten-free
Dairy-free
Saves Well

TIME TO PREP 20 minutes
TIME TO COOK 40 minutes
SERVES 4

NUTRITIONAL INFORMATION
Calories: 493
Fat: 22 g
Sodium: 485 mg
Carbohydrate: 38 g
Fibre: 11 g
Sugar: 18 g
Protein: 38 g

ALSO WORKS WELL WITH
Courgette, Turnip, Celeriac

If you're searching for a hearty dish to impress a crowd, look no further. Swedenoodles' resilience makes them ideal for serving with this classic Italian chicken dish – they won't break up on your guests' plates! The veggie's soft, buttery texture soaks up the flavours of the stewed tomatoes, herbs, garlic and onions, ensuring this dish a spot in your weekly dinner rotation, too.

3 small swedes, peeled, spiralized with BLADE D, *noodles trimmed*

Cooking spray

1 teaspoon garlic powder

Salt and pepper

45g almond flour

600g skin-on, bone-in chicken thighs

2 carrots, diced

1 large red pepper, diced

1 medium yellow onion, peeled, spiralized with BLADE A, *noodles trimmed*

2 large garlic cloves, finely chopped

¼ teaspoon chilli flakes

½ teaspoon dried rosemary

125ml dry white wine (I like Sauvignon Blanc)

2 (400g) cans no-salt-added chopped tomatoes

225ml reduced-salt chicken stock

1½ teaspoons dried oregano

1 bunch of fresh basil, roughly chopped

If you prefer chicken breasts over thighs, you can substitute them. Just let them cook a bit longer – 25–30 minutes – and use only four.

1 Preheat the oven to 220°C/425°F. Line a baking sheet with baking paper. Lay out the swede noodles on the baking sheet, spacing them apart. Spray them with cooking spray and season with the garlic powder, salt and black pepper. Bake for 20–30 minutes or until al dente.

2 On a large plate, season the almond flour with salt and black pepper. Season the chicken all over with salt and black pepper, then dredge it in the flour, pressing to adhere.

3 Place a large frying pan over a medium-high heat and coat with cooking spray. When water flicked onto the pan sizzles, add the chicken in a single layer, working in batches if necessary. Cook until browned on the outside, about 5 minutes on each side. Transfer to a plate and set aside.

4 Add the carrots, pepper, onion, fresh garlic, chilli flakes and rosemary to the pan. Season with salt and black pepper. Cook for 5 minutes or until the vegetables are softened. Add the wine and simmer for 5 minutes or until reduced by half. Add the tomatoes and their juices, stock and oregano.

5 Return the chicken to the pan, nestling it into the vegetables. Spoon some sauce over each piece of chicken, then reduce the heat to medium-low and simmer for about 20 minutes or until the chicken is cooked through.

6 Using tongs, transfer the chicken to a large plate. Add the cooked swede noodles to the frying pan and toss to coat. Cook for 2 minutes or until the flavours are melded.

7 Using tongs, divide the swede pasta among four plates and top each with chicken. Garnish with the basil and serve.

Swede Baked Ziti
with Mushrooms and Kale

Vegetarian
Gluten-free
Saves Well

TIME TO PREP 25 minutes
TIME TO COOK 35 minutes
SERVES 4–6

NUTRITIONAL INFORMATION
Calories: 320
Fat: 18 g
Sodium: 794 mg
Carbohydrate: 20 g
Fibre: 5 g
Sugar: 8 g
Protein: 22 g

ALSO WORKS WELL WITH
Sweet Potato, Potato

You'd be hard-pressed to find an Italian person – or maybe any person – who doesn't love baked ziti and lasagne. But what you might find are people who don't regularly eat these dishes because of their high calorie, fat and carbohydrate counts. This Inspiralized version calls for swede noodles instead of rigatoni or penne pasta. I promise you won't miss it – the swede holds its own against the melted cheeses. The mushrooms and kale squeeze in extra vegetables and nutrients, and add an earthy flavour to this comforting ziti.

Cooking spray

1 tablespoon extra-virgin olive oil

2 garlic cloves, finely chopped

1 small onion, diced

335g curly kale, chopped

480g baby portobello mushrooms, sliced

Salt and pepper

1 medium swede, peeled, spiralized with BLADE C, *noodles trimmed*

1 (400g) can chopped tomatoes

2 teaspoons dried rosemary

2 teaspoons dried oregano

½ teaspoon chilli flakes

225g ricotta cheese

100g Parmesan cheese, grated

175g mozzarella cheese, grated

Meat lovers can add crumbled sausage or turkey mince to this dish for extra flavour and protein.

1 Preheat the oven to 200°C/400°F. Coat a medium baking dish with cooking spray.

2 Heat the olive oil in a large saucepan or casserole dish over a medium-high heat. When the oil is shimmering, add the garlic and onion and cook for 3–5 minutes or until the onion is translucent. Add the kale and mushrooms, season with salt and black pepper and cook for 5 minutes or until the kale is wilted. Transfer the mixture to a medium bowl.

3 Add the swede to the same pan and cook for 5 minutes or until it begins to soften. Return the kale mixture to the pan and toss thoroughly to combine. Stir in the tomatoes, rosemary, oregano and chilli flakes. Increase the heat to medium-high and bring to a simmer, then remove the pan from the heat.

4 Meanwhile, in a medium bowl, stir together the ricotta, Parmesan and 115g of the mozzarella. Add the mixed cheeses to the pan with the swede and toss to combine.

5 Transfer the mixture to the prepared baking dish and top with the remaining mozzarella. Cover with foil and bake for 20 minutes. Remove the foil and bake for a further 10 minutes or until the swede is al dente and the cheese is golden brown. Serve immediately.

Sweet Potato

When you're shopping for sweet potatoes to spiralize, you may see signs for 'sweet potatoes' and 'yams'. What's the difference? Both are tuberous root vegetables, but they actually *aren't* related, and depending on which area of the world you live in, they may be entirely different.

Yams are most commonly identified by their blackish or brown, rough, thick skin and white, purple or reddish flesh. They're a bit starchier than sweet potatoes and drier – not as ideal for the spiralizer. The two major types of sweet potatoes you'll find in supermarkets are firm and soft. Firm potatoes have golden skin and paler flesh, and can be a little bit waxy and more difficult to spiralize. The soft ones have a copper skin and orange flesh. (You may find this variety labelled as a yam, although technically it is not.) When you are selecting a sweet potato for spiralizing, look for the latter type. If you're unsure which it is, scratch the skin to reveal the colour of the flesh. I prefer to use these in my recipes, as they become creamy, fluffy and moist when cooked. The potato should be medium to large in size and as tubular as possible. One more thing: Don't ever boil sweet potatoes – they'll turn into mush on your plate and break apart!

NUTRITIONAL BENEFITS: Sweet potatoes are an excellent source of vitamins A, B6 and C. They also contain iron, which is a necessary mineral to maintain adequate energy levels, and magnesium, essential for healthy arteries and nerve function. Sweet potatoes have a lower glycaemic index and are more nutritionally dense than traditional white potatoes, making them a better option for maintaining a healthy diet.

PREPARATION AND STORAGE: Peel the sweet potato, if you prefer. Slice off the ends to leave flat, even surfaces. Store in an airtight container in the fridge for up to 5 days. Sweet potato noodles can be frozen for up to 8 months for future use.

BEST BLADES TO USE
- Blade A
- Blade C
- Blade D

BEST COOKING METHODS
- Sauté over a medium-high heat for 5–7 minutes
- Roast at 220°C/425°F for 10–15 minutes

Tandoori Chicken
over Sweet Potato Rice

～ Gluten-free
～ Paleo
～ Dairy-free
  Saves Well

TIME TO PREP 35 minutes
TIME TO COOK 35 minutes
SERVES 4

NUTRITIONAL INFORMATION
Calories: 329
Fat: 21 g
Sodium: 111 mg
Carbohydrate: 20 g
Fibre: 4 g
Sugar: 5 g
Protein: 16 g

ALSO WORKS WELL WITH
Butternut Squash, Turnip, Kohlrabi

If you're ever in the mood for a super-well-seasoned, somewhat spicy piece of chicken, make it tandoori. Of Indian origin, tandoori chicken is traditionally prepared with yogurt. In this version, we use coconut cream to keep it dairy-free and to add a lightly sweet flavour in a subtle sauce that coats the sweet potato rice. While the classic is marinated and cooked on a skewer for hours, this quick version requires only an oven and a frying pan, and is done in about an hour.

120ml coconut cream (see page 19)

½ teaspoon onion powder

1 teaspoon garlic powder

1 teaspoon ground turmeric

1 teaspoon cayenne pepper

1 teaspoon paprika

½ teaspoon ground cumin

½ teaspoon ground coriander

Juice of ½ lemon

Salt and pepper

4 skin-on, bone-in chicken breasts or legs and thighs

1 tablespoon extra-virgin olive oil

2 garlic cloves, finely chopped

2 medium sweet potatoes, peeled, spiralized with BLADE D, then riced (see page 16)

125ml reduced-salt chicken stock

2 tablespoons chopped fresh coriander

20g sliced blanched almonds

1 Preheat the oven to 230°C/450°F. Line a baking sheet with baking paper.

2 In a medium bowl, stir together the coconut cream, onion powder, garlic powder, turmeric, cayenne, paprika, cumin, coriander and lemon juice. Season with salt and black pepper. Transfer to a large resealable plastic bag or container. Add the chicken and turn to coat. Set aside to marinate for 20 minutes at room temperature or up to 2 hours in the fridge.

3 Remove the chicken from the marinade, allowing the excess to drip off. Transfer to the prepared baking sheet and bake for 25 minutes or until charring on the outside and cooked through.

4 Heat the olive oil in a large frying pan over a medium-high heat. When the oil is shimmering, add the garlic and cook for 30 seconds or until fragrant. Add the sweet potato rice and stock, cover and cook for 7 minutes or until softened. Stir in the coriander and almonds.

5 Divide the rice among four plates and top each with a piece of chicken.

Sweet Potato Pizza Pan

Vegetarian
Gluten-free
One Pot
Saves Well

TIME TO PREP 25 minutes
TIME TO COOK 35 minutes
SERVES 4

NUTRITIONAL INFORMATION
Calories: 315
Fat: 15 g
Sodium: 812 mg
Carbohydrate: 35 g
Fibre: 5 g
Sugar: 15 g
Protein: 13 g

ALSO WORKS WELL WITH
Swede, Potatoes

If you'd like to re-create pizza with your spiralizer, you have options. You can make a mini pizza with a spiralized bun, or regular pizza by creating a larger version of the bun. But if you're craving pizza and need it now, this simple frying pan version is all you need. With cooked spiralized sweet potatoes covered in plentiful seasonings, toppings and cheese, there's not much more to it. You may be tempted to eat the whole thing yourself, so grab a friend to share it!

1 tablespoon extra-virgin olive oil

3 medium sweet potatoes, peeled, spiralized with BLADE C, noodles trimmed

1 teaspoon garlic powder

Salt and pepper

350ml marinara pasta sauce or tomato sauce

½ teaspoon dried oregano

145g mozzarella cheese, grated

45g black olives, pitted and sliced

½ small red onion, thinly sliced

1 small green pepper, thinly sliced

2 tablespoons chopped fresh basil, to garnish

1 tablespoon grated Parmesan cheese, to garnish

1 Preheat the oven to 220°C/425°F.

2 Heat the olive oil in a 25cm frying pan over a medium-high heat. When the oil is shimmering, add the sweet potato noodles and season with the garlic powder, salt and black pepper. Cook for about 5 minutes or until beginning to soften.

3 Pour the marinara sauce over the noodles, sprinkle with the oregano and layer the mozzarella on top. Top with the olives, onion and pepper.

4 Bake for 20–25 minutes or until the cheese is melted and golden.

5 Garnish with the basil and Parmesan before serving.

If there's excess sauce in the frying pan once the pizza's out of the oven, pour some out before serving or sop it up with some crusty wholegrain bread.

Chorizo-Sweet Potato Buns

with Tomato and Pepper Jack

≋≋
≋≋
≋≋ Gluten-free

TIME TO PREP 25 minutes
TIME TO COOK 15 minutes
SERVES 4

NUTRITIONAL INFORMATION
Calories: 403
Fat: 30 g
Sodium: 462 mg
Carbohydrate: 18 g
Fibre: 5 g
Sugar: 3 g
Protein: 15 g

ALSO WORKS WELL WITH
Swede, Potato

Essentially, this dish is an open-faced grilled cheese for adults. The chorizo releases its fats into the pan, which the sweet potato noodles soak up as they cook, setting up this yummy bun. The spiciness and sweetness are tied together by the soft, warm tomato, while the gooey melted cheese finishes everything off under the grill. The pepper jack brings notes of jalapeño chillies, garlic, rosemary and sweet peppers, creating a seriously good spiralized sandwich.

2 chorizo links, casings removed

1 large sweet potato, peeled, spiralized with BLADE D, *noodles trimmed*

½ teaspoon garlic powder

½ teaspoon paprika

Salt and pepper

2 large eggs, beaten

2 tablespoons olive oil

4 slices of beef tomato

4 slices of pepper jack (online) or Gouda cheese

1 avocado, sliced

Chopped fresh coriander, to garnish

Be sure the chorizo is really crumbled. If there are large chunks remaining, it will be difficult to keep the bun bound.

---

1 Heat a large non-stick frying pan over a medium heat. When water flicked onto the pan sizzles, add the chorizo and cook, crumbling the meat with a wooden spoon, for 5–7 minutes or until browned. Using a slotted spoon, transfer the chorizo to a medium bowl, reserving any fat in the pan.

2 Immediately add the sweet potato noodles to the pan and season with the garlic powder, paprika, salt and pepper. Cook for 5–7 minutes or until the noodles are softened and lightly browned. Transfer to the bowl with the chorizo and leave to cool for 1–2 minutes. Stir in the eggs, tossing to coat.

3 Fill four 175ml ramekins halfway with the noodles. Cover each with a piece of foil or greaseproof paper, pressing it down firmly onto the noodles to compress them. Chill for at least 15 minutes to set.

4 Heat 1 tablespoon of the olive oil in a large non-stick frying pan over a medium heat. When the oil is shimmering, add the buns, two at a time, flipping each out of its ramekin into the pan and patting the base until the bun falls out. Cook for 3 minutes or until set, being sure to push in any stray noodles. Carefully flip and cook for a further 2–3 minutes or until the buns are completely set and browned on both sides, flattening with the back of the spatula. Repeat with the remaining olive oil and buns.

5 While the buns are cooking, preheat the grill. Line a baking sheet with baking paper.

6 Transfer the buns to the prepared baking sheet. Top each with a tomato slice, then a cheese slice. Grill for 2 minutes or until the cheese has melted.

7 Remove from the oven, top with avocado and garnish with coriander.

Vegetarian Full English Breakfast

Vegetarian
Gluten-free
Dairy-free

TIME TO PREP 10 minutes
TIME TO COOK 15 minutes
SERVES 4

NUTRITIONAL INFORMATION
Calories: 328
Fat: 9 g
Sodium: 588 mg
Carbohydrate: 58 g
Fibre: 11 g
Sugar: 17 g
Protein: 16 g

ALSO WORKS WELL WITH
Potato

When I studied abroad in London, I made an effort to try all the classic British meals. From toad-in-the-hole to Eton mess, I tasted everything. One of the meals that most surprised me was the full English breakfast – I couldn't believe how much food it was! But now I am a believer in the expression 'Eat like a king for breakfast, a prince for lunch and a pauper for dinner'. Eating a big, hearty breakfast revs your metabolism first thing in the morning and fuels your body for whatever the day may bring, helping reduce your chances of overeating later because of hunger pangs. This spiralized vegetarian re-creation of the classic substitutes sweet potato noodles for toast or hash browns, making it more fun to eat *and* cleaner.

1 tablespoon extra-virgin olive oil

2 medium sweet potatoes, peeled, spiralized with BLADE D**, noodles trimmed**

½ teaspoon garlic powder

Salt and pepper

425g canned vegetarian baked beans

450g button mushrooms, quartered

2 garlic cloves, very finely chopped

60ml reduced-salt vegetable stock

2 vine tomatoes, cut into four 1cm thick slices

¼ teaspoon dried thyme

Cooking spray

4 whole large eggs

1 Heat the olive oil in a large frying pan over a medium heat. When the oil is shimmering, add the sweet potato noodles and season with the garlic powder, salt and pepper. Cook for 7 minutes or until al dente. Divide among four plates.

2 Meanwhile, put the baked beans in a small pan and bring to a simmer over a medium heat, then reduce the heat to low to keep warm until ready to serve.

3 Place a medium frying pan over a medium-high heat. When water flicked onto the pan sizzles, add the mushrooms and garlic, season with salt and pepper and cook for 2 minutes or until the mushrooms begin to release moisture. Add the stock,

cover and cook for 5–7 minutes or until the mushrooms are wilted. Transfer to the serving plates with the sweet potato noodles, dividing the mushrooms evenly.

4 Add the tomato slices to the pan in which you cooked the sweet potato noodles and season with the thyme, salt and pepper. Cook for 2 minutes on each side, flattening with a spatula, until seared and heated through. Add to the plates.

5 Spray the same pan with cooking spray and crack in the eggs, keeping the yolks intact. Cook until the whites are set on the bottom, 3–5 minutes. Place one egg on each plate.

6 Finally, divide the simmering baked beans among the plates and serve.

Mexican Eggs
in Pepper Cups

Thanks to Pinterest, eggs in pepper cups had their fifteen minutes of fame. Most feature a thin pepper slice with a fried egg neatly baked inside, resembling a flower. I've tried these myself and, while adorable, they're not exactly satisfying. Instead, this recipe utilizes the *entire* pepper and includes sweet potato noodles, which will both surprise your brunch guests and leave them feeling satisfied! The Mexican flavours add life to this modest breakfast dish, and the gorgeous presentation is still totally Pin-able.

Gluten-free
Vegetarian
Dairy-free (opt.)
Low-cal

TIME TO PREP 10 minutes
TIME TO COOK 25 minutes
SERVES 4

NUTRITIONAL INFORMATION
Calories: 228
Fat: 12 g
Sodium: 287 mg
Carbohydrate: 18 g
Fibre: 4 g
Sugar: 6 g
Protein: 11 g

ALSO WORKS WELL WITH
Potato, Parsnip

Cooking spray

4 medium peppers

1 tablespoon extra-virgin olive oil

1 large sweet potato, peeled, spiralized with BLADE D*, noodles trimmed*

½ teaspoon garlic powder

½ teaspoon chilli powder

½ teaspoon dried oregano

Salt and pepper

75g cotija or feta cheese, crumbled

4 whole large eggs

2 tablespoons chopped fresh coriander, to garnish

The egg might not look like much after it's cracked into the pepper cup, but it will fluff up. If you're using large peppers, you can cut a little more off the top, or you can use two eggs. You can also slice off the tops after baking if you want a perfectly filled pepper.

1 Preheat the oven to 200°C/400°F. Coat a medium baking dish with cooking spray.

2 Slice the tops off the peppers and discard. Carefully remove the white flesh and seeds from the pepper using a paring knife. If your peppers are uneven on the bottom, slice off a thin piece so they sit flat, keeping them intact. Stand the peppers up in the baking dish and bake for 10 minutes.

3 Meanwhile, heat the olive oil in a large frying pan over a medium-high heat. When the oil is shimmering, add the sweet potato noodles and season with the garlic powder, chilli powder, oregano, salt and black pepper. Cook for 7–10 minutes or until al dente.

4 Stuff the sweet potato noodles into the peppers along with half the cheese, dividing them evenly. Crack one egg into each pepper, keeping the yolks intact, and return to the oven for 12–15 minutes or until the egg whites are just set.

5 Remove the peppers from the oven and immediately garnish with the remaining cheese, coriander and cracked black pepper.

Creamy Chipotle Sweet Potato Pasta
with Chicken and Seasoned Corn

Gluten-free
Dairy-free

TIME TO PREP 25 minutes
TIME TO COOK 20 minutes
SERVES 4

NUTRITIONAL INFORMATION
Calories: 464
Fat: 23 g
Sodium: 1950 mg
Carbohydrate: 39 g
Fibre: 6 g
Sugar: 9 g
Protein: 32 g

ALSO WORKS WELL WITH
Butternut Squash, Swede

One of the cardinal rules of being healthy when eating out is to avoid any recipes with 'creamy' in the title. Traditionally, food that is creamy has some amount of butter, sugar, cream or flour. But it's not hard to re-create those sorts of dishes using alternatives, such as cashew cream. Thanks to that trick, this chicken dish is undeniably decadent. . . without the decadence!

For the corn
1 large ear of sweetcorn
Salt
½ teaspoon chilli powder
1 tablespoon fresh lime juice

For the chicken and pasta
1 tablespoon extra-virgin olive oil
4 skinless, boneless chicken breasts, pounded
¼ teaspoon garlic powder
Salt and pepper
1 large sweet potato, peeled, spiralized with BLADE C, noodles trimmed

For the sauce
30g raw cashews, soaked in water for at least 2 hours (preferably overnight) and drained
1 tablespoon coconut oil, melted
3–4 tablespoons hot sauce
1 teaspoon garlic powder
1 teaspoon paprika
1 tablespoon fresh lemon juice
1 tablespoon apple cider vinegar
Salt

1 tablespoon finely chopped fresh coriander, to garnish

1 Place the sweetcorn in a medium pan and add water to cover and a pinch of salt. Bring to the boil, then reduce the heat to medium-low and simmer for 5 minutes or until the kernels are easily pierced with a fork. Drain. When the sweetcorn is cool enough to handle, slice the kernels off the cob into a medium bowl. Add the chilli powder and lime juice. Toss to combine.

2 Heat 1 tablespoon olive oil in a large frying pan over a medium-high heat. Season the chicken with the garlic powder, salt and pepper. When the oil is shimmering, add the chicken and cook for 3–5 minutes on each side or until golden and cooked through. Transfer to a plate and cut into slices.

3 Immediately add the sweet potato noodles to the pan. Season with salt and pepper and cook, tossing frequently, for 10 minutes or until al dente.

4 Purée the cashews in a high-speed blender or food processor until creamy. Add the remaining ingredients for the sauce and pulse until combined. If necessary, add water, 1 tablespoon at a time, until the sauce reaches the desired consistency. Transfer to a small pot and keep warm over a low heat.

5 Divide the sweet potato noodles among plates and pour over the sauce. Add the chicken and seasoned corn and garnish with coriander.

Braised Short Ribs
over Sweet Potato Pasta

≈≈ Gluten-free
≈≈ Dairy-free
≈≈ One Pot
Saves Well

TIME TO PREP 15 minutes
TIME TO COOK 3 hours
SERVES 4

NUTRITIONAL INFORMATION
Calories: 496
Fat: 20 g
Sodium: 432 mg
Carbohydrate: 26 g
Fibre: 5 g
Sugar: 9 g
Protein: 38 g

ALSO WORKS WELL WITH
**Courgette, Butternut
Squash, Swede, Turnip**

I never truly appreciated short ribs until recently. The tender meat of the dish practically melted on my tongue, with the pasta carrying the hearty sauce. I remember every bite of that meal and in this spiralized version, the sweet potato pasta may be even more delicious than the original, thanks to its inherent sweetness. You'll want to make this dish for a special occasion or a loved one – it's exquisite.

3 tablespoons extra-virgin olive oil

4–6 beef short ribs (about 900g)

Salt and pepper

4 garlic cloves, sliced

1 small onion, diced

2 carrots, diced

2 celery sticks, diced

3 tablespoons tomato purée

350ml red wine (I like Cabernet Sauvignon)

Leaves from 2 sprigs of rosemary

Leaves from 1 sprig of thyme

2 bay leaves

350ml reduced-salt beef stock, plus extra as needed

2 medium sweet potatoes peeled, spiralized with BLADE C or D, noodles trimmed

½ teaspoon garlic powder

1 tablespoon chopped fresh parsley

~~~~~~~~~~~~~~~~~~~~~~~~~~~~

Top the finished plates with shaved Parmesan cheese, if you eat dairy, or make the vegan Parmesan on page 204.

~~~~~~~~~~~~~~~~~~~~~~~~~~~~

1 Preheat the oven to 190°C/375°F.

2 Heat the olive oil in a casserole dish or large ovenproof saucepan over a medium-high heat. Season the short ribs on both sides. When the oil is shimmering, add the ribs and cook until golden brown on the outside and beginning to crisp, about 3 minutes on each side. Remove and set aside.

3 Immediately add the garlic, onion, carrots and celery to the casserole and season. Sauté, stirring often, until the vegetables soften, about 5 minutes. Add the tomato purée and stir to coat for 1 minute. Add the wine and simmer for 1 minute until it has reduced by one-quarter. Add the rosemary, thyme, bay leaves and broth.

4 Increase the heat to high and bring the stock to the boil. Return the short ribs to the casserole, submerging them halfway. Cover and transfer to the oven. Braise for about 2½ hours or until the meat is fork-tender and falling off the bones. Every 45 minutes, check to make sure the ribs are still about halfway submerged, adding more stock as needed. Remove and discard the bay leaves from the short ribs before serving.

5 Before serving, place the sweet potato noodles in a large frying pan and season with the garlic powder, salt and pepper. Cook over a medium high heat, working in batches if necessary, for 7 minutes or until al dente.

6 Divide the noodles among four plates, add the short ribs and spoon the sauce over the top. Garnish with the parsley.

Creamy Spinach and Artichoke Sweet Potato Pasta

≈ Vegan
≈ Vegetarian
≈ Gluten-free
Paleo
Dairy-free
Low-Cal

TIME TO PREP 25 minutes
TIME TO COOK 25 minutes
SERVES 4

NUTRITIONAL INFORMATION
Calories: 246
Fat: 13 g
Sodium: 756 mg
Carbohydrate: 26 g
Fibre: 10 g
Sugar: 8 g
Protein: 8 g

ALSO WORKS WELL WITH
Swede, Turnip, Carrot, Celeriac

Spinach and artichoke is a popular combination – on pizza, as a dip, in sauces and in casseroles. Whatever the presentation, it's usually chock-full of cream, cheese and butter. Spinach is an excellent source of vitamin K and protein, and artichoke hearts are high in antioxidants and dietary fibre – why muck up these nutritional benefits with those processed ingredients? With this spiralized pasta, we highlight the health benefits and keep them top of mind, adding even more with sweet potatoes and cauliflower. This dish is ideal for cosying up with on cold winter nights when you need something warm, comforting and satisfying.

1 medium head cauliflower, chopped into florets

½ teaspoon garlic powder

2 tablespoons nutritional yeast

125ml reduced-salt vegetable stock

½ teaspoon dried oregano

Salt and pepper

1 tablespoon extra-virgin olive oil

2 medium sweet potatoes, peeled, spiralized with BLADE C, noodles trimmed

1 (400g) can halved artichoke hearts, drained and patted dry

1 garlic clove, sliced

200g spinach

1 teaspoon chilli flakes

For a deeper flavour, roast the artichoke halves for 20 minutes at 220°C/425°F with a tablespoon of extra-virgin olive oil, salt and pepper. Add them to the pasta after cooking the spinach.

1 Bring a large pan of water to the boil over a high heat. Add the cauliflower and cook for about 10 minutes until easily pierced with a fork. Drain and transfer to a food processor. Add the garlic powder, nutritional yeast, stock and oregano. Season with salt and black pepper and pulse until creamy. Taste and adjust the seasoning to your preference.

2 Meanwhile, heat the olive oil in a large frying pan over a medium-high heat. When the oil is shimmering, add the sweet potato noodles and season. Cook for 7 minutes or until al dente. Remove from the pan and set aside.

3 Immediately add the artichokes to the frying pan and season with salt and black pepper. Cook for 3 minutes or until warmed through. Add the garlic and spinach and cook for 3 minutes or until fragrant and just wilted. Return the sweet potato noodles to the pan and pour over the cauliflower sauce. Toss to combine thoroughly.

4 Divide among four plates and garnish with the chilli flakes.

Turnip

Turnips have a bit of a bad reputation, but I'm here to change all that. I'll admit that when served raw or plain, they do have a bitter taste. But with the right seasonings, sauces and accompaniments, you won't even recognize them – in a good way!

Turnips are a healthy, low-calorie vegetable that should be built into your healthy diet, because they're easy to find, spiralize and adapt into any pasta or noodle dishes! The noodles have a soft, velvety texture when heated and are durable enough for dressings and sauces to cling to well.

When picking out your turnips at the supermarket, feel for ones with smooth skin. The turnip should be firm with a purple-tinged top. The smaller the turnip, the more palatable the flavour, so aim for one that's 5cm in diameter – it'll spiralize well and be super tasty. Avoid any shrivelled turnips or those with major blemishes.

NUTRITIONAL BENEFITS: A medium turnip provides 54 per cent of your recommended daily amount of vitamin C, an immunity-boosting nutrient! Turnips are also high in fibre, which is helpful for weight loss and maintenance. Store in an airtight container in the fridge for up to 7 days.

PREPARATION AND STORAGE: Peel the turnip entirely and slice off the ends to leave flat, even surfaces.

BEST BLADES TO USE
- Blade C
- Blade D

BEST COOKING METHODS
- Boil for 2–3 minutes
- Sauté over a medium-high heat for 5–7 minutes
- Roast at 220°C/425°F for 10–12 minutes

Turnip alla Vodka

At restaurants, I've always steered clear of the creamier pasta dishes, even before I was Inspiralized. I much prefer a dusting of Parmesan or a dollop of ricotta to 225ml cream. With too much cream, you lose the taste of the noodle! So I've always had a love-hate relationship with vodka sauces. . . until now. This lightened-up version offers that iconic, luxurious texture and taste, without the processed ingredients and sugar rollercoaster. Instead, you get *healthy* fat and a little bit of protein from the cashew cream. The sauce lets these turnip noodles shine. Grab some bread – something tells me you'll want to soak up every last drop!

Vegan
Vegetarian
Gluten-free
Dairy-free
Low-cal

TIME TO PREP 15 minutes plus 4 hours to soak the cashews

TIME TO COOK 20 minutes

SERVES 4

NUTRITIONAL INFORMATION
Calories: 248
Fat: 14 g
Sodium: 766 mg
Carbohydrate: 20 g
Fibre: 4 g
Sugar: 9 g
Protein: 6 g

ALSO WORKS WELL WITH
Swede, Courgette

30g raw cashews, soaked for at least 4–5 hours, drained

Reduced-salt vegetable stock, as needed

1 tablespoon extra-virgin olive oil

1 large garlic clove, finely chopped

¼ teaspoon chilli flakes

½ red onion, diced

1 (400g) can chopped tomatoes

½ teaspoon dried oregano

½ teaspoon dried basil

60ml vodka

2 turnips, peeled, spiralized with BLADE D, **noodles trimmed**

Salt and pepper

25g vegan Parmesan cheese (see page 204)

2 tablespoons chopped fresh curly parsley

1 Place the cashews in a high-speed blender or food processor and pulse until creamy. Add the stock 1 tablespoon at a time as needed until the sauce reaches a smooth consistency, similar to a vodka sauce or alfredo.

2 Heat the olive oil in a large frying pan over a medium-high heat. When the oil is shimmering, add the garlic, chilli flakes and onion and cook for 3 minutes or until the onion is soft and translucent. Add the tomatoes, oregano, basil, vodka and turnip noodles and season with salt and black pepper. Reduce the heat to low and simmer for about 5 minutes or until the alcohol cooks off.

3 Stir in the cashew sauce and Parmesan and cook for a further 1 minute or until the turnip noodles are al dente.

4 Divide the pasta among four plates and garnish with the parsley.

Cauliflower Steak
over Roasted Garlic Tomato Turnip Noodles

Cauliflower steak is the vegetarians' best-kept secret, but ever so slowly it's starting to make its way onto restaurant menus and into home kitchens everywhere. They can be seasoned lightly or dramatically, depending on what kind of dish you're trying to create. With the proper accompaniments, you can enjoy a steak dinner without the steak! Here the warm, thick and hearty star of this dish sits atop a bed of roasted garlic tomato turnip pasta, adding Italian flair and completing a robust meal that's fully vegetarian.

Vegan
Vegetarian
Gluten-free
Paleo
Dairy-free
Low-cal
Saves Well

TIME TO PREP 25 minutes
TIME TO COOK 50 minutes
SERVES 4

NUTRITIONAL INFORMATION
Calories: 279
Fat: 12 g
Sodium: 1333 mg
Carbohydrate: 40 g
Fibre: 9 g
Sugar: 18 g
Protein: 9 g

ALSO WORKS WELL WITH
Butternut Squash,
Parsnip, Sweet Potato

1 head of garlic, outer skin peeled

1 tablespoon plus 1 teaspoon extra-virgin olive oil

1 large head cauliflower

Salt and pepper

For the sauce and pasta

1 tablespoon extra-virgin olive oil

1 small red onion, finely diced

1 tablespoon tomato purée

¼ teaspoon chilli flakes

½ teaspoon Italian seasoning

2 (400g) cans chopped tomatoes

Salt and pepper

2 tablespoons roughly chopped fresh basil

2 large or 3 medium turnips, peeled, spiralized with BLADE D, noodles trimmed

2 tablespoons vegan Parmesan cheese (see page 204), to garnish (optional)

1 Preheat the oven to 200°C/400°F and set a rack in the centre.

2 Slice off about 5mm from the top of the head of garlic so that you can just see the tops of the cloves. Drizzle the exposed part with 1 teaspoon of the olive oil. Wrap the garlic in foil and set on a baking sheet. Roast for 40–50 minutes or until lightly caramelized and very soft when pierced with a knife or fork. Remove from the oven, remove the foil and set aside to cool, then peel all the cloves.

3 While the garlic is roasting, line a baking sheet with baking paper. Remove the leaves from the head of cauliflower and, using a sturdy, large knife, slice the cauliflower from top to base into four 2cm thick 'steaks'. Season each with salt and pepper.

recipe continues

4 Heat the remaining 1 tablespoon olive oil in a large frying pan over a medium-high heat. When the oil is shimmering, add the cauliflower steaks in a single layer, working in batches if necessary. Sear for about 1 minute on each side or until golden, then transfer to the prepared baking sheet. Roast for 15–20 minutes or until tender and cooked through.

5 Meanwhile, make the sauce and pasta. In the same pan you used to cook the cauliflower, heat the olive oil over a medium-high heat. When the oil is shimmering, add the onion and cook for 3–5 minutes or until soft and translucent. Add the tomato purée, chilli flakes and Italian seasoning and cook for 1 minute, stirring to combine. Add the tomatoes and season with salt and pepper. Increase the heat to high and bring to the boil, then reduce the heat to medium-low and simmer for 20 minutes or until reduced by one-quarter.

6 Transfer the sauce to a food processor, along with the roasted garlic cloves. Blend until creamy. Taste and adjust the seasoning to your preferences.

7 Return the frying pan to a medium heat, pour in the sauce and fold in the basil. Add the turnip noodles and toss to coat. Cover and cook for 5–7 minutes or until warmed through and al dente.

8 Divide the turnip noodles among four plates and top each with a cauliflower steak. Garnish with vegan Parmesan, if you like.

~~~~~~

If you'd like to make your own Italian seasoning blend instead of using a pre-made shop-bought one, combine ⅛ teaspoon each of dried rosemary, dried oregano, dried basil and dried parsley.

~~~~~~

White Beans, Escarole and Turnip Noodles
in Parmesan Stock

Gluten-free
Low-cal
Saves Well

TIME TO PREP 15 minutes
TIME TO COOK 15 minutes
SERVES 2

NUTRITIONAL INFORMATION
Calories: 213
Fat: 8 g
Sodium: 300 mg
Carbohydrate: 26 g
Fibre: 10 g
Sugar: 7 g
Protein: 10 g

One of my mother's best dishes was her white beans and escarole in a salty chicken stock. Whenever I came home from university, I'd ask her to make it for me. This spiralized version adds turnip noodles to soak up the flavours from the buttery beans, earthy escarole and Parmesan-infused stock. Not quite a soup, not quite a pasta, this dish is something I like to whip up in a pinch for lunch or a late dinner.

1 tablespoon extra-virgin olive oil

1 large garlic clove, finely chopped

Pinch of chilli flakes

1 bunch escarole, rinsed and chopped into 5cm pieces

1 large turnip, peeled, spiralized with BLADE C, *noodles trimmed*

225ml reduced-salt chicken stock

Salt and pepper

75g canned white beans, rinsed and drained

2 tablespoons grated Parmesan cheese

1 Heat the olive oil in a large frying pan over a medium heat. When the oil is shimmering, add the garlic and chilli flakes and cook for 30 seconds or until fragrant. Add the escarole, turnip noodles and stock and season with salt and black pepper. Cover and cook for 5–7 minutes or until the escarole is wilted and the noodles are al dente. Using tongs, transfer the escarole and noodles to bowls, dividing them evenly and reserving the stock in the pan.

2 Immediately add the beans and Parmesan to the stock and remove from the heat. Stir constantly until the beans are warmed through, about 2 minutes.

3 Spoon the beans and Parmesan stock over the noodles and serve immediately.

Pan-seared Pork Chops
with Mushroom Gravy and Turnip Noodles

The difference between bone-in and boneless pork chops is astounding – with the former, the flavours intensify as the meat soaks in the juices released from the bone. If you're not a meat-eater, I apologize for that descriptive sentence, but if you are – this dish has it all. The turnip noodles' earthy taste complements the mushrooms and holds up to the gravy, just like real pasta. If you don't eat meat, omit the pork chop and make this sauce with vegetable stock – it will taste like a marsala!

Gluten-free
Paleo
Dairy-free
Low-cal
Saves Well

TIME TO PREP 20 minutes
TIME TO COOK 35 minutes
SERVES 4

NUTRITIONAL INFORMATION
Calories: 229
Fat: 10 g
Sodium: 158 mg
Carbohydrate: 12 g
Fibre: 2 g
Sugar: 5 g
Protein: 21 g

ALSO WORKS WELL WITH
Celeriac, Courgette, Swede

---

1 tablespoon extra-virgin olive oil

2 bone-in pork chops, about 1cm thick, fat trimmed

¼ teaspoon paprika

Salt and pepper

1 small onion, peeled, spiralized with BLADE A, noodles trimmed

2 garlic cloves, finely chopped

225g sliced chestnut mushrooms

125ml reduced-salt chicken stock

225ml light coconut milk

1 teaspoon dried thyme

2 medium turnips, peeled, spiralized with BLADE C, noodles trimmed

2 tablespoons finely chopped fresh parsley, to garnish

1 Heat the oil in a large frying pan over a medium heat. Season the pork chops with paprika, salt and pepper. When the oil is shimmering, add the pork chops in a single layer, working in batches if necessary, and cook for 3–4 minutes on each side or until browned. Transfer to a plate and tent with foil to keep warm.

2 Add the onion noodles, garlic and mushrooms to the pan and season with salt and pepper. Cook until the onions are caramelized, about 10 minutes. Add the stock and scrape up any browned bits from the base of the pan. Stir until the liquid has evaporated, about 5 minutes. Add the coconut milk, thyme, salt and pepper. Cook for 7–10 minutes, until thickened. Transfer to a bowl and set aside.

3 Immediately add the turnip noodles to the pan, season with salt and pepper, cover and cook for 5–7 minutes or until noodles wilt and are al dente, uncovering occasionally to toss. Add the mushroom gravy and toss for 1–2 minutes or until the turnips are coated and everything is warmed through.

4 Plate the pork chops and stir any collected juices into the noodles. Pour the noodles and sauce over the pork chops and garnish with parsley.

Turnip Risotto
with Crispy Pancetta and Chives

When I first discovered how to make rice out of spiralized vegetables, I experimented with about a dozen types of dishes, from stuffed peppers to burrito bowls. I can tell you with confidence that the dish most similar in consistency to the real thing is risotto. The spiralized 'rice' fluffs up when cooked with stock, collecting flavour. It's much faster than traditional risotto – and much simpler! Adding pancetta here infuses flavour into every bite of turnip. Everyone will think you slaved over the hob for hours!

〰〰 Gluten-free
〰〰 Dairy-free (opt.)
Low-cal
Saves Well

TIME TO PREP 10 minutes
TIME TO COOK 15 minutes
SERVES 4

NUTRITIONAL INFORMATION
Calories: 186
Fat: 12 g
Sodium: 755 mg
Carbohydrate: 9 g
Fibre: 2 g
Sugar: 5 g
Protein: 9 g

ALSO WORKS WELL WITH
Kohlrabi, Butternut Squash, Sweet Potato

225g pancetta, diced

2 garlic cloves, finely chopped

2 tablespoons finely chopped shallot

½ teaspoon chilli flakes

2 large turnips, peeled, spiralized with BLADE D, *then riced (see page 16)*

Salt and pepper

225ml reduced-salt vegetable stock

10g fresh chives, finely chopped

50g Parmesan cheese, grated (see Tip)

1 Cook the pancetta in a large frying pan over a medium heat for 7 minutes or until browned, flipping. Transfer to a kitchen-paper-lined plate to drain. Reserve 1 tablespoon of the rendered fat in the pan and discard the remainder.

2 Add the garlic, shallot and chilli flakes to the pan with the pancetta fat and cook for 30 seconds or until fragrant. Add the turnip rice, season with salt and black pepper and cook for 2 minutes or until the rice is beginning to soften. Add the stock and cook for a further 5 minutes or until the rice is al dente.

3 Fold in the half the pancetta, half the chives and the cheese. Remove the pan from the heat and stir constantly to melt the cheese completely.

4 Divide the risotto among four bowls and top with the remaining pancetta and chives.

If you eat don't eat dairy, stir in 120ml coconut cream (see page 19) instead of the Parmesan.

White Potato

We all know that potatoes are buttery, creamy and rich. Their starchy goodness is undeniably addictive and universally complementary to all types of meals. If you're trying to convince a stubborn friend or family member to try spiralizing but he or she is a 'meat and potatoes' kind of person, this chapter is the obvious place to start. There's a whole lot more to potatoes than chips, mash and crisps!

There are many varieties of potatoes, and we use a lot of them in this chapter. Some of my favourites to spiralize are the Russet and Yukon Gold. The differences among these are their starch and sweetness levels, but they all spiralize easily and make plentiful noodles. For example, Russet potatoes have an earthier, mild flavour, while red-skinned potatoes are slightly more sweet – but both carry moderate levels of starch.

Keep in mind as you're preparing your recipes that when potatoes are peeled and/or spiralized, they quickly oxidize (a chemical reaction that happens when their flesh is exposed to oxygen, resulting in browning and black spots). To avoid this, you have two options: wait to spiralize the potato until right before it's used in the recipe or, after you spiralize, place the noodles in a bowl of cold water and set it in the fridge for up to 24 hours.

NUTRITIONAL BENEFITS: Potatoes are high in vitamin B6, potassium and copper, all of which help lower blood pressure and support basic metabolic function.

PREPARATION AND STORAGE: Peel the potato, if liked, and slice off the ends to leave flat, even surfaces. Store in a container filled with water in the fridge for up to 24 hours. Potato noodles can be frozen for up to 8 months for future use.

BEST BLADES TO USE
- Blade A
- Blade B
- Blade C
- Blade D

BEST COOKING METHODS
- Sauté over a medium-high heat for 5–7 minutes
- Roast at 220°C/425°F for 10–15 minutes

Potato-wrapped Roasted Carrots
with Moroccan Black Lentils and Feta

Vegetarian
Gluten-free
Dairy-free (opt.)
Saves Well

TIME TO PREP 15 minutes
TIME TO COOK 50 minutes
SERVES 4

NUTRITIONAL INFORMATION
Calories: 389
Fat: 21 g
Sodium: 324 mg
Carbohydrate: 45 g
Fibre: 9 g
Sugar: 9 g
Protein: 14 g

ALSO WORKS WELL WITH
Sweet Potato, Swede

If you're a reader of the *Inspiralized* blog, you might have seen that for Halloween, I created potato-wrapped carrots that resembled mummies. I knew I wanted to turn them into a full meal. This dish squeezes in complex carbohydrates (the good kind!), and has a comforting taste enhanced by Moroccan-spiced black lentils and salty feta. Wrapping the carrots is an impressive presentation and also adds nutrients. If you want to try this recipe but don't want to deal with that intricacy, cook the potato noodles separately and stir them into the lentils.

200g uncooked black Beluga lentils, rinsed

475ml reduced-salt vegetable stock, plus extra as needed

Leaves from 1 sprig of thyme

450g heirloom or heritage carrots, scrubbed clean (unpeeled) and patted dry

2 large red potatoes, or 1 medium Yukon Gold potato, spiralized with BLADE D, untrimmed

1½ tablespoons extra-virgin olive oil

½ teaspoon ground cumin

Salt and pepper

For the dressing
1 tablespoon fresh lemon juice

1 teaspoon honey

3 tablespoons extra-virgin olive oil

½ teaspoon ground cumin

¼ teaspoon ground cinnamon

¼ teaspoon ground ginger

¼ teaspoon smoked paprika

¼ teaspoon ground coriander

⅛ teaspoon cayenne pepper

1 bunch of fresh coriander, chopped, to garnish

75g feta cheese, crumbled

1 Preheat the oven to 220°C/425°F. Line a baking sheet with baking paper.

2 Place the lentils, stock and thyme in a medium saucepan. Bring to the boil over a medium-high heat, cover, then reduce the heat to low and simmer for 20–30 minutes or until the lentils are tender but not mushy. If the liquid evaporates before the lentils are cooked, add more stock, 60ml at a time.

3 Lay out the carrots on the prepared baking sheet, spacing them apart. Roast for 15 minutes or until slightly tender. Remove and set aside until cool enough to handle. Then, working from end to end, twirl the potato noodles around the carrots.

4 In a small bowl, whisk together the oil and cumin. Brush the mixture over the carrots and season with salt and pepper. Return the carrots to the oven to roast for a further 30–40 minutes or until fork-tender.

5 Meanwhile, make the dressing. Whisk together all the ingredients for the dressing in a small bowl. Taste and adjust the seasoning to your preferences.

6 Serve the carrots over the lentils. Drizzle with the dressing and garnish with the coriander and feta.

Choose the longest spiralized potato noodles possible, discarding any extra noodles that are too short to wrap around the carrot or saving them for another use.

Asparagus, Egg and Potato Noodles
with Kale

≈ Vegetarian
≈ Gluten-free
Paleo
Dairy-free

TIME TO PREP 10 minutes
TIME TO COOK 15 minutes
SERVES 2

NUTRITIONAL INFORMATION
Calories: 365
Fat: 26 g
Sodium: 86 mg
Carbohydrate: 25 g
Fibre: 5 g
Sugar: 3 g
Protein: 11 g

ALSO WORKS WELL WITH
Sweet Potato

On those nights when you get home late from a long day at school, tiring meetings at work or an exhausting fitness class, this dish is for you. There's no point in making a big meal before you go to bed – your body doesn't need that much fuel to sleep. Instead, this quick recipe offers all you need to nourish yourself and turn in feeling light: leafy greens, protein-packed eggs, complex carbohydrates and fibre-filled asparagus.

3 tablespoons extra-virgin olive oil

8 large asparagus spears, ends trimmed

Salt and pepper

1 medium Russet potato, spiralized with BLADE D, noodles trimmed

¼ teaspoon garlic powder

⅛ teaspoon paprika

200g kale leaves, roughly chopped

Cooking spray

2 whole large eggs

To turn this dish into a more filling meal, add avocado and/or some bacon.

1 Heat 1½ tablespoons of the olive oil in a large frying pan over a medium heat. When the oil is shimmering, add the asparagus and season with salt and pepper. Cook for 5 minutes or until the asparagus is bright green and fork-tender. Divide between two plates.

2 Heat the remaining olive oil in the same pan. When the oil is shimmering, add the potato noodles and season with the garlic powder, paprika, salt and pepper. Cover and cook for about 5 minutes or until mostly wilted. Stir in the kale, cover and cook for a further 5 minutes or until the noodles are al dente. Divide the mixture between the plates with the asparagus.

3 Immediately coat the frying pan with cooking spray and set it over a medium-high heat. Crack in the eggs and cook until the whites are just set but the yolks are still runny, about 3 minutes.

4 Transfer an egg to each plate and serve immediately.

Half and Half Pasta

≈≈ Vegetarian
≈≈ Gluten-free
     Saves Well

TIME TO PREP 10 minutes
TIME TO COOK 15 minutes
SERVES 2

NUTRITIONAL INFORMATION
Calories: 382
Fat: 20 g
Sodium: 367 mg
Carbohydrate: 39 g
Fibre: 6 g
Sugar: 5 g
Protein: 14 g

If you know someone who is resisting becoming Inspiralized, beg for one more chance – and then make this recipe. This pasta is exactly what it sounds like: half courgette, half potato noodles! The latter offers a familiar starchiness that your regular pasta-loving pal will welcome. When the Parmesan cheese melts and coats both noodles together, he or she will only know that dinner tastes delicious. Oh, and here's a pro tip: peel the courgette before spiralizing – without the green, it will look more like the real thing!

2 tablespoons extra-virgin olive oil

2 garlic cloves, very finely chopped

¼ teaspoon chilli flakes

1 medium Russet potato, peeled, spiralized with BLADE D, noodles trimmed

Salt and pepper

1 large courgette, spiralized with BLADE D, noodles trimmed

50g Parmesan cheese, grated

Finely chopped fresh parsley, to garnish

1 Heat 1 tablespoon of the olive oil in a large frying pan over a medium heat. When the oil is shimmering, add the garlic and chilli flakes and cook for 30 seconds or until fragrant. Add the potato noodles, season with salt and black pepper and toss to combine. Cover and cook, tossing occasionally, for 7 minutes or until al dente. Remove from the pan and set aside.

2 Immediately add the courgette noodles to the pan and cook, tossing occasionally, for 3–5 minutes or until al dente.

3 Return the potato noodles to the pan. Drizzle over the remaining 1 tablespoon oil and toss to combine thoroughly. Turn off the heat, fold in the Parmesan and toss until the cheese has melted.

4 Garnish with parsley and serve immediately.

For the *most* stubborn of non-believers, you can replace the potato noodles with regular pasta. Baby steps!

Pan con Tomate
with Serrano Ham

≈≈≈ | Gluten-free
≈≈≈ | Dairy-free
≈≈≈ | Low-cal

TIME TO PREP 10 minutes
TIME TO COOK 30 minutes
SERVES 2

NUTRITIONAL INFORMATION
Calories: 272
Fat: 15 g
Sodium: 52 mg
Carbohydrate: 26 g
Fibre: 3 g
Sugar: 2 g
Protein: 6 g

My childhood friend Sarah and I have birthdays within three days of each other, and for years, we've celebrated together. We both studied in Europe during our first year of university, and that year we met up in Barcelona, the land of tapas. We discovered that one of the most ubiquitous and inexpensive tapas is *pan con tomate* ('bread with tomato'). We ate so much that by the end of our visit, we were in a carb coma. This spiralized version replaces the bread with a potato noodle bun and adds a little something extra with the ham. Bring on the cava!

4 teaspoons extra virgin olive oil

1 Russet potato, peeled, spiralized with BLADE D***, noodles trimmed***

¼ teaspoon smoked paprika

Salt and pepper

1 large egg, beaten

1 large ripe tomato

1 garlic clove, smashed and chopped

2 thin slices of Serrano ham

To make this dish vegetarian, omit the ham and sprinkle a little bit of smoked sea salt on top.

1 Heat 2 teaspoons of the olive oil in a large non-stick frying pan over a medium heat. When the oil is shimmering, add the potato noodles and season with the paprika, salt and pepper. Cook for 5–7 minutes or until the noodles are softened and lightly browned.

2 Transfer the noodles to a medium bowl and leave to cool for 2 minutes. Stir in the egg and toss to coat.

3 Fill two ramekins halfway with the noodles. Cover each with a piece of foil or greaseproof paper, pressing it down firmly onto the noodles to compress them. Chill for at least 15 minutes to set.

4 Heat the remaining 2 teaspoons oil in the same pan over a medium heat. When the oil is shimmering, add the buns two at a time, flipping each out of its ramekin into the pan and patting the base until the bun falls out. Cook for 3 minutes or until set on the bottom, being sure to push in any stray noodles. Carefully flip and cook for a further 2–3 minutes or until the buns are completely set and browned on both sides, flattening with the back of the spatula.

5 While the potato buns cook, using the largest holes on a box grater, grate the tomato. Smear each potato bun with the garlic, then spoon on the grated tomato. Top each bun with a slice of ham and serve.

Loaded Potatoes
with BBQ Sauce

Gluten-free
Low-cal

TIME TO PREP 15 minutes
TIME TO COOK 20 minutes
SERVES 4

NUTRITIONAL INFORMATION
Calories: 261
Fat: 16 g
Sodium: 359 mg
Carbohydrate: 28 g
Fibre: 4 g
Sugar: 2 g
Protein: 11 g

ALSO WORKS WELL WITH
Sweet Potato, Swede

Twice-baked loaded potatoes are essential for the football party spread. With melted cheese and bacon, something about them is just perfect for fun and celebrating. This spiralized version is a healthy spin that omits the traditional butter and soured cream. The potato noodles are shareable and almost resemble nachos! Does that make them even more perfect for sport-watching? Maybe.

4 bacon rashers

4 red potatoes, peeled, spiralized with BLADE D, noodles trimmed

½ teaspoon garlic powder

¼ teaspoon chilli powder

Salt and pepper

1 large avocado

1 tablespoon fresh lime juice

¼ teaspoon paprika

30g Cheddar cheese, grated

30g Monterey Jack cheese or mature Cheddar, grated

2 spring onions, green parts only, sliced

2 tablespoons bottled barbecue sauce

1 Preheat the grill.

2 Cook the bacon in a large frying pan over a medium-high heat, flipping occasionally, for about 10 minutes or until browned and beginning to crisp. Transfer to a kitchen-paper-lined plate to drain. Reserve 1 tablespoon of the rendered fat in the pan; discard the remainder.

3 Add the potato noodles to the pan with the bacon fat and season with the garlic powder, chilli powder, salt and pepper. Toss to combine and cook for about 7 minutes or until al dente. Transfer the potato noodles to a medium baking dish.

4 Meanwhile, use the back of a fork to mash together the avocado and lime juice in a medium bowl until no large chunks remain. Season with the paprika, salt and pepper.

5 Mound together the potato noodles in the centre of the baking dish. Crumble half the bacon over the noodles and sprinkle with the cheeses. Grill for 2 minutes or until the cheese is melted and bubbling.

6 Remove from the oven and immediately top with the spring onions. Crumble the remaining bacon over the top. Drizzle with barbecue sauce and finish with dollops of the avocado mash.

Recipes by Category

Recipe Title	Gluten-Free	Paleo	Vegetarian	Vegan	One Pot	Saves Well	Dairy-Free/optional	Low-Cal	No Cook
Crabless Crab Cakes with Green Apple Guacamole	X		X				X		
Creamy Roasted Butternut Squash Soup with Apple Noodles	X	X	X	X			X		
Apple-walnut Muffins	X	X	X			X		X	
Curried Apple Egg Salad Wrap	X		X					X	X
Ginger Pear and Apple Sangria			X				X		X
Spiced Lamb Skewers with Beetroot Noodles	X								
Tahini Beetroot Noodle Bowl with Falafel	X		X				X	X	
Chicken Tagine with Apricot Golden Beetroot Rice	X								
Green Curry Golden Beetroot Noodle Bowl	X	X	X	X					
Oven-fried Goat's Cheese with Figs, Bitter Greens and Beetroot Noodles	X		X						
Grams's Tuna and Macaroni Salad	X						X	X	
Sun-dried Tomato, Chicken and Broccoli Pasta	X					X	X	X	
Prawn Tom Kha with Broccoli Noodles	X				X		X		
Butternut Squash Rice and Beans	X		X	X		X	X	X	
Pumpkin-rosemary Alfredo with Crispy Prosciutto	X	X				X	X		
Butternut Squash Ravioli with Sage and Toasted Pine Nuts	X		X					X	
Butternut Squash Noodles with Almond Ricotta and Coconut Bacon	X	X	X	X			X		
Pear, Pomegranate and Roast Turkey Salad with Butternut Squash and Maple-sesame Vinaigrette						X	X		

Recipe Title	Gluten-Free	Paleo	Vegetarian	Vegan	One Pot	Saves Well	Dairy-Free/optional	Low-Cal	No Cook
Winter Lasagne with Brussels Sprouts and Chicken Sausage	X					X			
Teriyaki Mini Meatballs over Roasted Spring Onions and Butternut Squash Noodles						X	X		
Oven-fried Avocado Tacos with Chipotle Cream	X	X	X				X	X	
Butternut Squash Noodles with Butter Beans and Sun-dried Tomato Cream Sauce	X		X	X			X	X	
Crunchy Bok Choy and Cabbage Salad	X	X	X			X	X	X	X
Spanish Cabbage Stew with Cod and Saffron	X	X					X	X	
Spicy Cabbage and Carrot Detox Soup	X	X		X		X	X	X	
Cabbage Buddha Bowl with Chickpea-avocado Mash and BBQ Tahini	X		X	X			X		X
Roasted Carrot Noodles with Smoked Salmon, Avocado and Creamy Herb Dressing	X	X					X		
Garlic-miso Soup with Carrot Noodles, Seaweed and Tofu	X		X	X			X	X	
Mum's Matzo Ball Soup with Carrot Noodles			X				X	X	
Za'atar Chickpeas over Radicchio and Carrot	X		X				X	X	
Slow-cooker Spiced Lentils and Cauliflower over Carrot Rice	X	X	X			X	X	X	
Stuffed Cabbage Rolls with Celeriac Rice and Adzuki Beans	X		X	X		X	X		
Chicken and Celeriac Rice Soup	X	X				X	X	X	
Celeriac Spaghetti and Vegetarian Meatballs			X			X	X		
Buffalo Wings with Celeriac Slaw	X								
Thai Steak Salad						X	X		
Hoisin Salmon with Courgette Slaw							X		

Recipe Title	Gluten-Free	Paleo	Vegetarian	Vegan	One Pot	Saves Well	Dairy-Free/optional	Low-Cal	No Cook
Green Goddess Courgette Pasta	X		X	X		X	X		X
Dairy-Free Clam Chowder with Courgette Noodles	X						X	X	
Italian-Style Chicken Sliders	X	X				X	X	X	
Chocolate Chip Courgette Noodle Bread with Coconut Cream Icing	X	X				X	X		
Greek-Style Prawn Scampi	X						X	X	
Minestrone with Courgette Noodles	X		X	X	X	X	X		
Gluten-Free Chicken Parmesan over Courgette Noodles	X								
Seared Scallops over Courgette Noodles with Roasted Pepper Sauce	X	X					X	X	
Courgette Ravioli with Tomato Basil and Cashew Cheese	X	X	X	X			X	X	
Avocado BLT Courgette Pasta	X	X					X		
Lemon Halibut with Summer Squash Gratin and Tomato Coulis	X	X					X		
Cauliflower Pizza with Courgette, Ricotta, Corn and Pesto	X		X					X	
Vegetable Ribbon and Barley Salad with Basil-feta Vinaigrette	X		X			X		X	
Sausage and Peppers with Courgette Noodles	X	X				X	X		
Turkey, Spinach and Hummus Cucumber Noodle Roll-ups	X						X	X	X
California Roll Sushi Bowl with Ginger-carrot Dressing							X	X	
Lamb-feta Burgers with Greek Cucumber Noodle Salad	X								
Chicago-style Carrot Dogs with Spiralized Pickles			X	X		X	X	X	
Kohlrabi Spaghettini Aglio e Olio	X		X			X	X	X	
General Tso's Cauliflower with Kohlrabi Rice			X				X	X	

Recipe Title	Gluten-Free	Paleo	Vegetarian	Vegan	One Pot	Saves Well	Dairy-Free/ optional	Low-Cal	No Cook
Spicy Kohlrabi Tortilla Soup with Prawns	X				X	X	X		
Fried Green Tomatoes with Avocado Ranch Kohlrabi	X	X	X				X		
Chicken Mole with Kohlrabi Rice	X	X				X	X		
Kale and Quinoa Salad with Pickled Onions and Caesar Dressing	X		X				X	X	X
Wedge Salad with Caramelized Onions, Mushroom Bacon and Greek Yogurt–balsamic Dressing	X		X						
No-cheese French Onion and Lentil Soup	X				X	X	X		
Almond-crusted Lemon Sole with Tomato, Sweet Onion and Caper-parsley Salad	X	X					X		
Rosemary, Olive and Onion Frittata with Rocket Salad and Parmesan Vinaigrette	X		X				X	X	
Parsnip-chive Waffles and Gluten-free Oven-fried Chicken	X	X					X		
Hearty Beef Stew with Parsnip and Carrot Noodles	X					X	X	X	
Avocado 'Toast' with Cherry Tomato Jam	X	X				X	X		
Parsnip Pasta with Caramelized Leeks and Ham	X					X	X	X	
Broccoli Raab and Sausage Parsnip Pasta	X					X	X	X	
Grilled Halloumi, Lentils and Rocket with Roasted Fennel and Pear Noodles	X		X						
Chai-Spiced Pear Porridge	X		X	X			X	X	
Pear Noodle Bowl with Maple-roasted Acorn Squash and Pomegranate Dressing	X		X	X			X	X	
Cinnamon and Pecan Pear Noodle Pancakes	X	X	X				X	X	

Recipe Title	Gluten-Free	Paleo	Vegetarian	Vegan	One Pot	Saves Well	Dairy-Free/optional	Low-Cal	No Cook
Easy Pork Chops with Shredded Brussels Sprouts, Kale and Pear Noodle Salad	X	X				X	X		
Spiralized Shakshuka	X	X	X		X		X	X	
Turkey Picadillo with Green Pepper Noodles	X	X				X	X		
Quick Steak and Pepper Stir-Fry						X	X	X	
Pepper Taco Pan	X					X	X		
Roasted Pepper Chicory Salad with Anchovy–white Bean Dressing and Soft-baked Eggs	X						X		
Summer Ratatouille	X	X	X	X	X	X	X	X	
Foil Pouch Sea Bass	X	X					X	X	
Hot-and-sour Soup with Mooli Noodles			X		X	X	X	X	
Black Radish and Orange Salad with Radicchio and Salmon Cakes	X								
Ginger-crab Fried Mooli Rice							X	X	
Watermelon Radish Nourish Salad with Lemon-ginger Vinaigrette and Vegan Parmesan	X	X	X	X			X		X
Grilled Steak with Mustard Greens and Radish Noodles	X	X					X		
Clear Immunity Soup with Mooli Noodles	X	X	X	X	X		X	X	
Thai Almond and Pork Curry with Swede Noodles	X	X					X		
Swede Gratin with Leeks	X	X	X	X			X		
Mussels over Swede Pasta	X						X	X	
Chicken Cacciatore over Swede Noodles	X					X	X		
Swede Baked Ziti with Mushrooms and Kale	X		X			X			
Tandoori Chicken over Sweet Potato Rice	X	X				X	X		
Sweet Potato Pizza Pan	X		X		X	X			

Recipe Title	Gluten-Free	Paleo	Vegetarian	Vegan	One Pot	Saves Well	Dairy-Free/ optional	Low-Cal	No Cook
Chorizo–Sweet Potato Buns with Tomato and Pepper Jack	X								
Vegetarian Full English Breakfast	X		X				X		
Mexican Eggs in Pepper Cups	X		X				X	X	
Creamy Chipotle Sweet Potato Pasta with Chicken and Seasoned Corn	X						X		
Braised Short Ribs over Sweet Potato Pasta	X				X	X	X		
Creamy Spinach and Artichoke Sweet Potato Pasta	X	X	X	X			X	X	
Turnip alla Vodka	X		X	X			X	X	
Cauliflower Steak over Roasted Garlic Tomato Turnip Noodles	X	X	X	X		X	X	X	
White Beans, Escarole and Turnip Noodles in Parmesan Stock	X					X		X	
Pan-seared Pork Chops with Mushroom Gravy and Turnip Noodles	X	X				X	X	X	
Turnip Risotto with Crispy Pancetta and Chives	X					X	X	X	
Potato-wrapped Roasted Carrots with Moroccan Black Lentils and Feta	X		X			X	X		
Asparagus, Egg and Potato Noodles with Kale	X	X	X				X		
Half and Half Pasta	X		X			X			
Pan Con Tomate with Serrano Ham	X						X	X	
Loaded Potatoes with BBQ Sauce	X							X	

Acknowledgements

You know when you take a photo to capture a gorgeous sunset on the beach or a bright skyline in a big city like New York, and then you go home and share those pictures with a friend or loved one? As you look at the photos with that person, you start to realize that the pictures don't adequately capture what you saw and felt in that moment. Scrolling through the photos, you exclaim, 'The photos don't do it justice!' Well, that's how I feel when someone asks me about Inspiralized. Words like 'blessed' and 'grateful' immediately come to mind, but they don't do this feeling justice!

Every day, I get to help thousands of people find their healthy stride through spiralizing. Ironically, over these past three years, the Inspiralized community has helped *me* attain the healthiest, happiest and most inspired version of *myself*. Their daily encouragement means more to me than they'll ever know. So first, to all of my loyal, kind readers and followers – *grazie*!

Aside from my #inspiralizedsquad, there are a few others who have supported me along this path and helped me grow Inspiralized bigger than I ever thought I could, and for that, I'll always be thankful.

To the Clarkson Potter team, thank you for ensuring this cookbook has a special place in the kitchens of so many home cooks. Doris, thank you for taking a chance on this Inspiralized dream of mine. Kate, Carly and Erica, thank you for showing the world what this cookbook can do. To everyone behind the scenes (Stephanie, La Tricia, Amy, Mark, Alex and Heather), this book is as much yours as it is mine, and I hope you feel as proud as I do – what a labour of love!

And of course, thank you to my editor, Amanda Englander, for getting me and letting me be me! You took my haphazard spiralized recipe list and birthed it into this stunning must-have cookbook. You held my hand when I needed it and pushed me out there alone when I was ready. Thank you for being in my corner and teaching me to embrace 'shimmering oil' and the Oxford comma. Cheers to many more champagne lunches with great news!

Alyssa Reuben (Sedrish!), thank you for being my sounding board and standing up for me and this crazy vision of mine. The unbelievable opportunities that keep coming my way since my first cookbook would not have happened if it weren't for your trust in me. I can't wait to see what *Inspiralize Everything* brings. Next stop: world domination.

They say it 'takes a village', and it couldn't be truer! Thank you to the photography crew that brought life to my printed words. Even though I spiralize every single day, they'll never look as good as you've made them look in this book! Evan Sung, thank you for managing the show with absolute Zen-like composure. You're a true star, a pro and now a life-long friend. Your ability to make my home-cooked healthy meals look like something you'd find on a plate in a Michelin-star restaurant is uncanny, and I cherish these photos almost as much as our laughs on set! Undoubtedly, this wouldn't have happened without the support of the rest of the team – prop stylist Carla Gonzalez-Hart, you scrunch up napkins and lay down spoons with such artistic precision, it amazes me, and food stylist extraordinaire Suzanne Lenzer, I'm happy to have worked with such a talented woman, but most important, one who shares in my belief that a little olive oil, salt and pepper is all you need.

Laura Arnold, thanks for testing all of the recipes in this cookbook, especially so quickly, and I hope you've been #inspiralized and dig the final product.

Meaghan, Meaghan, Meaghan. Meaghan Prenda, I love you like family! Among other things in my life (like my wedding, the Inspiralizer and overall work-life balance), this cookbook truly would not have been possible

without you. Your commitment to Inspiralized and me is humbling, and I am so grateful to have you on my team every single day to laugh and eye-roll with, vent to, bounce ideas off of, and to answer 'those' emails with a smile. I'm so excited for what's to come with this little brand we're building together, and I'll forever be thankful for your kindness and hustle.

Felicia, you'll always be my little sister, and I'll always want to make you proud. I'm so happy you moved in next door in Jersey City so we can spend more time together, procrastinating on our workouts and drinking Karen Specials. Thank you for Inspiralizing all of your friends, because we all know you're more popular than I am. I love you so much, Feesh. And a special shout out to Ben, who should be on the payroll, he promotes Inspiralized so much! You guys are a great team, and I can't wait to see what life brings us all. Wink, wink.

Dad, since my first book, you've become my business partner and the father-in-law to the love of my life. I'm blessed to have you along in this Inspiralized journey. As I grow older, I realize more and more how alike we are, and I'm proud to be like you! I'm so happy I followed your footsteps into entrepreneurship. This life is so much better! And as this book publishes, we'll be celebrating your sixtieth birthday. Happy birthday, Dad!

Mum. WO-man. You're my best friend, and Inspiralized would never have happened without you. Literally, you discovered spiralizing and brought it to me, but aside from that, you have been there for me every single step of the way, supporting and encouraging me. I know you believe in me and I carry that confidence with me in every aspect of my life. Thank you for welcoming Lu into the family last year and making me feel loved and cared for every day of my life. I can only dream of being as good of a mother as you are one day!

Grams and Pops. Your love and faith is beautifully infectious, and we need more of it in the world. Grams, thank you for being there for Poppy during this past beyond-tough year. I know you pray for everyone in our family, and it's those prayers that keep us together. You're the sweetest woman in the world, and I find inspiration in my everyday from the lessons you've taught me. Pops: Although devastatingly scary, your struggle with cancer has only proved that you're the strongest man in the world. You've been through too much and continue to live life to its fullest with a optimistic perspective and a love for family and the good things in my life (like food!). I love you so much, and I have you in my heart everywhere I go.

Lu. I could fill this cookbook with how much thanks I'd like to give to you. Instead, I figured I'd immortalize a portion of the vows I wrote and made to you on our wedding day, by printing it in this cookbook – because after all, this cookbook is filled with anecdotes and inspiration from our lives together!

For those of you who don't know, Lu comes home almost every day to me still working at my desk on Inspiralized, another dream of mine he made happen. In our apartment, there's a little hallway where I can't see Lu until he turns the corner and enters the living room, where my desk is. In the three seconds it takes for you to open the door and get into the apartment, my heart skips a beat the moment I hear your keys open the lock, and I get butterflies in my stomach because, even though it's only been eight hours since I saw you last, I get so excited to see you, kiss you, and have you back in my arms. I want to feel that same way every single day of my life, forever.

Thank you for completing me, baby. I love you.

Index